ISLAM AND ARABS
IN EARLY AMERICAN THOUGHT
The Roots of Orientalism in America

*Dedicated to
Professor Muhammad Al-Imadi,
gentleman, intellectual, friend.*

ISLAM AND ARABS
IN EARLY AMERICAN THOUGHT
The Roots of Orientalism in America

by

Fuad Sha'ban

Published in Association with
Duke University Islamic and Arabian Development Studies

THE ACORN PRESS
Durham, North Carolina

First published 1991

Library of Congress Cataloging-in-Publication Data

Shaban, Fuad, 1935-
    Islam and Arabs in early American thought : roots of orientalism in America / Fuad Sha'ban.
        p.   cm.
    "Published in association with Duke University Islamic and Arabian Development Studies."
    Includes bibliographical references and index.
    1. Middle East—Foreign public opinion, American. 2. Islam—Public opinion. 3. Public opinion—United States—History—19th century. 4. Middle East—Study and teaching—United States—History—19th century. 5. Islam—Relations—Christianity. 6. Christianity and other religions—Islam. I. Duke University. Islamic and Arabian Development Studies. II. Title.
    ISBN 0-89386-029-8 (hc)
    DS63.2.U5S33 1990
    303.48'273056–dc20   89-82248
                                                                          CIP

Printed in the United States of America

CONTENTS

FOREWORD

This study by Dr. Fuad Sha'ban is weighted with a special relevance and urgency by the congruence of several events occurring during the last few decades. One of these events, found in the United States, has antecedents which can be traced as far back as the founding of Plymouth Colony. I refer to contemporary millenarianism, which has become enmeshed in the web of a Christian quest for Zion, thereby contorting our perception of Islamic and Arab affairs. This phenomenon has been explored and popularized by Edward Said's *Orientalism*. In the present work by Professor Sha'ban it is explored in greater depth by analysis of both literary and religious texts and behavior from our colonial beginnings to the time of Ulysses S. Grant.

It is well known to anyone who has studied the diffusion of Islam and Arab civilization in the West that both confront a seemingly ineradicable antagonism. It is common to trace this feeling to the Crusades of the 12th and 13th centuries which generated a paranoic repugnance toward Islam. This was reflected in canto 28 of Dante's *Inferno* which consigns Mohammad and Ali to the ninth *bolgia* along with the most dangerous sowers of discord and disunity (*seminator di scadalo e di scisma*). Mohammad is regarded as the figure who promoted the greatest schism in the Christian world, and his punishment—being split from chin to crotch— is the cruelest described in the *Inferno*. Allegorical though it is, the *Inferno* was undoubtedly a reflection of mediaeval thought; the Crusades were in progress, though waning, during Dante's lifetime and were undoubtedly the single most momentous international event of the period. This attitude, more latent than explicit in recent times, was resuscitated by Salman Rushdie's *Satanic Verses* (1988), in which much of the metaphoric and allegorical vituperation of the Middle Ages was restored in contemporary literary garb. This stunning reminder of an almost forgotten period of hatred accounts for much of the Muslim world's reaction to the Rushdie book.

There are many reasons for this perception of Islam by Christendom and the West. A third Abrahamic monotheism, emerging after only eight centuries, incorporated some of the doctrine of its two predecessors and claimed to be the final and superior divine revelation. Unlike the older faiths of Hinduism, Buddhism, Judaism, and the secular faiths of Taoism and Confucianism, it was activated by a dynamic zeal for global propagation which directly confronted the same Christian impulse. Christian territoriality was threatened by the dynamism as Islam spread in Asia and Africa and to the very threshold of Vienna. It destroyed the possibility of a world coterminous with Christendom. It continues today to manifest a vigor and zeal which other major religions have lost.

The ancient antagonism between the Christian West and Islam continues to be evident in the contemporary world. It is well developed in a variety of sources and is traced through some strands of literature by Edward Said in his *Orientalism* and in politics and print and audiovisual media by such works as *Split Vision* edited by Edmund Ghareeb, *The TV Arab* by Jack Shaheen, Michael W. Suleiman's *The Arabs in the Mind of America*, Edward Said's *Covering Islam*, and Grace Halsell's *Prophesy and Politics*. Its nadir in the realm of political disinformation was reached when Amos Perlmutter, writing in the *Wall Street Journal* of October 4, 1984 ("The Containment Strategy for the Islamic Holy War"), characterized the bombing of the American Embassy in Beirut as being "under the banner of an Islamic *jihad*." "It is," he continued, "a general Islamic war waged against the West, Christianity, modern capitalism, Zionism and communism all at once." American policy must "decide that our war against Moslem populism is of the utmost priority, not the long-term struggle against the Soviet Union." He thus raised the threat of holy war (*jihad*), a complex doctrine now loosely used by Muslem militant groups but the application of which is repudiated by most of the Muslem world. This assertion of the universal enmity of Islam is gross hyper-generality of the complex political positions of forty-six avowedly Islamic nations and one billion Muslems scattered over the globe. Its defiance of history is suggested by a few events selected from many. Morocco was the first nation to recognize the sovereign independence of the United States and has remained a friendly nation ever since. Iran under the Shah was a close ally and a bulwark of American policy in the area. Pakistan has had close military and economic ties with the United States since 1953. Malaysia and Indonesia have had cordial relations; Bangladesh has had close economic aid-receiving ties. The Gulf States, especially Oman and Saudi Arabia, have been important economic and strategic partners with the United States. Egypt and Lebanon have maintained postures of friendship. Syria in its revolt against French occupation in the 1940s took the American Constitution as its model. Jordan remains a constructive influence in the quest for peace in the Middle East. The Perlmutter assertion is the culmination of centuries of defamed imagery.

Added to this seven-century-old legacy of suspicion, if not hostility, are several new contemporary factors. The first of these is the Arab-Israeli conflict, which results in massive campaigns of disinformation and vituperation damaging to Islam and to the Arab image. The second is the rise of Arab militancy and bellicosity, the consequence of frustration over Palestine, but seemingly supporting (however unfairly) misconceptions of terrorism, belligerence, and intransigence. Distortion of the concept of holy war (*jihad*) is symbolic of this. In its most profound sense, *jihad* is man's internal struggle between good and evil. The third factor, dealt with so comprehensively by Professor Sha'ban, is peculiar to American culture. It is the phenomenal rise in the United States in visibility and political power of evangelical fundamentalist Protestant Christianity with its emphasis on the Old Testament and on "biblical inerrancy," i.e., the literal interpretation of Scripture perceived as the infallible word of God. This doctrine emphasizes the special status of Israelites and Zion and warns that divine retribution will be meted out to whoever disagrees. This is coupled by what might be called the Judaization of Christianity, in which the Judaic antecedents of Christian doctrine and Jewish genealogy of Christ and the Holy Family are given so much emphasis that the distinctions between the two religions are blurred, if not lost. The propagation of these ideas by highly effective television preachers, the foremost of whom has been the Reverend Jerry Falwell, powerfully reinforces earlier misconceptions by linking Judaism and Christianity and, by implication, isolating Islam as the enemy of both. Since these ideas touch the very essence of the Arab-Israeli dispute, namely, the status of Palestine and Jerusalem, they are hardly conducive to increasing an empathy for Islam or for Arabs. O. Kelly Ingram has analyzed this phenomenon as Christian Zionism (*The Link*, Vol. 16, November 1983).

This Old Testament literalism is limited to a small, but effective, portion of American Protestant evangelicals found mostly in the South and Southwest. The statement of policy adopted unanimously by the National Council of Churches in 1980 is quite different from the fundamentalists' views and is very similar to the Vatican's position. Both the Roman Catholic and the Orthodox churches show a greater appreciation of Islam and an affinity with Arab culture. The existence of the Pontifical Institute of Arabic Studies and the policies enunciated by the Second Vatican Council, as well as the Twenty-Four Declarations issued by the Vatican-Muslim Conference in Libya in 1976, make this clear. The

Roman church embraces within its fold a variety of Eastern Orthodox rites, in some of which Arabic is the liturgical language. Ironically, the Crusader legacy and the conquest of Spain, both occurring in the context of an undivided Christendom, have not resulted in a theological or institutional antagonism towards Islam in the Catholic Church. That feeling now resides in the evangelical fundamentalist realm. Telling evidence of this can be seen in the official Vatican stand on Palestinian rights, Jerusalem, the nonrecognition of the State of Israel, and Vatican pronouncements on Islam. A recent comprehensive review of the Vatican's position was given by Archbishop Renato R. Martino, Permanent Observer of the Holy See to the United Nations, "The Holy See and the Middle East" at a Fordham University Colloquium, April 10, 1989. The Vatican's stand is in stark contrast with fundamentalist views on these issues. This view is shared totally by Greek Orthodoxy and, to a lesser extent, by the Episcopal and Presbyterian churches.

The vision of Zion portrayed in the present work of Dr. Sha'ban shows the depth of these beliefs which have now come to the fore in the context of the Arab-Israeli question. It reveals a dimension which has heretofore been eclipsed, or at least isolated, from the political context of our times. He shows us incontrovertibly that fundamentalist views of Zion are not new, but are deeply rooted in American 19th century literary and religious sources. They are strengthened by antecedent views of the Crusades against the "infidel" allegorized in the *Inferno* and are given new meaning and strength by contemporary events which plunge them into the maelstrom of global politics. The consequence is that the emotional circumstances sustaining a Western alienation with Islam and Arabs are given new meaning. American attitudes towards Islam and Arabs are not the consequence of Palestinian desperation over the 1948 establishment of Israel. It is the millenarian attitude, embedded in Old Testament prophesy linked with the quest for a New World Zion fantasized in such place names as Salem, Sinai, Nazareth, Providence, New Jerusalem, Bethel, Mount Olive, New Bethlehem, Zion, and similar New World communities that distorts our perceptions. The appeal is dangerously subliminal. The New Jerusalem of fantasy is materialized in the recreation of the Old Jerusalem. Since 1948 much Christian doctrine, prayers, and hymns have been modified to eliminate suggestions of Jewish blame for the crucifixion of Christ. A comparable expurgation of the myth of Zion and its equation with contemporary Israel is needed before Islam can be placed in its proper historical and theological relationship with Judaism and Christianity.

But the identification and classification of sources of thought and the construct of their patterns of relationship is a critical step in correcting false imagery. Dr. Sha'ban has gone beyond the "Orientalist" exposition in revealing the profundity of this attitude and the web of relationships in literature and religion.

For those interested in widening the appreciation of Islamic and Arab culture, this is not a revelation which can be greeted with joy or with equanimity, even though its masterful and objective exposition must be regarded with respect and admiration.

Ralph Braibanti
James B. Duke Professor of Political Science
Duke University
King Faisal Distinguished International Lecturer
American-Arab Affairs Council

May 1990

PREFACE AND ACKNOWLEDGMENTS

Certain basic factors in the history and culture of the West have contributed to the formation of an awesome and authoritative institution known as Orientalism. As a result of the cumulative efforts of this institution, the Orient has become the object of intense and uncompromising feelings in the West.

In a seminal work on the subject, Edward Said describes Orientalism historically and materially as "the corporate institution for dealing with the Orient—dealing with it by making statements about it, authorizing views of it, describing it, by teaching it, settling it, ruling it: in short, Orientalism is a Western style for dominating, restructuring, and having authority over the Orient."[1] Orientalism, accordingly, is the generic term which describes the Western approach to the Orient and which designates "that collection of dreams, images, and vocabularies available to anyone who has tried to talk about" the Orient.[2]

American Orientalism—as distinguished from European (principally French, British, and German Orientalism)—has derived from those as well as native sources. While drawing on the basic premises presented by Said, of Orientalism as discourse and as knowledge for domination, I will explore and analyze the factors in American history and culture responsible for the institution which I call American Orientalism.

American Orientalism is a phenomenon which finds expression in certain attitudes and behavior towards the Orient and Orientals. It is an American experience stemming from a historically-conscious process of self-analysis which has been reflected in America's relations with things Oriental. American Orientalism is, in short, a national cultural dialogue which derives from European background, heritage and influence on the one hand, and, on the other, stems from particularly American factors and experience.

The Orient as dealt with here is the geographical area which consists of present-day Turkey, Iran, the Levant, Arab North Africa, and other Muslim African territories. In the nineteenth century this is what was referred to in the West as the Ottoman Empire and its Eastern Muslem dominions, including North Africa. The term "Orientals" refers to the peoples who live in this geographical area. In the West they were variously called Turks, Muhammadans, Arabs, and Muslems. The most important part of this Orient for Americans in the nineteenth century was the Holy Land and its immediate surroundings, and it is this Orient which was the main object of American Orientalist thinking and behavior throughout the century. Spiritually, Americans felt very close to this Orient; indeed they identified themselves with the Holy Land from the times of the earliest settlements established by English immigrants in the New World, as will be seen in the course of this study. In a sense, Paris and London were no closer to the Orient than Salem, Massachusetts or Salt Lake City.

America developed a definite Orientalist cultural attitude from its beginning and, with variations and a change in direction, has sustained it ever since. In order to treat the development of this attitude, it will be necessary to isolate from American cultural history some of the important concepts and beliefs which were essential to the formation of American social and political thinking. Considered separately, these national concepts and beliefs may seem irrelevant to the treatment of American Orientalism, but their combination, interaction, and progress shaped America's self-image and, by contrast, its image of the Orient and consequent attitude.

From the very beginning, immigrants to the New World considered themselves chosen people and America the land of promise. With Independence, this concept took on added significance and the new state became the symbolic Kingdom of God. This, very briefly, was the basis of American Orientalism. It was, so to speak, the westward expression of an American Orientalist dialogue. At the beginning of the nineteenth century a group of events and experiences gave added dimensions and a redirection to American Orientalism; America went to war against the North African Muslim states; commercial and diplomatic relations were gradually established between America and the various dominions of the Ottoman Empire; there was a surge of missionary enthusiasm and operations carried out by Americans in these dominions, especially in the Holy Land; the Oriental tour became a popular American activity. As a result of these events and of other contributing factors, the symbolic Kingdom of God in America was replaced by a more physical aspiration to establish that Kingdom in the Holy Land. The early immigrants looked forward to the establishment of God's American Israel in the New World. Many enthusiastic nineteenth-century Americans were dedicated to the fulfillment of the vision of Zion in the Holy Land. All shared the firm belief that they, as Americans, were destined to play a principal role in such an undertaking.

Although the treatment of these factors and activities seem to arrange them in neat and separate compartments, it is important to realize that this is done for the sake of clarity, not oversimplification. In reality, they were interrelated and interdependent. The dependence of American activities in the Orient on the formative factors in American history on the one hand, and, on the other, the interaction and overlapping of these activities, are what gave American Orientalism its continuity and steady growth into a complete and self-sustaining institution by the end of the nineteenth century.

American discovery of the Orient came at a time when America's concept of itself as the ideal state was at its height, and when the nation was launching itself on the world scene as a power to be reckoned with. The United States was also experiencing a religious revival which permeated most sectors of the society. These two factors were vital in shaping America's attitude to and treatment of the "others." This was particularly true in America's dealing with the Orient. Americans were applying to their external relationships—neighbors especially—the concept of Manifest Destiny. This stance was particularly applicable in the case of the Orient, where the American missionary enterprise was well established.

Manifest Destiny, Adventist, and Millennial tendencies, patriotic enthusiasm, missionary zeal, all went into play when Americans flocked to the Holy Land and decided to extend to it the "blessings" they enjoyed back home. The transfer of the American "Land of Promise" to the "Promised Land" was inevitable and the rebuilding of the City of the Great King was a vision to be fulfilled in obedience to the will of God. Everything seemed to fall into place within a providential plan. The discovery of the New World was perceived as part of that plan, as was the rediscovery of the Holy Land. Throughout the first three centuries of the life of the American nation, its people saw everything they did as part of that plan; in the nineteenth century its outlines became much clearer with the central position occupied by a vision of Zion as it was to be realized in the Holy Land, and with Americans taking part in bringing about the great event. Looking back to the beginning of creation, Americans saw their continent as ready and waiting for the fullness of time, and looking at the many contemporary signposts they envisioned the Coming Kingdom ready to be born in New Jerusalem. In both contexts, they recognized their central position as the seed of Abraham and beneficiaries to the promise. A tendency to extend American values and beliefs to the rest of the world was an integral part of American Orientalism. Orientals were the "others" to whom "we" Americans should extend the blessings we enjoy. The religious missionary enterprise was not the only expression of this tendency; there were various other expressions in politics, economics, the military, and the sciences. But in spite of the variety of expressions, there was a commonality in the American Orientalist experience which could be seen in the behavior of American tourists, diplomats, missionaries, and others in the Orient, as well as in statements made by fellow Americans back home. The following chapters will attempt to present a comprehensive and integrating study of various aspects of this experience.

In the final analysis, American Orientalism is the total and combined awareness by Americans of the Orient and its peoples, and the attitude towards the Orient which resulted from the American cultural makeup and actual contact with the Orient. Some of this awareness derived from the extensive knowledge and materials about Islam and Muslims which were available to Americans of all walks of life. Such a body of information was one of the factors which preconditioned the American attitude to the Orient and Orientals. So did the widespread popularity of the *Arabian Nights* and its imitations. In fact, because of this kind of literature, the Orient often represented to Americans a world of dreams and romance.

Given the nature of these preconditioning factors in American cultural development and education, when Americans traveled to the Orient they were in most cases seeking to fulfill the vision of Zion or the dream of Baghdad. This is the focal point of American Orientalism as it appeared in the nineteenth century. I have quoted profusely from a variety of texts with the aim of letting Americans speak in their own voices; the material used is drawn not only from the writings of prominent American statesmen, intellectuals, and men of letters, but also from those of the common man. These writings illustrate the pervasiveness of the Oriental motif in American life.

I have not attempted to treat American Orientalism beyond the nineteenth century because, first, as a modern institution its existence has not been in doubt, and, second, American Orientalism during the present century has merged with international political issues which lie beyond the scope of this work. It is obvious, however, that the modern development of American Orientalism is to a great extent a continuation of the formative stages dealt with here. It seems obvious to me also that by the end of the Civil War, when American officers and soldiers flocked to Egypt, American Orientalism had become an active, though perhaps not an organized, institution.

As an Arab Muslem, I have approached this subject with some trepidation. Much of the material I have dealt with is obnoxious to me, but I hope that I have not allowed my feelings to interfere with an objective treatment of the subject.

I have consistently used the spellings Muhammad, Al-Qur'an, and Muslem because they are closer to the Arabic pronunciation. I realize that "Muslem" is not the usual rendition, but it is, in my view, the correct one. I have, however, retained the original spelling of these words in quoted texts.

During the years spent on this research, I accumulated debts of gratitude to many people. The Bibliography will serve as a partial acknowledgment to those who preceded me in dealing with some aspects of this subject.

In 1982–83 when I was Visiting Scholar at Duke University, on sabbatical from Damascus University, James B. Duke Professor Ralph Braibanti, Director of Islamic and Arabian Studies at Duke, invited me to hold the position of Senior Research Fellow, also providing me with office accomodations, secretarial assistance, and occasions to participate in the Outreach Lecture Program. I am grateful for this opportunity and the amenities. Most of all, I am grateful for Professor Braibanti's continued interest in my research and for the many hours of discussions with him which clarified a number of points and made this work a pleasure. Down through the years, my association with Professor Braibanti has been an inspiration.

While at Duke University I also had many interesting sessions with Professors Clarence Gohdes, Louis Budd, and Buford Jones. Their ideas and comments were very useful to me, even when we disagreed on some points. Professor Budd also read the manuscript, made many helpful suggestions, and wrote the Introductory Essay. I am very grateful to each of these scholars.

The Perkins Library at Duke University is an ideal venue for serious research, not only by virtue of its large collection of material, but also for the helpful attitude of its staff. Many persons, especially those working in the Reference, Manuscripts, Rare Book, Documents, and Interlibrary Loan Departments, cheerfully offered their expert assistance to provide the material needed. I am grateful to the Manuscript Department for permission to quote from the "Bergh" and "Andrews" papers.

I also wish to mention with gratitude the Administrations of the Universities of Damascus and the United Arab Emirates for their support, and my colleagues and students at both institutions for sharing their reactions to some of the ideas dealt with in this work.

While working with original material on missionary activities, my search led me to the collections of the Office of History of the Presbyterian Study Center at Montreat, North Carolina. I am grateful to the Curator for allowing me to use their facilities and holdings for my research.

I wish also to thank Mrs. Marion Salinger, Ms. Wendy Simonetti, and Mrs. Rebecca Royal McLoughlin for preparing the manuscript for publication.

Finally, I am grateful to my wife, Mary, and our children, Marwan, Sami, Rana, and Omar, for the patience they exercised throughout the process of research and writing. Mary also typed several versions of the manuscript, proofread and corrected many errors, and made helpful comments and critiques.

Fuad Sha'ban

May, 1990   Al-Ain, United Arab Emirates

INTRODUCTORY ESSAY

In 1878 a now forgotten humorist caught the public's fancy with "A Threnody," which began:

What, what, what
What's the news from Swat?
Sad news,
Bad news
Cometh by the cable led
Through the Indian Ocean's bed,
Through the Persian Gulf, the Red
Sea and the Med-
Iterranean—he's dead—
The Akhoond is dead!

The third of its four irregular stanzas best typifies its condescension:

Mourn, city of Swat,
Your great Akhoond is not,
But laid 'mid worms to rot—
His mortal part alone, his soul was caught
(Because he was a good Akhoond!)
Up to the bosom of Mahound.
Though earthly walls his frame surround
(Forever hallowed be the ground!)
And skeptics mock the lowly mound
And say He's now of no Akhoond!"
His soul is in the skies—
The azure skies that bend above his loved
metropolis of Swat.
He sees, with larger, other eyes,
Athwart all early mysteries—
He knows what's Swat.

"A Threnody" came from George T. Lanigan(1845–1886), a "literary comedian" who, as one way of earning his keep, wrote poems for the Sunday edition of the *New York World*.[1] Other newspapers across the country applauded it; an anthologist reprinted it later in the same year (and it still appears in several collections of light verse). Eugene Field, a well-remembered newspaper poet and humorist, would complain during the presidential election of 1884:

> When the writer has written with all of his might
> Of Blaine and of Cleveland a column or more,
> And the editor happens along in the night
> (As he generally does betwixt midnight and four)
> And kills all the stuff that that writer has writ,
> And calls for more copy at once, on the spot—
> There is none for the writer to turn on and hit
> But that distant old party, the Akhoond of Swat.

"A Threnody" carried the epigraph: "The Akhoond of Swat is dead—London Papers of January 22, 1878." Very few readers knew or would care to learn more about him. It was enough that a tiny, faraway, presumably benighted territory had regarded him as a potentate. Two or three years later when Mark Twain, projecting the anthology that became his *Library of Humor*, planned to include material by Lanigan, he fumbled for the title of the poem on "that Eastern savage that died."[2] He would also plan to quote "A Threnody" in *Following the Equator*, although the book as printed would simply list the Akhoond of Swat among the "sumptuous" names of India.

That adjective underlines the important clue. Americans had reacted, from a haze of ignorance, to an unusual name. In spite of their ethnic mixture, they were quick to find comedy, more playful than malevolent, in a proper name outside their official tradition. If they had heard that the Akhoond—the spelling wavers according to the system of transliteration—had been named Abdul Ghafur they might have guessed a Muslim origin before laughing again, but only a rare expert could have pinpointed Swat more closely than Twain. If scolded for ethnocentrism, they would have protested that they saw no harm in the fun. When Lanigan elsewhere defined a "Musselman" as a "man of strength" he intended neither harm nor compliment.

Professor Fuad Sha'ban's *From Plymouth to Appomatox: The Genesis of Orientalism in America*, by mapping the contours of nineteenth-century attitudes, presents the serious setting for the literary comedians (as scholars have agreed to call them), who once lightened the columns of metropolitan as well as small-town newspapers with verse, anecdotes, sketches, and jokes. For the image of the Muslim they were both a result and a cause. Hungry for subjects because of a revolving deadline, they were driven to exploit any motif that might amuse readers. Petroleum Vesuvius Nasby (born David R. Locke), best known for his grassroots political humor, varied his repertoire with *The Morals of Abou Ben Adhem*, which hid a Yankee in a white turban and flowing black robe; the "imposture was a very safe one, for his auditors knew as little of Persia as he did."[3] Nasby also meant no harm. His con man did give sound, if florid, crackerbarrel advice free of charge.

Alert to every saleable technique and idea, the literary comedians honed parody into one of their slickest genres, and they inevitably used it upon the vogue of Orientalism among British authors. Abou Ben Adhem, every constant reader knew, borrowed his name from a famous, kindly poem by Leigh Hunt. As the literary comedians came to depend on a breezy irreverence of tone, the "Dream of Baghdad" made an especially inviting target, familiar to all. To prove the popularity that the Arabian Nights cycle enjoyed during the nineteenth century would be to labor the obvious; any skeptic needs only to scan the Union Catalogue from the Library of Congress for the myriad editions in English for various levels of readership. Though exotic fantasy is always vulnerable, its shapes spun out of Orientalism raised expectations so high that the honest traveler or stay-at-home realist would also feel driven to deflate them.

But the literary comedians were as much cause as effect, since they encouraged the currency of stereotypes. During the Crimean War they could poke fun at all sides.[4] Muslems, however, presented an attractive victim in the United States because they had few advocates to protest the distortion inherent in comedy. Furthermore, they allowed surefire laughs based on Western pride in a technology that made other cultures look backward, if not stupid. Beneath the guffaws, darker attitudes operated. The obligatory joking about the cruelty reported of Ottoman rulers may do credit to American humaneness, or may merely open another path for gallows humor—still, a reader today can also suspect a vicarious sadism. More certainly, the frequent joking about slave maidens, dancing houris, and harems appealed to prurient appetites that gentility kept hidden at home. (Few American males discussed the Mormons without an inner tingle about polygamy.) The Middle Eastern travel books of George W. Curtis and Bayard Taylor likewise titillated Victorian repression by sketching scenes forbidden to their own pallid novels.

Insularity is still stronger and broader than humor as a barrier to objective insights. Even those minds stretched across a nearby national boundary by the social sciences can relapse into fatigue as if they were to explore outer space. I know too little about other cultures to judge whether the United States is egregiously insular (and not merely by its tendency to monopolize the word "American"), but every country or tribe resists adjusting to the variety of humankind around the globe. Perhaps just because peoples do vary so wondrously, we keep retreating to stereotypes, to rigid images of "the others"—to use Professor Sha'ban's phrase.[5]

Not everyone in the United State has as yet managed to accept the distinctiveness of Western Europe or, closer to home, South and Central America; and Canada attracts tepid interest on the few campuses where it is studied by its close neighbor. Nevertheless, ignorance about the Muslem is astonishing for its tenacity among Americans. How many of them today would feel embarrassed by George William Curtis' once popular *Nile Notes of a Howadji* (1851)? It claimed hegemony for the West because the "Egyptians and Easterns" were "imbeciles"—"picturesque and handsome" but too torpid to copy the "clean, and comely, and comfortable" society he hailed from. "That the East will never regenerate itself, contemporary history shows."[6] Curtis, an active progressive at home, ignored contemporary Egyptian politics and religion. His reveries focused on its deepest layers of antiquity so soulfully that its descendants looked all the more degenerate.

His own descendants can judge him forgivingly because his blindness had several causes. New World democracy welcomed any opportunity to cheer onward the struggles for national liberation elsewhere, such as from the Austro-Hungarian Empire and, still more avidly, from the decaying Ottoman Empire. Specifically, the British and American literati grew bitterly anti-Turkish in behalf of Greek independence. In general, the dominant voices of the New World preached Protestantism as a beneficent cultural force. This article of faith justified elevating Jesus Christ far above Muhammad as a model for conduct. It also encouraged what a recent analyst calls "the Protestant Passion"—the "driving force of American history"—which created an "insatiable desire to redeem mankind from sin and error."[7] Though emphasizing the missionary impulse, Professor Sha'ban does not exaggerate its many-tiered influence, from intellectuals like Curtis on down to the barely literate millions whose only important book was the Bible—perhaps absorbed mostly through sermons and Sunday-school lessons. The mental and emotional expropriation of Palestine for Christianity was made explicit. Implicitly, the Bible was interpreted to glorify the social and economic values of the middle class. That synthesis of religion and the western work-ethic was echoed in the McGuffey Readers for all grades of the elementary schools.[8] Islam posed a further, active, and urgent challenge to the millennialists who preached that the Kingdom of God would not return to earth until all the heathen had been converted.

Historians of ideas can offer false comfort by diagramming a previous cast of mind. Since we can identify its mistakes, we have presumably overcome them. But the nineteenth-century blindness toward the Muslem persists. A black historian of ideas may give the soundest explanation by adding the factor of racism. After forbidding any official dogma, the polity of the United States developed a "civil religion," which he labels "Americanity." It has worked out a "mutually accommodative relationship" with Christianity and Judaism to establish a "semi-secular" creed that "grants to civil power the support and respectability of religion." Americanity includes faith in the altruism of its Manifest Destiny within global politics, where it carries the old white man's burden.[9] I add that Americanity has grown dangerously ahistorical. While regularly invoking a lofty past and promising a noble future, it learns little from the actual course of history.

Discussions of the mass mind tend to shift blame away from the intelligentsia. However, Professor Sha'ban treats the figures of the literary canon only briefly because he wants to reflect the spread of constituencies. Moreover, critics too easily take the presently canonical authors as representative or influential for their time. Herman Melville's *Clarel*, ignored in 1876, is now given great cultural significance. On the other hand, Washington Irving, whose prestige at one time could scarcely be exaggerated, has shrunk to a story or two in college anthologies and only a few specialists know about *Mahomet and His Successors*. Overall, the situation can oblige either the sanguine or gloomy observer. Many canonical authors enter briefly into Professor Sha'ban's pages because they did perceive a world beyond the Anglo-Saxon, European horizon. Yet they seldom wrote directly, much less empathetically, about the Muslem countries. As for the belletristic travelers to the Middle East, like Curtis or Taylor or Charles D. Warner, they misled or blinded the public more than they enlightened it.

Mark Twain offers the richest example among today's standard authors. Now mediating between high and low culture, he had aimed at a mass audience, and he remains so popular as to command interest for any subject. Yet the academicians discuss him more seriously each year, willing to forgive his ties to the literary comedians. He makes a fine reflector in both senses of the metaphor. He picked up mass attitudes accurately and quickly, and in turn he emitted and certainly affected them. While epitomizing misperceptions of the Muslem, in his final years he approached and perhaps contributed to a sounder insight.

Samuel L. Clemens began his climb toward Mark Twain in newspaper offices, which trained him as a spokesman to, if not for, Americanity. Along with politics, his reminiscences of boyhood include Bible tracts, which were often enlivened by drawings to arouse a child's imagination, and *The Innocents Abroad* casually remembers "that picture of the Queen of Sheba visiting Solomon." Furthermore, young Sam Clemens swallowed his doses of the McGuffey Readers dominated by solemn moralizing, but spiced with selections like "*The Arab and His Horse*." He had many other chances of encountering such tales, including those used by newspapers as a filler, for example. His autobiography remarks about a friend's son that "being seven years old, he was of course acquainted with the *Arabian Nights*," and *Following the Equator* (ch. 39) recalled those lively visions "when you were a boy and steeped your spirit in the tales of the East." Risen to a practicing journalist, Twain now and then drew on the "Dream of Baghdad" for a familiar example or comparison. In 1867, exclaiming over the first girlie musical in New York City, he built up to the "whole tableau resplendent with columns, scrolls, and a vast ornamental work, wrought in gold, silver and brilliant colors—all lit up with gorgeous theatrical fires, and witnessed through a great gauzy curtain that counterfeits a soft silver mist! It is the wonders of the Arabian nights realized."[10]

His first acclaimed book, *The Innocents Abroad* (1869), vibrated with his tension between fantasy (more exotic than pious in his case) and the disillusionment that struck many a Christian pilgrim to the Middle East. Though Twain brought along images from his Sunday-school classes, his latent agnosticism soon let him toy with them sardonically. But ethnic stereotypes, themselves overlapping, intersected confusingly with religious groupings. In the 1860s Twain was still mindlessly anti-Semitic, that is, Anti-Judaic. While in Palestine he did wonder, however, if the Israelites of the Old Testament had not been Arabs on every other count.[11] Fortunately for the total results anyway, perplexity seldom blocked him from producing the copy he needed to make a living.

Muslems perplexed Twain enough on their own. Ashore in Morocco on the voyage out, he exulted about finding the "true spirit" of the Arabian Nights. Such romanticizing could not last, and his more recent travels in the Sandwich Islands should have inoculated him against it. He soon reported that the ruler of Morocco was a "soulless despot," as was Abdul Aziz, the Sultan of the Ottoman Empire. Because Syria was suffering under "inhuman tyranny" (–I wish Europe would let Russia annihilate Turkey a little"), he decided that its "people are naturally good-hearted and intelligent, and with education and liberty, would be a happy and contented race" (ch. 42). Nevertheless, other Arabs were inherently "savages," and Muslems were mired in "paganism." Whether from genetic or religious inferiority, the Middle East wallowed in dirt and foul odors that clouded any romance. There is no need to pile up examples of his jovially harsh humor, such as claiming that his towel and cake of soap "would inspire respect in the Arabs, who would take me for a king in disguise." Inevitably, he hinted at the prurient side of exoticism, most notably in his "Slave Girl Market Report" from Constantinople. His praise of the legendary Crusaders, intended tactically to soften his sarcasms about Protestant smugness, sounded fervent when set next to his slurs about the Arabs he saw.

Twain's little-known O'Shah letters in 1873 partly deserve their obscurity, but it may also result from later lack of interest in their subject. Because he was already in England, the *New York Herald*, which prided itself on its foreign coverage, hired him to write up the state visit of Nasr-Ed-Din of Persia. More than Twain let on here, he realized that the European powers were maneuvering for spheres of influence or, more crassly, for economic penetration of the Middle East. But in joking about British efforts to "impress" the Shah, he essentially ignored imperialism. By then a professional humorist, he met the expectations of the *Herald*, which puffed each of his five O'Shah ("O, pshaw"?) letters with jaunty editorials about a "passionate child of the East" and his "pampered despotism."[12]

Twain dutifully condescended from democratic heights. Emphasizing Oriental ignorance and cruelty rather than glamor, he featured a "splendid barbarian, who is lord over a few deserts and a modest ten million of ragamuffins." For instance, the Shah "never sees any impropriety in chopping a subject's head off for the mere misdemeanor of calling him too early for breakfast." Wryly if not confusingly, after declaring "our religion is the right one, and has fewer odd and striking features than any other," Twain did concede that, remembering how "our ancestors used to roast Catholics and warm their hands by the fire, the Persians "are really our brothers after all." In a better apology, he equivocated later that the humor in the letters "was not his but was added by a *Herald* employee without authorization."

The critics who revere *Adventures of Huckleberry Finn* are startled to learn that while Twain was finally finishing his masterpiece during the summer of 1883 he also put major effort into "*1,002^d Arabian Night*." Having completed over 20,000 words and 131 drawings, he wanted to publish it, perhaps anonymously, "right after Huck." But everybody who read the manuscript discouraged him, surely because its parody of Scherezade's longwindedness is self-destructing. Nobody since then has perceived literary or comic merit in "*1,002^d Arabian Night*."[13] Nor do its raucously cheerful yet superior tones lead to a sounder acceptance of Islam; curiously, its reader finds no reason to suspect that the author had ever visited the Middle East. Soon, however, Twain's comedy did call for much more serious thinking, although he left no glaring clue as to why, in the early 1890s he would already turn skeptical about western imperialism or would apply to Islam his gift for soaring beyond nativist and even anthropocentric vision.

Tom Sawyer Abroad (1894) has never rated as a major novel. Therefore only children and scholars know that its first chapter ridicules the by making Tom fail to convince Huck and Jim that Christianity should "go and take the land away from the people who own it." That sympathy for the rights and customs of the living inhabitants colored the trio's adventures in North Africa and Egypt. Also, when drawing on five tales from the Arabian Nights, *Tom Sawyer Abroad* leaned toward friendly irony and workaday problems rather than romanticism.[14] Therefore *Following the Equator* (1897) may backslide when its India chapters invoke the Arabian Nights for atmosphere. Still, while primarily conscious of Hinduism, it now and then notices the Muslem culture and Mughal tradition much more respectfully than readers of *The Innocents Abroad* could anticipate. Twain was slowly becoming a shrewd cosmopolitan. The "Conclusion" of *Following the Equator* presented as its epigraph: "I have traveled more than anyone else, and I have noticed that even the angels speak English with an accent."

Twain was growing away not only from Protestant insularity, but also its optimism. In 1898 he wrote forty-five somber quatrains modeled on Edward Fitzgerald's *Rubaiyat*, without parody.[15] About the same time he began struggling with his dark, relativistic manuscripts centered on a "Mysterious Stranger." After 1900 he boldly confronted the expansionism of the industrialized powers. The title of his most effective essay, "To the Person Sitting in Darkness," was made savagely ironical. During the final ten years of his life he accused Western missionaries as the sometimes naive, sometimes willing agents of greed that destroyed alien cultures in the name of progress. Still, Twain's admirers must always pull up short of hagiolatry on any score. For instance, in order to attack Mary Baker Eddy as a new religious despot he would argue that "Christian Science, like Mohammedanism, is restricted to the unintelligent, the people who do not think."[16]

The ultimate, dangerous reality is that someone so capable of elemental human warmth (as well as venom) and so venturesome as Twain could not reach an adequate, stable objectivity toward the Muslem. Though he learned to reject the missionarying animus, he kept honoring the Manifest Destiny of the United States as the embodiment of progress for supposedly benighted societies. Though his experiences on the silver and gold frontier, and then in Hawaii, should have awakened him, the "Dream of Baghdad" was so bewitching that he could never clear his eyes or even stop resenting the mundane people and places he found instead. Or, sometimes hungry for applause instead of just royalties, he sagged into a literary comedian again. Like Lanigan and other hacks, he could not resist exploiting the stereotypes the public liked to see. In the overall accounting for Twain's career, his flexibility of heart and mind helps to explain why he has lasted up into our times, beyond a horde of competitors, and how he did move toward a genuine empathy with "the others." Nevertheless, Americans at best moved toward such a perception so erratically that Professor Sha'ban would perceive the need for this study.

He combines objectivity with empathy because his Middle Eastern origins are balanced by education in the United States and close personal bonds. Fully aware of British and European Orientalism, he does not indict Americans as being particularly misled. Rather, he strikes an engaging tone; avoiding sardonic irony or even scolding, he allows readers to form their own verdict. While comprehending the pressures that pit nations against each other, he concentrates on the operative attitudes within the United States, not its rivalries. But his Introduction outlines his demonstrable insights so capably that no Foreword needs to anticipate them. It needs only to regret that he had to be heroically selective about a subject radiating in many rich directions.

Surely Professor Sha'ban, while examining the United States, has made Oriental culture clearer to the West. His book warns once more that the world is round, that intellectual sins will orbit back to punish their source. The conscience of nineteenth-century westerners must have suffered, at some level, for excluding the Muslim from shared humanity. Their descendants can do for themselves not the penance but the boon of learning better, because reality is more satisfying and safer than ignorance or fantasy. Professor Sha'ban will help them meet the Muslim with sound curiosity, openness, and pleasure.

Louis J. Budd
James B. Duke Professor of English
Duke University

May 1990

1

A PLACE FOR MY PEOPLE
The Pilgrims in the New World

"I will appoint a place for my people Israell, and I will plant
them, that they may dwell in a place of their owne, and
move no more." (Second Samuel; 7:10)
John Cotton, "God's Promise to his Plantation."

Puritan beliefs and the Puritan way of life have had a continuous and
lasting influence on prevailing American religious, as well as secular,
tendencies and in the shaping of American history. This influence can be
seen in the evolution of the American governmental system, in social
behavior and habits, in the various religious movements such as the
Great Awakening and the Revivals, in the missionary tendencies of the
American nation, and in the sociopolitical attitudes of Americans
towards the "others,"—Muslems and Arabs in particular. The influence
of Puritanism on the development of American thinking is best described by the modern American religious historian Sidney E. Ahlstrom,
who says that "the architects of the 'Puritan way' [were]...in a very real
sense the founders of the American nation," and that "Puritanism, for
weal or woe, provided the theological foundation and molded the
prevailing religious spirit in virtually all the commonwealths which
declared their independence in 1776. With lasting effects and hardly less
directness it conditioned the people's social and political ideals."[1]

It is indeed in the Puritan beginnings of the American nation that we
should look for the formative factors which shaped America's image of
itself, its self-awareness and analysis, and, by contrast, its awareness of
and attitude towards the Arab world, its land and people.

It is unnecessary for the present study to relate the story of the settlement of the New World and the subsequent religious, political and social
developments of the American people. The story is well-known and has
been documented many times over by able historians.[2] However, it is
important to present a number of ideas and themes in order to explore
the way in which they contributed to the shaping of the American con-

1

cept of Arabs, Muslems, and their part of the world. This selection is not the result of a random process, neither is it inclusive; only a few of the most influential and popular ideas will be treated. The aim of this analysis is to show how these ideas have influenced, in varying degrees, the basic attitude of Americans toward the Arabs and Muslems, and how this attitude shaped their behavior when they came into contact with them.

Briefly, the selection includes the following ideas:

1. The existence of an overall providential plan within which the Puritans and Pilgrims saw their immigration to the New World and the role which was assigned them by God.
2. The conviction that those Protestants who emigrated from Europe (especially from England), and settled in the New World were God's people, chosen by divine ordinance to escape the corruption and iniquities of the Old World.
3. The settlers in America enjoyed a convenantal relation with the Creator and were thus partners in a divine mission.
4. As convenanted people, Americans saw their religious community as the Church of Visible Saints and considered the members of that community to be citizens in the Kingdom of God.
5. Partnership in the covenant implied the awesome duty of enlightening and saving the rest of the world.

These ideas are by their very nature visionary and idealistic. They continued to shape the behavior and attitude of American private individuals and public figures, at least until the end of the nineteenth century. Furthermore, in spite of an idealistic and visionary nature—perhaps one should say *because* of it—these ideas frequently resulted in encouraging a superior, sometimes racist, attitude towards the rest of mankind.

The Pilgrim Fathers and the Providential Plan

The principle of a providential plan is a central concept in Puritan theology and behavior. Puritans saw every detail in their daily life, indeed in life generally, as the unfolding of a providential plan which existed from the beginning of time. That is to say, the hand of Providence governs their actions and their destiny, as well as the shape and existence of things in the universe. Nothing happens in vain; everything leads to a preconceived goal. In Puritan diaries and journals—Samuel Sewall's *Diary* is a good example—it can be seen to what extent the belief in Providence influenced the thinking of the Puritans and their way of life. It was within the framework of this providential plan that the Pilgrims saw their journey to the New World. As agents of God's will, the Pilgrim Fathers considered the founding of their communities in the New World as a sign of manifest, divine election and favor.[3]

The literature shows that from the selection of a particular group of people to emigrate to the New World to the choice of a special place for them—and the roles assigned them in the new life—all was considered to be part of the will of God. When John Cotton wrote his essay on "God's Promise to His Plantation," he quoted on the title page this passage from the Scriptures: "Moreover I will appoint a place for my people Israell, and I will plant them, that they may dwell in a place of their owne, and move no more (2 Sam. 7. 10.)."[4] Cotton presented the concept clearly when he told the settlers that "the appointment of a place for them...is the first blessing," and every single step from their selection to "the placing of a people in this or that country is from the appointment of the Lord."[5]

The first ecclesiastical historian of the new nation, Cotton Mather, deemed it necessary, later in the seventeenth century, to keep these thoughts alive in the memory of "the posterity of those that were the *undertakers*, lest they come at length to forget and neglect the *true interest* of New England." Mather's "reminder" elucidated this point:

> Briefly, the God of Heaven served as it were a *summons* upon the *spirits* of his people in the English nation; stirring up the spirits of thousands which never saw the *faces* of each other, with a most unanimous inclination to leave all the pleasant accommodations of their native country, and go over a terrible ocean, into a more terrible *desert*, for the pure enjoyment of all his ordinances.[6]

The immigrants settling in the New World, like the Protestants of Europe, believed in a providential plan. But what gave the concept added poignancy is that the immigrants, as well as their descendants, firmly believed that they held a special position in this plan. They were, as it were, hand picked, chosen by God for the fulfillment of His will. Thus it is that the Pilgrims and the subsequent generations of Americans were constantly applying to their situation the religious analogy of the "chosen people." The leader of one of the earliest groups of settlers, John Winthrop, saw the analogy even in God's punishment inflicted on his followers. "It may be by this means," he said, that God will induce them to repent of their former sins, and through that punishment save them from the "desease, which sends many amongst us untimelie to their graves and others to hell, soe he carried the Israelits into the wildernesse and made them forgett the flesh potts of Egypt, which was sorie pinch to them att first but he disposed to them good in th'end. Deut. 30.3.16."[7]

In the early religious dissenting movements and controversies, contending parties used these scriptural analogies to lend strength and credibility to their respective arguments. In *The Letters of Roger Williams to Winthrop*, for example, Williams saw the situation of his party and their case in the light of the persecuted "people of God, wheresoever scattered about Babel's banks, either in Rome or in England, etc." But to Winthrop, Williams said,

> Your case is the worst by far, because while others of God's Israel tenderly respect such as desire to fear the Lord, your very judgement and conscience leads you to smite and beat your fellow servants, expel them from your coasts, etc., and therefore, though I know the elect shall never finally be   forsaken, yet Sodom's, Egypt's, Amalek's, Babel's judgements ought to drive us out, to make our calling out of this world to Christ, and our election sure in him.[8]

In a different context, the case of the Christian settlers as God's chosen was used by Increase Mather to explain the intervention of divine power on the side of the settlers in their fights with the Indians. It was cause for prayer and rejoicing, he said, to realize "how often have we prayed that God would do for us as in the Days of Midian, by causing the Heathen to destroy one another, and that the Egyptians might be set against the Egyptians. The Lord hath answered that Request also." The Indian heathens were, in answer to the prayer of the settlers, killing each other, "yea not only such Indians as do pretend Friendship to the English...but also some of those that were once in Hostility against us, did help to destroy their own Nation, Friends and Kindred, that so they might do Service for us."[9]

If the settlers in the New World conceived of themselves as the chosen people of Scripture, it was only natural that their leaders should be portrayed as the Prophets and personalities of the Old and New Testaments. Many analogies of this kind can be seen in the writings of Americans down through the centuries. One interesting case is the eulogy by Increase Mather for the Governor of New England where the latter is described on his deathbed "like Jacob, [he] first left his council and blessing with the children gathered about his bed-side; and, like David, 'served his generation by the will of God.'" For the Governor's epitaph, Mather saw fit that "the words of Josephus about Nehemiah, the governor of Israel, we will now use upon this governour of New-England, as his Epitaph."[10]

This concept of Americans as God's people remained a constant factor in the thinking of American religious as well as lay leaders, although at times it took on certain variations and colorings to fit particular situations. Even George Washington, a man not known to mix religion with politics, in his "Address to the Hebrews of Savannah," compared the situation of the Israelites with that of the European emigrants to America. Washington expressed his hope that just as God had delivered the Israelites from oppression in Egypt,

> and planted them in the promised land, whose providential agency has lately been conspicuous in establishing these United States as an independent nation, still continue to water them with the dews of heaven, and to make the inhabitants of every denomination participate in the temporal and spiritual blessings of that people whose God is Jehovah.[11]

The analogy of the "Chosen People" was to play an important part in the tremendously popular Puritans;emulated by missionariesmissionary enterprise of the nineteenth century. A modern historian of American thought, Perry Miller, sums up the concept in the following words: "For many decades the Puritan colonies had been geographically set apart; the people had been thoroughly accustomed to conceiving of themselves as a chosen race, entered into specific covenant with God."[12]

The Covenant with God's Chosen People

The idea of a people "entered into specific covenant with God" had a strong hold on the minds and imaginations of Americans of successive generations. As a general rule, Protestant theology assumed that those who believed in the true Church of Christ had a special relationship with the Creator, referred to as the Covenant of Grace. The covenant implied not only God's favor by election, but also, and just as importantly, that demanding duties were enjoined upon the believers as a result of that election. For American Puritanism the covenant and its conditions were binding upon Americans, not simply as it related to religious affairs and devotions but daily life itself was expected to be governed by the covenant. Throughout the first three centuries of the history of the American nation, there were frequent statements which confirm this belief. Thus the Covenant has to be taken seriously if one is to understand the shape given by the Puritans to their religious as well as social and political institutions, leading to and including the American Declaration of Independence, the Constitution and the system of government.

The importance of this special relationship with the church and with God has been rightly emphasized by many historians of American religion. Sidney Ahlstrom, speaking of the Puritans, says that "the clue to their understanding of regeneration, as well as to their theories for ordering the church and society, is the *covenant*. It was around this point that the particular dogmatic interests of the English and later the New England Puritan theologians were oriented. Theirs was a *covenant theology*."[13] Ahlstrom quotes a contemporary Puritan, John Preston, who preached the principle that the covenant "is the ground of all you hope for, it is that that every man is built upon, you have no other ground but this, God hath made a Covenant with you, and you are in covenant with him."[14]

If this seems to suggest that the settlers had no choice but to be partners in the covenant, it is because it was so intended. Nor would they have had it any other way. The choice had been made for them by divine authority, and they willingly entered into the covenant. The best expressions of this covenantal relationship with God is found in the constitutions (sometimes called "compacts") of the earliest Puritan colonies in the New World. When he wrote the history of these communities, Cotton Mather spoke with total conviction of "the covenant whereto these Christians engaged themselves." As an example which should be emulated by other Christian communities, Mather "lay before all the Churches of God" the text of the Covenant of the Salem community "as it was then expressed and enforced."[15]

The text of the Salem Covenant,[16] as cited by Mather, illustrates the application of the concept of the Covenant to every aspect of life. It calls upon its members and followers to consider themselves to be the People of God, to renounce all ways of life contrary to the teaching of Jesus Christ, to act towards one another as he has instructed, to comport themselves decorously and in a brotherly fashion in church and society, to advance the gospel but not to offend others (including Indians), to obey their superiors and governors in church or state, to work and live as the stewards of the Lord and to bring up their children and influence their servants to acknowledge their relationship to God and the Covenant.

This, then, is the true covenant to which the first wave of settlers bound themselves. The conditions named therein were to regulate their relations with one another, with "those that are within or without," and with God. They were also to serve as the constitution for church and state, and, as we will see later, they were to figure in the subsequent formation of the political thinking and behavior of an independent America, beginning with the Founding Fathers. More important for the present study, this covenantal relation with God and the duties assumed by the people of the covenant, one of which was "to spread the light," were very instrumental in shaping the American attitude to, and perception of, other people—whether native Indians, Arabs, Muslims, or still others who stood outside the covenant.

Although they saw themselves as latter-day Israelites, the Puritans of New England did not rest their title to the chosen people simply on the similarity of their respective situations. They took the original promise made by God to Abraham as the basis of all subsequent covenantal partnerships. They thought of themselves as the "seed of Abraham" and beneficiaries to the promise given to him. They were also the faithful members of the true church of God; for a member of the community to qualify for the covenant and promise, membership in the church was a precondition.

A significant example of this connection between church membership and the covenant comes from one of the earliest records of the settlement of New England. Cotton Mather related how the new settlers at Salem, on their arrival in 1629 "resolved, like their father Abraham, to begin their plantation with 'calling on the name of the Lord.'" Although they had been advised to reach an agreement on the form of church government before they left for New England, all the immigrants could agree upon was the "general principle, that the reformation of the church was to be endeavoured according to the written word of God." Accordingly, they sought the advice of their "brethren at Plymouth" who gladly instructed them as to how they could find a lesson "in the laws of our Lord Jesus Christ, for every particular in their Church-order." Finally, and after obtaining the approval of the messengers of the church of Plymouth, "they set apart the sixth day of August, after their arrival, for fasting and prayer, for the settling of a Church State among them, and for their making a Confession of their Faith, and entering into an holy Covenant, whereby that Church State was formed."

The "Covenant of the Church State" was an establishment into which the whole community entered, once the general principles were agreed upon. It was, in a way, a communal baptism into the Church of Christ. But that was not enough. Every member of the community had to be admitted into the church through an individual profession of faith. "Some were admitted by expressing their consent unto their confession and covenant," some after submitting to oral (and some to written) examinations by giving answers to questions about religion "as might give satisfaction unto the people of God concerning them." Two points are paramount in this process: first, that the community was basically considered the "people of God" through an acceptance of the covenant of Abraham and "the children of the faithful were Church-members, with their parents; and that their baptism was a seal of their being so." Secondly, that every individual, before being admitted to a particular church, "should publickly and personally own the covenant; so they were to be received unto the table of the Lord."[17]

This early American formula of the covenant placed the American community, particularly confirmed church members, in a special position in the world, a position of which they were quite conscious from the beginning. With this special position firmly established, the association of the covenant, through descent from Abraham, gained in importance as Americans directed their efforts to evangelizing the rest of the world. To be qualified for the task, and to be a nation which partakes of divine favor and divine mission, devout Americans often identified themselves with biblical missionary characters and situations. But the most convincing connection used persistently was the succession from Abraham. In the context of nineteenth-century zeal for evangelizing the nations, Samuel Worcester presented this same argument in "Two Discourses" in 1805 (especially relevant because Worcester's "Discourses" were written in connection with missionary efforts). Briefly, his argument goes like this:

God treated all mankind in the way of the covenant, first through Adam, then Noah, then Abraham. "He made a covenant with Abraham" which he fulfilled by conferring His blessings on Abraham and all his posterity, and ultimately He bestowed this blessing on all humankind. "And in this way," said Worcester, "he continues to treat with mankind. All the blessings, which from generation to generation, he bestows upon the church and upon the world, are bestowed in pursuance of some existing covenant."[18] Since God said to Abraham "In thee all the nations shall be blessed," the blessings will eventually reach the whole world. There were conditions, however. A person had to be "of the faith" and to be baptized in the church through Christ. Baptism took the place of circumcision, a substitution deemed necessary to disprove the limitation of the promise to the Jews; and faith in the true church was a condition which gave Americans precedence over "nominal" Christians, Papists in particular. Worcester's conclusion drives the point home:

> For as many of you as have been baptized into Christ, have put on Christ. There is neither Jew nor Greek, there is neither bond nor free, there is neither male nor female; for ye are all one in Christ Jesus. And if ye be Christ's, then ye are Abraham's seed, and heirs according to the promise. If ye be Christ's, then are ye brought into a covenant relation to Abraham.[19]

The covenant is thus said to be in existence to the end of time and it includes all mankind—but those who accept Christ, and are of faith, are the children of Abraham; theirs is the responsibility of extending God's blessings to the rest of the world. Worcester therefore called on the American missionaries who were about to embark on their evangelical journey to the Holy Land to

> Go, and from the heights of Calvary and of Zion proclaim to the long lost tribes of Israel, to the followers of the Pseudo-prophet, to the bewildered people of different lands, tongues, and religions, the *fountains* there opened, for the cleansing of all nations—the banner there displayed, for the gathering of all people.[20]

The Journey As Pilgrimage to the Kingdom of God

For the religious-minded settlers in America and for prospective immigrants, journeys, pilgrimages and evangelical sojourning were not activities undertaken primarily for pleasure or even to satisfy intellectual curiosity. In fact, in the tradition of Protestant Christianity, the life of a Christian was considered a spiritual journey, a pilgrim's progress, aspiring to reach God's kingdom. Often this theme of the spiritual journey through life led to a symbolic holy land, as one can see from the titles *A Brief Account of my Soul's Travel Toward the Holy Land* (Isaac Penington) and *A Declaration to the World, of my Travel and Journey out of Egypt into Canaan through the Wilderness, through the Red Sea, from Under Pharoah* (Thomas Greene, 1659).[21] For the immigrants to the New World, the similarity which they saw between their conditions and those of the Israelites was not limited to the dangers faced in a new hostile environment; it actually became an extended spiritual metaphor in which biblical geography blended with real-life experiences and included the story of the flight from Egypt, crossing the desert and sea, and facing a vast inhospitable wilderness. On the eve of their departure to the New World, John Winthrop's followers listened to a sermon by John Cotton who, using the biblical association and idiom, assured them that "when God wrappes us in his ordinances and warns us with the life and power of them as with wings, there is the land of Promise."[22] And when William Bradford reflected on the miserable state of the Pilgrims after their voyage across the ocean, his language was reminiscent of scriptural experiences: Bradford recalled that "it is recorded in scripture as a mercie to the apostle and his shipwraked company, that the barbarians shewed them no small kindness in refreshing them, but these savage barbarians, when they mette with them (as after will appeare) were readier to fill their sides full of arrows then otherwise."[23]

In conclusion to this section of his *History*, Bradford asked: "what could now sustaine them but the spirite of God and his grace?" Should not the descendants of these settlers, asked Bradford, remember that their fathers were Englishmen which came over this great ocean,

> and were ready to perish in the wilderness.... Yea, let them which have been redeamed of the Lord, shew how he hath delivered them from the hand of the oppressour.[24]

The blend of realistic description of the pilgrims' plight with biblical idiom does not take anything away from Bradford's sincere sentiments and temporal concerns.

The same blend of sincere feelings, realism and biblical allusions informs Cotton Mather's description of the voyage and experience of the immigrants who arrived in New England in 1623, among whom "were diverse worthy and useful men, who were come to *seek* the welfare of this little Israel; though at their coming they were so diversely affected as the rebuilders of the Temple of Jerusalem: some were *grieved* when they saw *how bad* the circumstances of the friends were, and others were *glad* that they were *no worse*."[25]

But the Pilgrims were not daunted by the difficult circumstances which they faced; they were men of vision, and their aim was to "rebuild the Temple of Jerusalem." In the words of Vernon Parrington, "it was to set up a kingdom of God on earth that the Puritan leaders came to America."[26] This overriding concept of the kingdom of God within which the Puritans saw themselves as partners and co-workers with God is quite important for a proper understanding of American attitudes towards others who did not belong to the kingdom. It is also important because of the Puritan representation of the kingdom as a stage leading to more momentous events. The idea was recognized by William Bradford who, writing of the Pilgrims, said that

> A great hope and inward zeal they had, of laying some good foundation, or at least to make some way thereunto, for the propagating and advancing the gospell of the kingdom of Christ in those remote parts of the world; yea, though they should be but even as stepping stones unto others for the performing of so great a work.[27]

The idea of establishing the kingdom of God, or God's American Israel as it was called, was a dominant American religious vision throughout American history. In his excellent study, *The Kingdom of God in America,*

H. Richard Niebuhr describes the forms taken by this idea in American thought. "In the early period of American life," Niebuhr says, "when the foundations were laid on which we have all had to build, 'kingdom of God' meant 'sovereignty of God'; in the creative period of awakening and revival it meant 'reign of Christ'; and only in the most recent period had it come to mean 'kingdom on earth'."[28] In all of these stages, however, Americans considered themselves citizens of this kingdom, favored by the Governor and partners in a great enterprise; John Winthrop recognized this when he said that God may have "some great worke in hand whiche he hath revealed to his prophets among us."[29] American citizenship in this kingdom was never seriously challenged, and, consequently, as we shall see later, during the periods of Awakening, Independence and Revivals, Americans felt impelled by the sense of divine mission which comes with this citizenship to spread the light among other less fortunate nations.

Even while the first waves of Puritan settlers were busy establishing their new homes under very adverse conditions, they were constantly reminded of a sense of responsibility towards the "others", stemming from that special position which they assumed, in the providential plan. To be partners in the covenant and members of a chosen band in the church of grace brought certain privileges, but also heavier duties than those carried by ordinary men. The covenant was an essential condition for election and grace, but, once attained, this election puts the elect in a peculiar position vis-a-vis the rest of the world.

True Christians, and this is how the New England settlers saw themselves, are "the light of the world."[30] This is the way they were addressed in Scriptures: "Ye are the light of the world" (Math., v, 14). And the true Christian Church, the home of the Kingdom of God in the New World, is, to use Stephen Olin's phrase, the "depository and sole agent" of the Gospel.[31] This principle was essential for the Puritan settlers from the first day they set foot in the New World. John Winthrop's "Conclusions" advances practical, indeed very mundane, economic grounds for settling a "plantation in new England." The first justification, however, according to Winthrop, is "the propagation of the gospel to the Indian. Wherein first the importance of the worke tending to the inlargment of the Kingdome Jesus Christ;kingdom ofof Jesus Christ and winning them out of the snare of the Divell and converting others of them by their meanes."[32] Although other material grounds are advanced, spreading the light of the Gospel remains a top priority. This early missionary spirit is a forerunner to the zeal with which nineteenth-century American evangelists set out to convert the rest of the world. The missionary spirit, according to a nineteenth-century, devout American scholar, is "a vital element in Christian character [and] a fundamental principle of our holy religion. By an eternal law, whoever believes in Christ must proclaim him to others. Whoever embraces Christianity, must diffuse it." Finally, and that which is especially the lot of Americans, "whoever is converted to God, and through faith made a partaker of Christ's love, is by that very fact set apart to the work of saving others. He has a mission to fulfill in regard to the spread of religion."[33] This is how the settlers looked at their situation and at the rest of the world.

Just as the Pilgrims conceived of themselves as agents in God's plan to establish "His Kingdom," they and their descendants also assumed the inevitability of their mission to the rest of the world. Their church was the bearer of the true light and it was their duty to compete with the false missionaries of the "antichrist" in the New World, as their Protestant partners in the church were doing in the Old World. To be sure, one of the motives which prompted Winthrop and his company to establish a plantation in New England was "the Dilligence of the Papists in propagating their religion and superstition and enlarginge the kingdome of Antichrist thereby with all the manifest hazards of their persons and depe engagements of their estates."[34] The same conviction that theirs was the "true light" led nineteenth-century American missionaries to clash with the Roman Church and Islam in the Levant and in other parts of the world. They held to the belief that the Christian church as they conceived of it "is *the true light*, in distinction from all other systems, whether of religion or morals...[which] were for the most part positively and universally mischievous in their entire action and tendencies. They led to evil, and that continually."[35]

Prominent in this attitude are two characteristics which remained the hallmark of the American missionary enterprise and also distinguished the political attitudes of the newly independent nation in the nineteenth century. There is, for one thing, a sense of urgency and tremendous importance attached to this unique (perhaps even monopolistic) position of American Protestantism. Secondly, the missionary impulse, despite the dangers and pitfalls it involved, was optimistic of reaching fulfillment.

There was no doubt in the minds of the devout that God had elected this nation to be His agents in spreading the light. This was reflected time and again in the writings and sermons of American divines. "A sense of mission to redeem the Old World," says Frederick Merk, possessed the Pilgrim Fathers and their descendents which "appeared thereafter in successive generations of Americans" and remained unaltered.[36] One of these generations of mission-driven Americans was the mid-nineteenth-century generation; and looking in retrospect at the roots of the American nation, a nineteenth-century writer saw with conviction that "the character of our population shows us eminently that God has appointed us to be a missionary people," and drew a picture of America as a missionary nation, called by destiny to use the blessings of its geography, its freedom and security, to civilize "so motley a group of heathen and Mohammedan, Buddhist and Papist, white, colored and mixed, bond and free."[37]

A sense of urgency and importance, then, was the direct result of the appointment by God and of the worldwide application of that missionary commission. The New England Puritans and their American descendants considered the world in dire need of their help and believed that they were delegated by God to answer that need. How they undertook to fulfill the divine commission, and how they looked at the rest of the world—the "others"—will be considered and illustrated in detail in the treatment of the missionary enterprise.

2

THE STAR IN THE WEST
The United States as the Light of the World

Twice twenty years have roll'd away.
Since on this memorable day,
Was Independence born;
The child of heav'n—of earth the joy,
Whom no base *Herod* could destroy.
Though feeble and forlorn.
May all other nations, in time, too rejoice
To have, for their rulers, the men of their choice—
The King of all kings, but no other obey,
And blest *Independence* the *Universe sway*.
(William Ray, "Independence: An Ode"—1816)

The vision of the Puritan ideologues did not end with the establishment of the independent political state. In fact, in spite of the political atmosphere which characterized the polemics of the Revolution and Independence, many of the basic premises of the early American religious communities continued to inform the idiom and thinking of these two periods. The most obvious among these early premises are: the belief in the unfolding of divine will in the establishment of the United States of America; the covenantal nature of the new American system and the blend of religious and sociopolitical principles in this "ideal state"; and the compelling sense of mission felt by American nationalists toward the rest of the world. These premises, moreover, were all operating within the framework of an active awareness by Americans of the unique nature of their experiment in the history of man.

To begin with this last idea, there was general agreement that the new American situation was a unique experiment—never witnessed before in the annals of mankind. This point was emphasized by Americans from many walks of life who were overjoyed by the novelty of their experiment and the opportunities it held for them, for their nation's posterity and for the rest of the world. During the first few decades of Independence, intellectual visionaries such as the Connecticut Wits, as well as practical politicians, expressed this notion in no uncertain terms. "For our situation," Joel Barlow maintained, "is in many respects not only new to us, but also to the world." Realizing that the opportunities opened up to the new system would render it "as novel as it is important," Barlow reminded his generation that it was their duty to make full use of the opportunity; for, he said:

> There has been no nation either ancient or modern that could have presented human nature in the same character as ours does and will present it; because there has existed no nation whose government has resembled ours. A representative democracy on a large scale, with a fixt constitution, had never before been attempted, and has no where else succeeded. A federal government on democratic principles is equally unprecedented, and exhibits a still greater innovation on all received ideas of statesmen and lawgivers.[1]

This was the time for those "powerless potentates of reason" to watch the new developments and learn a lesson in political science and the principles of democratic government. The enthusiasm generated in the hearts of Americans was not limited to one group or class. Intellectuals, politicians, and religious extremists alike, saw the unique nature of their experiment, each in his own frame of reference.

God's American Israel

But this new nation, which evolved into what was considered the perfect state, was not only the fruit of the efforts of its founders. Although this country, "freedom's sacred temple," was "built by immortal patriot's hands,"[2] its patriots were only carrying out the will of God. The United States of America, to quote Timothy Dwight, was a happy state,

> by HEAVEN design'd
> To reign, protect, employ, and bless mankind;[3]

While recognizing their happy situation and their own part in bringing it about, these Americans were visibly conscious of the part played by the hand of Providence. They had no doubt whatsoever that a superior power had brought this new nation to such a perfect state; they were also quite certain that the same power had prepared them for a tremendous task.

The establishment of this ideal American state, moreover, was not seen only as the unfolding of a superior providential plan. Prophecies revered by the Christians were read into this momentous event. "God's American Israel," said another American intellectual, was the fulfillment of the vision of Noah and the realization of Deuteronomy (26:19) "to make thee high above all nations which he hath made, in praise, and in name, and in honor; and that thou mayst be an holy people unto the Lord thy God."[4]

Throughout the period of the Revolution and Independence there were frequent references by preachers, educators and politicians to the unfolding of a manifest divine plan in these auspicious events. According to this plan, America had been there from the beginning of creation, and was now opportunely thrust upon the world scene. The new nation, God's peculiar people, "after having been concealed for so many years from the rest of the world, was probably discovered in the maturity of time, to become the theatre for displaying the illustrious designs of Providence, in its dispensations to the human race."[5] The new state also inherited from its Puritan ancestors the firm conviction that its citizens were favored and selected by God to establish His Kingdom in this newly-independent territory and to extend that Kingdom to the rest of the world.

On other continents, the belief was that revolutions had been the outcome of accident—especially in Europe where sound judgment and human rights were preyed upon by caprice and tyranny. Empires were established on foundations of ignorance and self-interest. Not so on the "western continent."[6] This new experiment, unknown to human legislators anywhere else, "was imposed upon the fathers of the American Empire" by the Divine law-maker. A "beneficent providence, the God of order and justice," according to Barlow, brought to perfection the United States of America and provided it with the necessary qualifications to lead the rest of humanity from darkness to the new light.[7] The concept of light figures prominently in these qualifications and, without being ambivalent, takes on both secular and religious meanings in the writings of Americans. In a poem by William Ray, the figure of light is clearly within the Christian tradition, but it also speaks of Independent America as a phenomenon emerging from Jehovah's throne—"a star arising in the west."[8]

Such was the secularized, indeed the nationalized, Kingdom of God as Americans conceived it when they achieved their independence. America was qualified to assume the role of that Kingdom, and foremost among her qualifications was a system of governance which valued the ideals of the Enlightenment without sacrificing the age-old principles of obedience to God and church. Thus the authors of the Constitution found it natural that to be free and independent meant also to maintain "firm reliance on the Protection of Divine Providence."[9] The new system was to be a covenantal form of state; a covenant was drawn by the people to govern their experiment in statehood, but it was felt to be drawn before God, and in obedience to His will. The state of peace and happiness which was achieved by Americans, as seen by Joel Barlow, was a condition predicted in Scripture, where it was referred to as the millenial period. It was the "sun of glory [which illumined] JEHOVAH's throne."[10]

The ecclesiastical and sociopolitical covenant of the Puritans was dressed in the new garb of an eighteenth-century system of rational thought. A modern American historian describes the American nation at every stage of its early development as "the result of the consecutive unfolding of God's covenant with mankind, now come to a climax on this continent; for Americans the exercise of liberty becomes simply the one true obedience to God."[11] Obedience to God implied respect for the law and enjoyment of political and civil liberties. In spite of the insistence of the Founding Fathers on the separation of church and state and on the sanctity of individual religious freedom, there was then, and still is at present, a persistent, association between the ideals of the American political system and those of American Christianity.

The first advocates of separation of church and state and toleration of religious freedom regarded Protestant Christianity to be an essential ingredient for the success of the new experiment. Daniel Webster's well-known statement that Christianity "must ever be regarded among us as the foundation of civil society"[12] summed up the prevailing sentiment among his contemporaries and was echoed later by such statements as that made by President Eisenhower that "without God there could be no American form of Government, nor an American way of life." Eisenhower went on to call on the American people to pray to Almighty God "each day...to set and keep His protecting hand over us so that we may pass on to those who come after us the heritage of a free people, secure in their God-given rights and in full control of a government dedicated to the preservation of those rights."[13]

It was this underlying belief in the essential role of religion in the American experiment—a heritage of the first American political systems, called "compacts" or "covenants"—which prompted political as well as religious missionaries to equate the two components of religion and politics in their efforts to convert the rest of the world. Founders of the American Bible Society were conscious of this dichotomy in the American role when, in the Society's Constitution, they addressed "the People of the United States of America," urging them to recognize the "great political event" as a sign of God's favor and of the coming of the millenium.[14]

Citizens of the young state were often reminded of this happy blend of religion and politics in their national experiment and of the advantageous duties they shouldered. On the Fourth of July, 1812, Enoch

Lincoln delivered an Independence Day Oration in Worcester, Massachusetts, in which he said: "Fellow citizens! while we cling to our natural and social rights, let us be faithful to our civil duties. So shall our country rise unrivalled in wisdom; its population be numberless as the rays of the firmament and Heaven above exceed our felicity."[15] To emphasize the importance of American religious-political conduct for the achievement of America's mission, Lincoln called on his fellow citizens to "be tolerant to opinion," and to make freedom of expression and belief a means of attracting others to the new system. "The politician is a slave until Religion also be free," he said, and concluded that diversity of opinion could only lead to a unity of belief.

After Independence, and throughout the first half of the nineteenth century, many Americans were convinced that theirs was the ideal political state and the most likely setting for the Kingdom of God. Obviously, covenantal thinking was a dominant factor in American religious and political beliefs. In fact, Sidney Ahlstrom's statement that "as night follows day, 'covenant thinking' carried over into the Puritans' ecclesiastical and social thinking"[16] can very well be applied to American patriotic feelings after independence. The Puritan settlers' belief that they had been delivered from the iniquities and corruption of Europe to the land of promise was strengthened by the establishment of an independent state and American expressions of optimism and enthusiasm in the period which followed Independence. Lyman Beecher showed the typical national sentiment of his countrymen when he said that it was time for the American experiment to be made available to the rest of the world in order for it "to be emancipated and rendered happy."[17] Failing this, Beecher warned, "the whole creation shall groan and travail together in pain." In statements like this, the religious missionary idiom blends completely with the language of the enlightened social and political reformers.

The Unique Nature of the American Experiment

Advocates of the uniqueness of the American experiment did not have to look very far for proof that they were blessed by heaven with every qualification necessary for spreading the new system to the rest of the world. Geography, for one thing, provided convincing signs to prove the point. The continent of America, according to one writer, was so centrally situated that it made it possible for Americans to reach every part of the world with the light of the Gospel and of the American system. The author of an article in the *American Theological Review* (1859) expounded on the advantages of the geographical position of the United States, which, he said, being

> placed nearly between Africa and Europe on the east and Asia on the west, it attracts thither the adventurer and the oppressed from those lands, while it is so far removed from them all, as easily to keep aloof from their contentions. South America, too, is quite accessible. Indeed, radii drawn from our eastern, western, and southern shores, reach almost all Pagan, Mohammedan, and Papal lands, or rather most of them can be reached by nearly direct water communication.[18]

This happy geographical situation—the center of the world—would, according to the *American Theological Review,* enable Americans to extend "civilization and Christianity among degraded and benighted nations."[19]

This same central position, conversely, had the further advantage of insularity, one which protected the United States from invasion and from the corrupting influences of other, less civilized nations. The Founding Fathers realized this advantage even as they deliberated over the text of the Declaration of Independence. Addressing the Continental Congress which was drafting the Declaration, one of the delegates spoke of "the great gulph which rolls its waves between Europe and America," and which forms a line of "full and lasting defence"[20] to protect the newly-independent country. And at the meeting which endorsed the Constitution, Hamilton recognized the advantages of the geographical position of his country.[21] Insularity, then, worked for the dual purpose of reaching out with the light of civilization and of protecting the country against outside dangers.

The variety of climatic conditions, terrain, and natural resources was also an advantage which attracted immigrants from all corners of the world to the United States. Immigrants "from every region where oppression reigns or poverty blights" would flock to the United States where, the *American Theological Review* said, "our great rivers, with our fast extending railroads, enable them to penetrate into fertile regions, where industry insures them a competence, and their rights are secure." They would also find the variety of climate adapted to their constitutions, whether they come from the north or south regions. It also prepares Americans to go anywhere, "to carry thither and teach the principles of learning, liberty, and religion."[22] As for the great wealth in natural resources, the United States can accommodate more than "five hundred millions of people."[23]

In mineral wealth, the land had unexhaustible deposits of iron, lead, copper, and gold. With happy satisfaction, the writer exclaimed: "Half a million of years would be required to exhaust our fossil fuel, and the supply will surely be fully adequate to meet the largest wants of three hundred millions that may in a few centuries be congregated here."[24]

As early as 1809, Joel Barlow saw what came to be known half a century later as "Manifest Destiny," when he envisioned "the vast extent of continent that is or must be comprised within our limits, containing not less than sixteen hundred millions of acres, and susceptible of a population of two hundred millions of human beings."[25]

All of this wealth, and the fortunate geographical and political situation enjoyed by the newly created nation, were viewed as if planned by Providence for the benefit of mankind.

American Concern for the Rest of Mankind

One of the most enduring characteristics of nineteenth century American nationalism was its outward look and missionary nature. Founders and visionaries of the new American state (variously called "kingdom" and "empire") looked out to the rest of the world even as the groundwork of the new system was being laid. Only eleven years after Independence, Joel Barlow addressed the Connecticut Society of the Cincinnati on the Fourth of July, describing the great results expected of the "Federal Convention now sitting at Philadelphia." There was immense confidence in that body of legislators, he said, owing to their past services to the nation, but much more was expected: "If ever there was a time, in any age or nation, when the fate of millions depended on the voice of one, it is the present period in these states. Every free citizen of the American Empire ought now to consider himself as the legislator of half mankind." And if every American citizen would only view the opportunities open to him, he would rejoice at the results to be achieved by "one rational political system upon the general happiness of mankind."[26]

In political and religious, as well as in literary statements, it was firmly asserted that the happiness of America meant, by logical extension, the happiness of the rest of the world. This was expressed by another enthusiastic patriot in a versified, though not more poetic, form:

> Yet there, even there, Columbia's bliss shall spring,
> Rous'd from dull sleep, astonish'd Europe sing,
> O'er Asia burst the renovating morn,
> And startled Afric in a day be born;[27]

Both the American sacred Kingdom of God and American political democracy were brought together by nationalist visionaries as a model for the Old World and for uncivilized nations. This model was to beam the light of the Gospel and of freedom to the world. The blend has been fully described by H. Richard Niebuhr in his celebrated work, *The Kingdom of God in America*. "The institutionalization of the kingdom of Christ was naturally accompanied by its nationalization," Niebuhr said, and, he continued,

> The old idea of American Christians as a chosen people who had been called to a special task was turned into the notion of a chosen nation especially favored. In Lyman Beecher, as in Cotton Mather before him, we have seen how this tendency came to expression. As the nineteenth century went on the note of divine favoritism was increasingly sounded. Christianity, democracy, Americanism, the English language and culture, the growth of industry and science, American institutions—these are all confounded and confused. The contemplation of their own righteousness filled Americans with such lofty and enthusiastic sentiments that they readily identified it with the righteousness of God....It is in particular the Kingdom of the Anglo-Saxon race, which is destined to bring light to the gentiles by means of lamps manufactured in America.[28]

In retrospect, Niebuhr saw a "confusion of church and world," and a confounding of Christianity, democracy, Americanism, and all other American institutions.

There was little doubt in the minds of patriotic Americans that this new experiment was to be extended to the rest of the world. The *Theological Review* writer of 1859 put special emphasis on this aspect of America's mission to the nations. He said that "now that Providence has shown how applicable this system is to the whole human family, the descendants of the Pilgrims should be satisfied with nothing short of its universal extension."[29] And, as if to explain that by the "system" there were considerations other than religious, the writer went on to say that "our free political institutions furnish another evidence of our adaptedness and consequent duty to become a missionary nation."[30] America shared in the natural human, "love of unbridled liberty," but, the writer continued, "in this country, however, hitherto we have been able to subject liberty to law."[31] Furthermore, social equality, a progressive educational system, and many other advantages convinced many Americans they were qualified to extend the experiment to the rest of the world. Expressions such as these show how the sociopolitical developments in America became part of the religious belief that the new nation was directed by the hand of Providence.

Extension of the American system was to be for the good of mankind. That was the ideal of the missionary establishment and of the patriotic men who believed that theirs was a Revolution for the betterment of the human condition. Some propagators of the westward expansion of the United States also considered their efforts part of this reaching-out to the rest of mankind and not simply as acquisition of territory. In October, 1847, the editor of the *Public Ledger*, William Swain, put forth this idea very clearly:

> We are believers in the superintendence of a directing Providence, and when we contemplate the rise and amazing progress of the United States, the nature of our government, the character of our people, and the occurrence of unforeseen events, all tending to one great accomplishment, we are impressed with a conviction that the decree is made and in the process of execution, that this continent is to be but one nation, under one system of free institutions. This is said in no spirit of prophecy, but in the conclusion of reason,...and the natural tendency of the moral and physical elements at work.[32]

America's Manifest Destiny

The belief in the United States as the new ideal state—the religious as well as the secular Utopia—played a significant role in the movement known as Manifest Destiny. This concept meant, among other things, the extension of the benefits of the American experience to the neighboring areas. In fact, not all people could qualify to emulate the American system. Manifest Destiny also meant that it was *others* who were in need of the American helping hand, and the aim was not simply territorial expansion.

The intervention of Providence was at work in American efforts to "explode" old habits and establish new standards of morality and political conduct. This was to be achieved through spreading the light of the Gospel and of American Revolutionary ideas. In this sense the American Revolution was not American only; it was rather the property of mankind. Ezra Stiles described the new system in 1783 as a "recent political phenomenon of a new sovereignty arising among the soverign powers of the earth...[which] should be attended to and contemplated by all nations."[33] At about the same time, Joel Barlow enthusiastically described the great prospects which awaited the American nation. In a perfect blend of religious and sociopolitical missionary expression, Barlow called on all mankind to emulate the American model of government:

But now no more the patriotic mind,
To narrow views and local laws confined,
Gainst neighboring lands directs the public rage,
Plods for a clan or counsels for an age;
But soars to loftier thoughts and reaches far
Beyond the power, beyond the wish of war;
For realms and ages forms the general aim,
Makes patriot views and moral views the same
Works with enlighten'd zeal, to see combined
The strength and happiness of humankind.[34]

The "cause of political liberty," according to Niebuhr, was part of the whole humanitarian enterprise which characterized the American enlightenment of the nineteenth century.[35] Americans sincerely sought to bring their brand of enlightenment to the other peoples of the earth, especially to those who were "oppressed" and "in darkness." The theme of light beaming from America to the four corners of the world was a favorite topic with Americans through the centuries. Ray's poem, "Spreading the Gospel: Star in the West," was prefaced with Revelation, "And I will give him the Morning Star," but the substance of that light derived also from a patriotic stand when the poet wrote, predictively, that "a star is rising in the West!" The lamp, as another poem by Ray illustrates, was an instrument of the American enlightenment. Although "Virtue, Vice, Liberty and Oppression, are beloved and detested by the good and bad of all countries and nations," it was America who had

. . . .
caught the flame
O may it burn eternal!
. . . .
Where freedom's sacred temple stands,
Built by immortal patriots' hands.[36]

Liberty became synonymous with the American system itself—basically a system of government and life identified with God's covenant. This is the system of political and civil liberties which Ahlstrom saw as "simply the one true obedience to God."[37]

Yet it was not only the exercise of liberty which was considered by Americans to be the true obedience to God; the exercise had to be complemented with the spreading of liberty throughout the world. Timothy Dwight, Joel Barlow, William Ray, and countless other Americans joined in the exercise, which was also shared by such diverse nineteenth century American travellers to the Orient as David Dorr, an American slave from Tennessee; Richard Haight, a gentleman from New York; and William Lynch, a U.S. Naval officer. In the account of his journey "around the world," David Dorr said that "the author of this book, though a colored man, hopes to die believing that this federal government is destined to be the noblest fabric ever germinated in the brain of men or the tides of time. Though a colored man, he believes that he has the right to say that, in his opinion, *the American people are to be the Medes and Persians of the nineteenth century.*"[38]

William Lynch also exhibited a blend of American religious and national pride when, on the Sea of Galilee, he was able to lower the two boats carried there by his party. With the help of a group of Arabs, the boats were finally launched on the water and the Arabs cheered and shouted. But the Americans were Silent:

> From Christian lips it would have sounded like profanation. A look upon that consecrated lake ever brought to remembrance the words, 'Peace! be still!'—which not only repressed all noisy exhibition, but soothed for a time all worldly care.

> Buoyantly floated the two 'Fannies,' bearing the stars and stripes, the noblest flag of freedom now waving in the world. Since the time of Josephus and the Romans, no vessel of any size has sailed upon this sea, and for many, many years, but a solitary keel has furrowed its surface.[39]

And when the American flag was flown atop Lynch's camp on his insistence, he remarked that "for the first time, perhaps, without the consular precincts, the American flag has been raised in Palestine. May it be the harbinger of regeneration to a now hapless people!"[40]

It became apparent that by virtue of this new experience, America was deemed more qualified for the task of spreading the light than any other nation, including the Christian nations of Europe. Americans enjoyed, in addition to their immense natural resources, a fortunate geographical location and an ever-increasing population and a freshness of outlook and innocence which distinguished them from the people of the Old World. There were frequent comparisons of the American nation with European as well as Eastern countries. Europe was too steeped in her old ways, corrupt in morals, politics, and religion; her institutions were "to be suspected,... scrutinized, and brought to the test...of the general principles of our institutions, and the habits and maxims, that arise of them."[41] But whereas Barlow was willing to put European institutions to the test, Dwight's rejection of these institutions and everything European was total and uncompromising. Set against the American "Hesperian climes" and the "happy isles, and garden'd realms" which "display Th'advancing splendours of prophetic day," Europe, and the rest of the world for that matter, presented a sorry spectacle indeed.

Europe's energy was spent and her innocence lost; America was pure and in the prime of youth. Europe's social and political institutions were despotic and old fashioned; the American nation had devised a system which was to be a model for men everywhere. On the eve of the Revolution, an English immigrant (and a citizen of the world) announced the magnitude of America's undertaking and its effects on the future of mankind:

> The sun never shined on a cause of greater worth. 'Tis not the affair of a city, a county, a province, or a kingdom; but of a continent—of at least one-eighth part of the habitable globe. 'Tis not the concern of a day, a year or an age; posterity are virtually involved in the contest, and will be more or less affected even to the end of time by the proceedings now....

Small islands not capable of protecting themselves are the proper objects for government to take under their care; but there is something absurd in supposing a continent to be perpetually governed by an island. In no instance hath nature made the satellite larger than its primary planet; and as England and America, with respect to each other, reverse the common order of nature, it is evident that they belong to different systems. England to Europe: America to itself....[42]

Joel Barlow voiced a similar sentiment when he stated that "on the western continent the scene was entirely different from that of the eastern continent where the foundations of empires were laid in ignorance. The new task, he said, was unknown to legislators of other nations, and "was imposed upon the fathers of the American Empire."[43] Dwight's eloquent burst of pride in America is magnified by the subsequent picture he presented of Europe:

> Profusely scatter's o'er these regions, lo!
> What scenes of grandeur, and of beauty, glow.
> It's noblest wonders here Creation spreads'
> Hills, where skies rest, and Danubes pour cascades;
> Forests, that stretch from Cancer, to the Pole;
> Lakes, where seas lie, and rivers, where they roll;
> Landscapes, where Edens gild anew the ball,
> And plains, and meads, where suns arise, and fall.[44]

As for the Old World, Dwight said:

> Thrice wretched lands where, thousands slaves to one,
> Sires know no child, beside the eldest son;
> And kings no pleasure, but from subjects' woe.[45]

In conclusion, Americans saw in their new nation a true hope for humanity, and recognized their responsibilities to the whole world in secular, as well as in religious, terms. This feeling was very instrumental in shaping America's attitude toward other nations.

3

THE PROPHET'S PROGRESS
American Understanding of Islam

"Mahomet...should be read by anyone calling himself educated."

Bronson Alcott, Journals,
August 8, 1867

An important factor which contributed to the shaping of American perceptions of Arabs and Muslims may be described as that conglomerate
of accumulated knowledge and steady flow of information on Arabs,
Muslims, the religion of Islam, and the Prophet Muhammad which was
available to the American reading public prior to and during the
nineteenth century. The bulk of this knowledge came from biographies
of the Prophet of Islam, translations of and commentaries on the Qur'an,
and works dealing with the Arabs, Muslims, and Islam. There was of
course a good deal of related matter available to the general public
through more popular publications such as the travel book, the newspaper and the periodical article, works of literature, missionary writings,
and other works of general nature. Obviously, these works are by their
nature very diverse, scattered over a wide range of print sources and over
a long period of time. Thus any academic study of this body of knowledge has to be highly selective; and the selection process has been based
on the importance of the material, its contemporary popularity, and
range of circulation. The process, by necessity, has therefore omitted a
good deal of related material and highlighted what seem to be representative works on the subject. It should also be pointed out that the accumulated body of knowledge pertinent here, unlike that which stems, solely
from American history and thought, is not strictly American. We have
had to recognize that America was *heir* to a great deal of knowledge of
Islam and Muslims, and to a long-standing tradition of prejudice towards them, from its European background and ancestry. In fact, Americans continued to be influenced by European, especially British, treatments
of Islam and the Prophet Muhammad well into the nineteenth century.

Nevertheless, a certain degree of specifically American treatment of Islam and Arabs and the development of a national attitude towards them was recognizable by the second half of the nineteenth century. This is seen especially in two diverse activities: the missionary enterprise and the fairly unique movements of Transcendentalism, Free Religion and Universal Religion.

The movements known as Transcendentalism, Free Religion, and Universal Religion considered Islam as one of the major religions of the world and accorded it a more sympathetic, objective treatment than it had received earlier. In 1878, to cite one example, the *Index*, one of the later transcendental journals devoted to the principles of Free Religion, published an essay by L. K. Washburn under the title "Who are Christians?" in which the writer attempts an analysis of the true meaning of Christianity. Washburn emphasizes the true-spiritual Christian beliefs and the fundamentals of religion in contrast to what he considers the body of dogma which had attached itself to religion and actually became a substitute. In this analysis, Washburn makes an interesting, and relatively novel, remark on Islam. "The Mohammadan," he says, "has faith in one God, in his kindness and mercy, in his justice and love; he believes in moral and religious duty, in being upright and pure, in humanity and forgiveness, but he is not a Christian."[1] In speaking of the differences and similarities between Christianity, as it had come to be enunciated by the late nineteenth century, and other religions of the world—including Islam—Washburn says that all of these religions are based on belief in God, divine revelation, immortality of the soul, inspired men and books, the virtue of the human heart, freedom, right, truth, and progress.[2]

Washburn's essay, however, came in the latter part of the nineteenth century and was representative of a trend which was limited to a few intellectual circles. Islam and the Prophet had a long, rough road for over two and a half centuries before encountering a fairly tolerant attitude, and even this was on a limited scale.

Traditional Prejudice Against Islam

The prevailing atmosphere of prejudice towards Islam and the misconceptions which were perpetrated in Western and American writings can be illustrated indirectly by citing remarks which were critical of these misconceptions. One interesting reference came from the pen of a mission-minded and devout Christian, Theodore Dwight, in an article on the conditions of the negro peoples of Africa.[3] Dwight presents a historical description of the cultures of the African peoples, criticizing his fellow Americans in particular for the "erroneous impressions which prevail in the civilized world respecting the condition of the negro race in Africa."[4] He considers these erroneous impressions "discreditable to the intelligence of the age" and singles out "the people of the United States [who] are doubly blamable for the false views on this subject." Americans, Dwight says, inflicted many wrongs on their fellow beings and denied them "those intellectual faculties and moral qualities which the Creator has bestowed on the entire human family."[5]

To correct these misconceptions, Dwight offers his own views on Africa where, he says, "millions of pagan negroes, in different parts of that continent, have been for ages in the practice of some of the most important arts of life, dwelling in comfort and generally at peace; while many other millions have been raised to a considerable degree of civilization by Mohammadism, and long existed in powerful independent States." And although these states had undergone many violent changes, according to the writer, they were not "as many or great as those through which the principal nations of 'civilized Europe' passed during the same periods."[6] Dwight then proceeds to describe the condition of the peoples which had adopted Islam and had been for "a thousand years, mostly under the influence of Mohammedan institutions." These institutions he says,

> are everywhere similar, so far as they prevail, establishing fixed laws, customs, arts, and learning; and, although abounding in errors and evils on the one side, embracing benefits on the other which are not enjoyed by such portions of the negro race as remain in paganism. The Koran, as is well known, has copied from the Hebrew Scriptures many of the attributes of God and the doctrines of morality, with certain just views of the nature, capacities, duties, and destiny of man; and these are so faithfully taught, that they are conspicuous in the writings of many of the numerous authors in Mohammedan countries, and often displayed, in a more or less satisfactory degree, in the characters and lives of those educated in them.[7]

For Dwight, the prevalence of Islam and its encouragement of learning meant that "large portions of the African Continent lie open to the access of Christian influences through channels thus prepared by education."[8] It is clear from the article that the writer was disturbed by the treatment which was accorded by civilized Christian nations to the Negro race of Africa, especially to those peoples who had been raised to a civilized state by Islam. The praise of Islam and Muslim institutions stands out in this article, particularly because the main subject treated by the writer is not Islam.

The work of such authors as L. K. Washburn and Theodore Dwight was representative of a new climate of opinion towards Islam. Their attempts to dispel established notions and misconceptions indicate a degree of impatience with popularly disseminated perceptions. But in a wider context, these writers were protesting against an age-old Western treatment of Islam which the United States had inherited from its European background. To understand this treatment we must describe some of the more popular works on Islam and the Arabs available to the American reading public from the earliest settlements to the second half of the nineteenth century. These publications, had a lasting influence on American perceptions of Arabs, Muslims, and Islam, as well as on attitudes and behavior towards them. To a great extent, this perception was European—because of its presence in material transmitted from Europe to the New World. This can be seen from the catalogs of public and private libraries. For example, the *Catalogue of Books in the Library of Yale College in New Haven* (New Haven, 1755) includes some pertinent holdings—especially Sale's *Koran*, which was recommended reading for Juniors and Seniors. (A gift of books from Elihu Yale, at Cotton Mather's request, included many books on the East due to the fact that Elihu Yale had worked with the East India Company and had been governor of Madras.) Sale's *Koran* and Boulainevillier's *Life Of Mahomet* were available in public libraries by the middle of the eighteenth century.[9] The Qur'an and other works on Islam and the Arabs were often quoted during this time by many learned Americans. Some private collections were also noted.[10]

Translations of the Qur'an and Biographies of the Prophet

No detailed analysis of these foregoing works will be attempted here, but a description of the two most important will be helpful since they will be mentioned often in this study. Two translations of the Qur'an were in use in the United States from the second half of the seventeenth century forward. These are the translations made by Alexander Ross (1649) and George Sale (1734).[11] The first complete English translation of the Qur'an was done by Alexander Ross (1649), who rendered it from the French translation of the Sieur (Andre) De Ryer (1647). This rather inaccurate translation went into many printings in England and was included in volume II of Paul Rycaut's 1688 updated edition of Richard Knolles' famous *Turkish History*. Ross followed De Ryer's translation closely, copying the French translation's marginal notes from other European and Arabic sources. Ross' main contribution, however, is an "Address to the Christian Reader," a "Caveat or Admonition, for them who desire to know what use may be made of, or if there be danger in reading the ALCORAN," a confused, brief biography of the Prophet Muhammad and a description of the religious beliefs of Islam. The prevailing tone of this introductory matter is antagonistic and condemnatory, as is apparent in the address to the reader in which Ross says: "Thou shalt find it of so rude and incongruous a composure, so farced with contradictions, blasphemies, obscene speeches, and ridiculous fables....Yet is the whole esteemed so sacred, that upon the Cover therof is inscribed—*Let none touch it but he who is clean.*"[12]

This translation of the Qur'an enjoyed considerable popularity in the United Sates through the wide circulation of Paul Rycaut's edition of Richard Knolles' *Turkish History*. But more importantly, the first American edition of a translation of the Qur'an was that of Ross, which came out in Springfield, Massachusetts, in October of 1806. So although Sale's was to become the standard and more popular translation, and during the nineteenth century, Ross' translation must have been more widely known, and consequently his introductory material was influential in shaping early American concepts of Islam and Muslims.

George Sale's translation of the Qur'an came out in 1734. This is a more accurate translation than Ross' and includes many explanatory footnotes, biblical comparisons and analogies, and textual explications. Sale also provides the reader with a book-length "Preliminary Discourse" in which he introduces the religion of Islam, the Qur'an, and the Prophet Muhammad as he sees them. In spite of a slightly more tolerant attitude towards Islam and its sacred book, once again the basic theme is how to defeat Islam and convert Muslims to Christianity. Sale's suggestions include the following:

1. Avoid the use of force and compulsion (although at the time the Christian world was capable of that).

2. Avoid teaching doctrines which go against common sense. For whatever we may think of them, Muslims are no fools. (This was partly the reason for the dismal failure of Catholics in the confrontation with Islam.)

3. Treat Muslims humanely and avoid ill and harsh language in the controversy. (Sale rejects the all-too-common vindictive attacks on Islam and Muslims, and vows never to use them.)

4. Do not abandon any article of the Christian faith just to gain converts.[13]

Certain attitudes and tendencies that were common among Western writers in their treatment of Muslims and Arabs found their way to the works of American writers. Obviously they were of great influence upon the American public.[14]

With a surprising degree of unanimity, authors of works dealing with Islam and the Prophet Muhammad felt the need for an apology, or at least a justification, for writing on the subject. The various reasons they advanced revealed their preconceptions and attitudes. Many of them felt there was a public need for information on Islam and Muslems. Washington Irving, one of the first American writers to show interest in Oriental topics, says in his biography of the Prophet Muhammad that "some apology may seem necessary for presenting a life of Mahomet at the present day, when no new facts can be added to those already known concerning him."[15] Since Irving was planning a series of works on the Arabs in Spain, a biography of the founder of Islam seemed to be an appropriate introduction. In writing the life of the Prophet, he explains that his aim "has been to digest into an easy, perspicuous, and flowing narrative, the admitted facts concerning Mahomet, together with such legends and traditions as has been wrought into the whole system of Oriental literature; at the same time to give such a summary of his faith as might be sufficient for the more general reader."[16]

Similarly, the American biographer of the Prophet Muhammad, George Bush, thought that no new facts could be added to those already known. But whereas Irving, the man of letters, aimed at presenting the reading public with a "flowing narrative" of the life and legends of the Prophet, Bush, the religious historian, thought that "new theories and speculations, moral and philosophical, founded upon these facts, and many of them richly deserving attention, are frequently propounded to the reflecting, but they add little or nothing to the amount of our positive information."[17] What Bush proposes to do therefore is attempt "such a selection and arrangement and investigation of the leading particulars of the Impostor's history, as shall convey to the English reader, in a correct and concentrated form, those details."[18] There was a demand for this kind of material, and Bush thought that "such a work, discreetly prepared, would supply, if we mistake not, a very considerable desideratum in our language—one which is beginning to be more sensibly felt than ever, and the spirit of the age loudly required to have supplied."[19]

As for the sacred book of Islam, the first English translator of the Qur'an, Alexander Ross, provides an essay entitled "The Translator to the Christian Reader," in which he gives his reasons for offering the translation in English. Ross says: "There being so many sects and heresies banded together against the truth, finding that of Mohamet wanting to the Muster, I thought good to bring it to their colours, that so viewing thine enemies in their full body, thou maist the better prepared to encounter, and I hope overcome them."[20] Should the English reader be surprised "to find him [Muhammad] so to speak English, as if he had made some Conquest on the nation," Ross assures his reader, "thou wilt soon reject that fear, if thou consider that this his *Alcoran,* (the Groundwork of the *Turkish* Religion) hath been already translated into almost all Languages in Christendom...yet never gained any Proselyte, where the Sword, its most forcible, and strongest argument hath not prevailed."[21] Ross thought that since the Qur'an had been translated into many other European languages, it should be translated into English to strengthen people's faith in Christianity and to show the ugliness of the religion of the Turks, and to administer "an antidote to confirm...the health of Christianity."[22]

In George Sale's translation of the Qur'an, which became the standard reference on the sacred book of Islam and on the religion in general, the translator also offered reasons for its publication. Curiously enough, this translation, which was more accurate and scholarly in rendering the Qur'an into readable English, is prefaced with reasons which are far from objective and quite derogatory of Islam. Sale states that it is necessary to undeceive those who "by virtue of the ignorant and unfair translations of the Koran have entertained too favourable an opinion of the original."[23] According to Sale, "no danger can be apprehended from so manifest a forgery," yet the translation of the Qur'an would "enable us effectually to expose the imposture."[24] Obviously, even his standard translation was not intended to bring about a better understanding of Islam; the translator says, "if we entertain too favourable an opinion of the original we would be dignifying it."[25]

The Qur'an was not considered worthy of perusal and study for its own sake. These authors of works on Islam seemed to feel that by such derogatory remarks they were anticipating and rebuffing criticism of their work. At least that is what Ralph Waldo Emerson thought when he said of Simon Ockley's *History of the Saracens:* "And Simon Ockley's *History of the Saracens,* recounts the prodigies of individual valor with admiration, all the more evident on the part of the narrative, that he seems to think that his place in Christian Oxford requires of him some proper protestations of abhorence."[26]

Yet most Western writers on Islam and the Prophet claim objectivity in their treatment of the subject. Some of them recognize that previous authors were vindictive and acrimonious in their judgments and presentations of Islam and its Prophet. But in spite of the later claims and intentions of objectivity, the tendency to condemn Islam remains prevalent. A good example is the anonymous biographer of the Prophet who begins his *Life of Mahomet* with a long treatise on the virtues of objective biography and history,[27] yet proposes to use the life and experiences of the Arab Prophet as an example of evil and wickedness.

> Biography is at once a pleasing and interesting study. The lives of
> particular personages, whether they have been conspicuous for their
> vices or their virtues, cannot be persued by a rational enquierer
> without unspeakable advantage....There is something in the life of a
> Julius Caesar, or an Alexander the Great, which is peculiarly disgust-
> ing to unbeclouded reason, notwithstanding the high place they oc-
> cupy in the estimation of the world, while the life of a Belisarious, a
> Solon, or a Socrates cannot fail to be admired.[28]

Studying the lives of the most profligate and vicious people, according
to the biographer, would be useful; it would be more useful, in fact, than
the best sermon on moral virtues. "Viewing things in this light," he goes
on, "it was thought that an accurate, well digested life of Mohamet...
would be an acquisition to the Christian world, not unworthy the
perusal of those who are friends to revealed religion."[29]

The presupposition, then, even in what was claimed to be an objective
biography, is that the life of Muhammad is the best example of these
profligate vicious people and would offer a moral lesson for Christians.
The author then states that he would use only the relevant facts in the life
of Muhammad, and that he would "consult only the writings of such
men as could not be reasonably suspected of partiality or party spirit."[30]
At the same time he vows to follow the best principles of objective biography, especially by consulting only those authors who

> spoke of Mahomet occasionally, and with seeming indifference, as if
> they neither believed nor rejected what they have transmitted to us
> as historical facts. If the testimony of such men is not to be depended
> on, it would be difficult to point out any who are deserving of public
> credit.[31]

George Bush, the American biographer, states at the beginning of his
Life of Mohamet, as if in reference to such works as the anonymous biographer: "I have not, in speaking of Mohammad or his Koran, allowed
myself to use those approbious appellations and unmannerly expressions, which seem to be the strongest arguments of several who have
written against them."[32] But such appellations and expressions were the
rule, not the exception. In reference works such as dictionaries of
religions and encyclopedias, one cannot fail to discern the attitudes of
condemnation towards the Prophet Muhammad as a schemer and Islam
as an imposture. For example, the article on "Mohametans" in John
Hayward's *Book of Religions* begins by describing Islam as "a scheme of
religion formed and propagated by Mahomet,"[33] and ends on the following note from Dr. Joseph White:

> What raises Christ and his religion far above all the fictions of
> Mahomet, is that awful alternative of hopes and fears, that looking-

for of judgment, which our Christian faith sets before us. At that day, when time, the great arbiter of truth and falsehood, shall bring to pass the accomplishment of the ages, and the Son of God shall make his enemies his footstool,—then shall the deluded followers of the great Impostor, disappointed of the expected intercession of their prophet, stand trembling and dismayed at the approach of the glorified Messiah. Then shall they say, "Yonder cometh in the clouds that Jesus whose religion we labored to destroy; whose temples we profaned; whose servants and followers we cruelly oppressed!"[34]

Western writers on Islam generally give the Prophet Muhammad credit for the meticulous preparation and planning of the principles of Islam, and for laying the groundwork for its growth. This involves the denial of a divine inspiration and prophecy on the one hand; and, on the other, the portrayal of Muhammad as a cold-blooded man who secretly schemed for a new religion while biding his time for the appropriate moment to declare his beliefs. In the mildest of these biographies, Muhammad's "scheme" is mentioned briefly as a part of the general outline of Islam. Muhammad, says Hannah Adams,

> was endowed with a subtle genius and possessed of great enterprise and ambition. He aimed at the introduction of a new religion, and began his eventful project by accusing both Jews and Christians with corrupting the revelations that had been made to them from heaven. He maintained that the prophets, and even Christ himself, had foretold his coming, which he endeavoured to make out from the Arab version of Deut. ii. 2. Psalm 1. 2. Isa. xxi. 7. and John xvi. 7: in some of which he pretended that he was literally named, as likewise in other parts of the original gospels: and particularly that he was the *paraclete* promised by our Saviour in the text referred to.[35]

Hayward also begins his treatment of Islam by describing Muhammad as a schemer, but he goes a step further and refers to Muhammad's upbringing, childhood behavior, and domestic situation as factors which contributed to his formulation of the new religion. He states that "Mohamet descended from an honorable tribe, and from the noblest family of that tribe; yet his original lot was poverty." His good conduct and honesty secured for him the hand of a wealthy and respectable widow. This raised him to a station equal to the richest people of Mecca. Hayward continues, however, that

> soon after his marriage, he formed the scheme of establishing a new religion, or, as he expressed it, of replanting the only true and ancient one professed by Adam, Noah, Abraham, Moses, Jesus, and all the prophets, by destroying the gross idolatry into which most of his countrymen had fallen, and weeding out the corruptions and super-

stitions which the later Jews and Christians had, as he thought, introduced into their religion and reducing it to its original purity, which
consisted chiefly in the worship of one God.[36]

These are mild statements regarding the manner in which the Prophet
Muhammad supposedly planned the introduction of the new religion;
the anonymous biographer, on the other hand, sees a much more wicked
and cold-blooded intent in the making of Islam. According to this biographer, the facts of Muhammed's childhood poverty or of his origin are
immaterial to his scheme of religion; "the nature and circumstances of a
man's birth being wholly independent of himself, make no part of the
value of significance of his character."[37] Nor would "it ever detract from
the first infamy which he has brought upon himself in the eye of true
discernment, that he was the hated spawn of opulence and power."[38]

The biographer here is obviously refuting Thomas Paine's assertion
that great reformers came in most cases from humble origins. He accuses
Paine of adopting in his *Age of Reason* "the common blunder" that
Muhammad's parentage was obscure and mean, when he said that
"Moses was a foundling, Jesus Christ was born in a stable, and Mahomet
was a mule driver."[39] The biographer accuses Paine of being prepared
"at any time [to] barter his reputation, I had almost said his soul, for a
stroke at Christianity."[40]

Muhammad's plan, according to his biographer, must have been in
the making while he was still young, for, he says, the death of a husband
of Khadija, his rich employer, was "peculiarly favourable to the advance-
ment of his projected scheme."[41] Even Muhammad's well-known good
character and behavior are seen as a ruse to deceive the public, for "as he
rightly judged that the well known profligacy and wickedness of his life
would form insurmountable barriers in the way of his success, he
resolved to lead a life of seeming sanctity and actual retirement for two
years."[42] The picture of Muhammad which the reader derives from reading this anonymous biography is that of a scheming, patient, un-
scrupulous man who spent thirteen years preparing a secret plot, not
even shared by his wife. He began his preparation when he was twenty-
five years old, but the first time he disclosed it to his wife, Khadija, was
when he was thirty-eight. The biographer then draws the historical and
psychological conclusion that:

> I am not warranted to say, from any historical information to
> which I have had access, that he inherited from nature this govern-
> ment of himself. From the most minute attention to his life, con-
> sidered as a connected whole, I am apt to believe that he was either
> of a morose and sullen, or of an hasty, passionate temper; for the
> propagation of his religion by the sword has nearly as much the air

of rancor and revenge, as a determined resolution to push the advantages he had obtained. But before he sounded the minds of his countrymen, on which depended the probability of his success, his cunning and readywit no doubt pointed out the necessity of disguising his temper.[43]

A more subtle imputation of Islam and its tenets and principles to the personality of Muhammad is proposed by Henry H. Jessup in his *The Setting of the Crescent and the Rising of the Cross* (Philadelphia: 1899). Here the author compares the divine nature of Christ's teachings to the personal and earthly character of Islam which, he says, derives from the whims and fancies of Muhammad.

Propagation of Islam by the Prophet Muhammad also required, according to a majority of these writers, accurate knowledge and deep insight into the psychology and sociology of the Arabs. It also called for a detailed knowledge of Christianity and Judaism, as well as of the state of the Christian and Jewish communities in the East. Biographers of the Prophet Muhammad and writers on Islam make great efforts to analyze the social character of the peoples of the region in their attempts to find the right reasons for the rapid spread of Islam. According to Adams, "Mohammed contrived by the permission of poligamy and concubinage to make his creed palatable to the most depraved of mankind."[44] Hayward also states that

> his law was artfully and marvellously adapted to the corrupt nature of man, and, in a most particular manner, to the manners and opinions of the Eastern nations, and the vices to which they were naturally addicted; for the articles of faith which it proposed were few in number, and extremely simple; and the duties it required were neither many nor difficult, nor such as were incompatible with the empire of appetites and passions.[45]

Not only did Muhammad exploit the "gross ignorance" of the peoples of the East; some writers claim that he actually tried to preserve that state of ignorance by preventing the spread of science and learning. An article on Muhammad and Islam in the *New York Morning Herald* claims that it was the intentional policy of the Prophet of Islam to keep Muslims in abject ignorance.[46] And in Knolles' *Turkish History* Alexander Ross informs his readers that the masses of Muslims are not "permitted to read it [the Qur'an], but live and die in an implicit faith of what their Priests deliver; which indeed (as saith the learned *Grotius*) is a manifest argument of its iniquity: For the Merchandise may justly be suspected, which will not be sold, unless unseen."[47]

Islam and Christianity

The Prophet Muhammad, according to most Western writers, had a solid knowledge of the Christian and Hebrew religions and borrowed profusely from them, claiming to correct the errors and deviations which had developed in the practices of adherents of the two religions. Many of these writers dwell on the similarities between Islam on the one hand and Christianity and Judaism on the other, often to illustrate Muhammad's knowledge of these religions and subsequent borrowings. Bush devotes a considerable part of his *Life of Mahomet* to an exposition of these similarities,[48] and Adams says that Muhammad "aimed at the introduction of a new religion, and began his eventful project by accusing both Jews and Christians with corrupting the revelations that had been made to them from heaven."[49] Describing some of the beliefs of Muslems, Adams says: "As to the scriptures, they are taught by the Koran, that God in divers ages of the world gave revelations of his will in writing to his prophets, all of which are lost except the pentateuch, the psalms, the gospel, and the Koran, which were successively delivered to Moses, David, Jesus, and Mohammed."[50] And he explains the position accorded to the Qur'an in Islam by saying that all articles of faith are "professedly derived from the Koran, or Mohammedan bible, repeatedly referred to above. This book has been extolled as the standard of eloquence among the Arabians; and many learned Christian writers have admitted that it contains eloquent passages, but it has been asserted, that 'most of these are evidently borrowed from the writings of Moses and the prophets, and are written in a style similar to that of the Hebrew scriptures.'"[51]

Adams also points out one important similarity between Islam and the two other religions: the belief in one God and his prophets. He adds, however, that Muslims believe "that whenever this religion became neglected, or essentially corrupted, God informed and admonished mankind thereof by prophets, of whom Moses and Jesus were the most distinguished, till the appearance of Mohammed."[52] Adams, as well as other American writers on religion, recognizes the difference between Christianity and Islam on the position Jesus Christ holds in their beliefs. "The Koran," says Adams,

> asserts Jesus to be the true Messiah, the word and breath of God, a worker of miracles, a preacher of heavenly doctrines, and an exemplary pattern of a perfect life. Many Mohammedans deny that he was really crucified; but pretend that, to elude the malice of his enemies, he was caught up into paradise, and another person crucified in this stead; though this opinion is by no means universal. They believed that his religion was improved and completed by

Muhammed, who was the seal of the prophets, and was sent from God to restore the true religion to its primitive simplicity; with the addition, however, of some peculiar laws and ceremonies.[53]

These borrowings from the two great religions are seen by Josiah Brewer as the device used by Muhammad to appease Christians and Jews and entice them to his new religion. In 1830 Brewer wrote in his analysis of the "Religion of the Turks," that

the great outline of the Mahometan religion and of the ecclesiastical establishment of the Turks are well understood. 'There is no other God but God, and Mahomet is his messenger,' is the summary of their creed, which is forever on their lips. Accommodating himself somewhat to the pagan, Jewish and Christian nations of his age, but chiefly to the corrupt propensities of human nature, the great deceiver formed a system which has endured almost as long, and extended itself almost as widely as the religion of Christ.[54]

As to how the Prophet Muhammad acquired his knowledge of Christianity and Judaism, writers record that he would have had access to their main principles through some Christian and Jewish elements in Arabia and through his travels in Arabia and Syria. That he did travel as far north as Busra, a town near the present borders between Syria and Jordan, is sufficiently recorded in contemporary accounts. But Western writers send Muhammad on his trading journeys as far North and East as Persia and as far West as Egypt.[55] Arab contemporaries of the Prophet cite one particular trip made by Muhammad in his youth, in the company of his uncle Abu-Taleb, and a meeting with the Christian monk Bahira in the old Roman town of Busra. It is recorded that Bahira recognized the signs of prophecy on Muhammad's face and advised his uncle to take him back and protect him from the enemies of the true monotheism creed of Abraham.

Western writers credit Muhammad with studying the Jewish and Christian creeds for a considerable part of his life in preparation for formulating his religion. He is also said to have recognized the deep divisions and internal strife which plagued both Christians and Jews, and to have seen the corrupt state of the two religions. He capitalized on this situation and used both disaffected Jews and Christians to formulate his creed and execute his scheme, while at the same time gaining credibility with the two religious communities. In this regard, the incident of the meeting with the monk Bahira takes on various dimensions in Western literature. In one instance Bahira is said to be an uncle of Muhammad's wife Khadija.[56] In another, Muhammad's mother is said to be a Jew whose influence resulted in his adoption of the new creed. In fact, some writers go so far as to claim that Muhammad was actually a tool in the hands of these people.[57] Hayward asserts for example, that Islam "is a compound of Paganism, Judaism, and Christianity; and the Koran, which is their Bible, is held in great reverence. It is replete with absurd representations, and is supposed to have been written by a Jew."[58] These disaffected groups are said to have wanted to revenge themselves against the established church, which had become their enemy, even if that meant supporting the scheme of an imposter.[59]

One of the most active men in the American missionary field in Syria, Henry Jessup, attempts to clarify the matter in his own way. Realizing that a favorable feature to missionary efforts in the Muslem World is the Muslem "reverence for the Old and New Testament Scriptures," Jessup explains how Muhammad could have had access to the Scriptures. He says:

> It is said that during the lifetime of Mohammed, between the years 569 and 632, Warka, the son of Nofel, translated the Bible or some part of it into Arabic, but that the version is no longer to be found. It is unquestionable that Mohammed knew of the pentateuch and the Psalms, which are sometimes written together in Arabic manuscripts, and that he had knowledge of the Gospels. In general terms he speaks of these collectively as the Scriptures.[60]

Jessup concludes by stating that "it would be difficult to doubt that Mohammed found both the Old and New Testaments in the hands of the Arabs when he gave them his own book, which he pretended to be divine."[61]

Understandably enough, very few of the works written on Islam, the Prophet, or the Arabs had the purely objective aim of studying the subject for its own sake, much less with the intent of convincing the reader by presentation of its principles and arguments. Even those few which were objective were limited, generally speaking, to a readership of educated groups which indeed may be considered radical by contemporary standards. Most of the works had other goals in mind, which were, in most cases, explicitly identified by the authors.

Reasons for the Spread of Islam

One such goal was to explore the reasons for the wide appeal of Islam to so many millions of people, and the swiftness and suddenness of its expansion over a large geographical area of the habitable earth. Even in the nineteenth century, and in America, which was rather remote from any Islamic peril, there were scores of books and treatises on the expansion of Islam and many statistical tables counting the Muslem populations of the various parts of the world. It was always a matter which puzzled Westerners, including Americans, that there should be so many followers of the "false prophet." Many attempts were made to explain—indeed, explain *away*—this strange phenomenon. Another aim was to understand in order to refute (to defeat) Islam, and thereafter to be able to convert Muslims by persuasion and controversy. Since the Middle Ages religious polemics and debate were a well-established tradition in Western literature. The tradition of polemics against Islam on the ideological level began with the writings of the fifteenth-century religious scholar De Cusa, and continued as a genre of religious writing down to the end of the nineteenth century.

In particular, the mass appeal of Islam as a religion, and its worldwide dissemination, occupied many of the critical writers on Islam. It was always a matter which puzzled Christian Europe and required some answers. At the turn of the nineteenth century, an English writer, Edward Forster, posed the question by quoting the following words on the title page of his *Mohammedanism Unveiled*: "The extraordinary success, which has attended the imposture of Mahomet, has exercised the ingenuity of Christian writers; and yet does not appear to have been satisfactorily explained." Forster states that he himself had "for a considerable time...read and thought on the Mahometan apostacy, but...there remained still the painful conviction that some of its most important features were left wholly unexplained."[62] The question becomes very crucial to Forster's Christian beliefs, first because no satisfactory answer had yet been offered in spite of the numerous attempts, and secondly, because, as he puts it, "my persuasion was unshaken, that, whether the case were explicable or inexplicable by human judgement, the true elucidation would hereafter be vouchsafed, and would triumphantly justify the revealed wisdom and goodness of God."[63] An answer to the question, then, would reveal God's wisdom and would justify the ways of God to man.

What makes Forster's inquiry all the more interesting is that, unlike some of his American emulators, he recognizes the austerity of Islam and its lack of any ceremonial aesthetic appeal which is palatable to the senses. He says, Islam, with the

> pure and naked theism of its confusion of faith...is so abstract and unpalpable to be, of itself, inviting to the popular tastes or feelings. Since the world began, there is no instance beside, and while the world lasts, there will probably be no second instance, of a simple theism recommending itself, as such, to the popular choice. The laboured simplicity of its ritual, again, is, if possible, yet more repulsive, than the cold severity of its doctrine.[64]

Forster goes on to cite the strict duties of Islam: ablution, prayer, fasting, almsgiving, and pilgrimage, and feels this warlike fervor, combined with an austerity of discipline, holds little lasting attractiveness for the human spirit. Both in his fresh, new analysis of the creed, and in his conclusion, Forster merits attention for breaking new grounds in Western literature on Islam. This, despite the fact that, practically speaking, he has no answer to the question: "Mahometanism," he says, "has been largely progressive...while the permanence of its rigid and inviolable theism remains, after a duration of 1200 years, an unsolved, and apparently unsolvable phenomenon."[65]

Yet many American popular writers clung to the traditional explanation that Muhammad was able to spread his religion by the sword and by appealing to men's desires. Adams offers this simple explanation:

> This rapid and extensive spread of the Moslem faith has not only been urged as an argument in its favour, but been brought into competition with the propagation of Christianity. Two circumstances however must be brought into consideration. Mohammed contrived by the permission of poligamy and concubinage to make his creed palatable to the most depraved of mankind; and at the same time, allowing its propagation by the sword, to excite the martial spirit of unprincipled adventurers.[66]

Similarly, Hayward attributes the sudden success of Islam to the sword and the appeal to men's natural desires. He says:

> The terror of Mahomet's arms, and the repeated victories which were gained by him and his successors, were, no doubt, the irresistible arguments that persuaded such multitudes to embrace his religion, and submit to his dominion. Besides, his law was artfully and marvellously adapted to the corrupt nature of man, and in a most particular manner, to the manners and opinions of the Eastern nations, and the vices to which they were naturally addicted.[67]

Thus, although Hayward hints at some "irresistible arguments," he does not elaborate on them. Instead he emphasizes the "corrupt nature of man" and in particular that of the Eastern nations, as a factor to which Islam appealed. This is quite contrary to Forster's and Bush's conclusions.

George Bush sees the hand of Providence in the rise of Islam and its success; Islam is part of the divine plan for Christianity and the world. He considers the "life, character, and actions of its founder" the main key to understanding Islam and its progress. He finds several explanations for this phenomenon, all of which begin and end with divine dispensation. The corrupt and divided state of the Eastern Christian churches, the ignorance of the peoples of the area, and the fulfillment of prophecy are all cited as factors which account for the rise of Islam and, subsequently, for its expected fall. Bush's "grand object," he says, "has been to exhibit the Arabian prophet as a signal instrument in the hands of Providence, and to put the whole system of his imposture, with its causes, accompaniments, and effects, where it properly belongs, into the great scheme of the Divine administration of the world."[68] Bush cites as immediate causes the circumstances of the Roman and Persian Empires and Muhammad's personal experience and knowledge of these conditions. But in the final analysis, he sees only the working of the hand of Providence: "After all," he says:

> it is not improbable that Infinite Wisdom has so ordered it, that a veil of unpenetrated darkness should rest on the motives of the impostor, in order that a special providence may be recognised into the rise and establishment of this archdelusion in the world. In the absence of sufficient human causes to account for the phenomena, we are more readily induced to acknowledge a divine interposition.[69]

Islam in the Scheme of Creation

This look at Islam is very significant in that it reveals a totality of American perception of the Muslem Orient, and of itself, within the framework of one whole scheme of creation. The predominant belief was that the hand of Providence had brought forth the American plantation to begin with; the same hand was credited with the rise of America as the ideal Christian state, God's American Israel, upon whose actions the salvation of the whole world depended.

This totality in the American perception of the Orient as part of a divine plan was given expression in various statements. Two examples are particularly relevant to the attitude towards Islam. Bush's explanation of the rise and permanence of Islam attempts "to exhibit the Arabian prophet as a signal instrument in the hands of Providence, and to put the whole system of his imposture, with its causes, accompaniments, and effects, where it properly belongs, into the great scheme of the Divine administration of the world."[70] Now this scheme of divine administration of the world is the plan in which the Puritan settlers placed themselves as principal partners. Bush goes one step further in assigning to Islam a special place in this Providential plan, noticing the

> striking coincidence, that the period of Muhammed's retiring to the cave of Hera for the purpose of fabricating his imposture corresponds very nearly with the time in which Boniface, bishop of Rome, by virtue of a grant from the tyrant Phocas, first assumed the

> title of Universal Pastor, and began to lay claim to that spiritual
> supremacy over the church of Christ, which has ever since been ar-
> rogated to themselves by his successors.[71]

Although Bush does not agree with Dr. Prideaux that it is as correct to
apply "the epithet Antichrist to Mohammed" as it is to the "Romish
heirarchy," yet he thinks that the agreement of dates is worth noticing.

Protestant Christianity, especially American Christianity, which had
become for many missionaries the hope of the world, was to administer
the "final rites" to the tottering Papal and Muslem empires. The divine
scheme can be seen in all its fullness in the writings of missionaries,
political as well as religious, treated elsewhere in the present work. But
the second example of the American perception of the totality of this
scheme, and direct American participation in it, comes from the pen of a
person who may (with justice) be described as the American Orientalist
par excellence. Henry Jessup introduces his book on *The Mohammedan
Missionary Problem* by citing two striking coincidences: first, "at the
beginning of the seventh century there occurred two events of momen-
tus importance....One was the rise of the Mohammedan religion—the
other the christianization of the Saxon race in Britain."[72] Jessup realizes
that the two events are "geographically remote from each other" and are
"not often associated in the mind of the Christian student." Yet he
proposes to show how "they were providentially related in the most intimate manner, as bearing upon the welfare of the race and the future
development of Christ's kingdom in the world."[73]

The second "significant coincidence in history" which Jessup identifies and which is no less "providentially related" to the welfare of the
kingdom of Christ, comprises the two events which took place

> in the year 1492—the year in which Columbus discovered America,
> and thus opened a new field for the growth and development of that
> christianized Anglo-Saxon race which was destined to wield so
> mighty an influence upon the future of the Mohammedan nations—
> Ferdinand overthrew the last Spanish Mohammedan army at the
> gates of Granada, and the Muslems were driven back into Africa.[74]

In the light of these striking coincidences—the Christianization of the
Anglo-Saxon race and its extension to the American continent on the one
hand and, on the other, the rise of Islam and its overthrow in Spain—Jessup attempts "to show the evident plan and providence of God in the
past, present and future relations of the Anglo-Saxon Christian race to
the Mohammedan world."[75]

As for the past, Jessup describes the relations of Christianity with
Islam in extremely interesting terms of reciprocal exchange of services
orchestrated by the Great Master of the universe:

God has been preparing Christianity for Islam; he is now preparing Islam for Christianity. The Roman power and the Greek language prepared the way for the coming of Christ and the giving of the gospel to the world. Anglo-Saxon power and the Arabic language, the sacred language of the Koran, are preparing the way for giving the word of Christ, and Christ the Word, to the millions of the Mohammedan world.[76]

Jessup also characterizes the Muhammadan religion as a "scourge to the idolatrous Christians and the pagan systems of Asia and Africa" and suggests that, although a step forward for the pagan systems, it remains inferior to the spiritual, redemptive message of Christianity.

As for the working of this providential plan in the future, Jessup sees the combined efforts of the two Anglo-Saxon powers as the tool to be used in the accomplishment of the goals of the Church of Christ on earth.

Again, Jessup calls attention to the similar datelines of the Christianization of the Saxons in Britain and the emergence of the Muslim religion—all part of a Divine Plan. He foresees the fulfillment of a "Divine commission" for the world's salvation and for the survival of a common faith.

Like many of his countrymen, Jessup recognizes three basic ideas underlying the American Oriental attitude: first, the overwhelming task at hand in evangelizing the Muslim world and the feeling of urgency that accompanied the task; secondly, the sense of divine mission which weighed on the conscience of Americans as a result of their citizenship—here expressed in racial terms; and, thirdly, the deep confidence in the success of their mission because it constitutes part of the divine scheme for the whole world.

Other corollary ideas are also evident here and in the ensuing treatment of the "problem." To begin with, Jessup sees that there is a dilemma which confronts those who set about to convert Muslims and he attempts to write a prescription for its solution. There is also the definite conviction that not only is it the duty of Anglo-Saxon Christians to evangelize the Muslim world, but the Muslim world itself seems in dire need of the reforming influence of Christianity and is ripe for change, with the ultimate aim of conversion.

The Western Polemics of "Controversy"

The method of refuting Islam by argument and "controversy" was formally instituted as an intellectual exercise in Western religious literature in the mid-fifteenth century by the theologian-philosopher Nicolas de Cusa.[77] De Cusa wrote what he described as "a conference" in which

Christianity and Islam confront each other in a dialogue emphasizing the virtues of Christianity while presenting explications of Islam. It was hoped, that such an encounter would result in a wholesale conversion of the Muslem peoples. Born and raised in the Catholic tradition, de Cusa achieved great prominence as a clergyman-philosopher and in 1437–8 he was sent to Constantinople to attempt a reconciliation of the Eastern and Western Christian churches, so that together they might face the Ottoman peril. He had the opportunity to read extensively on Islam and made use of the Cluniac translation of the Qur'an, which was a complete distortion of the original.

What makes de Cusa's work important for a study of Western attitudes towards Islam and Muslems is that it established a tradition and a method which were imitated by successive generations of writers, American writers not excluded. It is significant that de Cusa rejected the older method of vicious attacks on Islam and proposed, instead, a "dialogue" which aimed at conversion through controversy. It should be noted, however, that nowhere in the controversy does Islam present any inherent virtue, and nowhere is it likely to gain the upper hand. The defeat of Islam is a foregone conclusion. Although the principle of the "dialogue" is established, the two arguments are spoken in one voice, that of the Christian and Western writer.

This supposed debate was to become an established form for Western Christian polemics on Islam. The argument takes more or less the following lines: Islam is credited with some merits, but these are all taken from Christianity and Judaism. The rest is "a heap of rubbish."[78] All merits, especially Islam's unitarian principle and respect for Christ, Moses and the other prophets, are used to advantage in striving to convert Muslems, whereas the "rubbish" (which is usually comprised of misquotations and misrepresentations of the Qur'an) is used to prove that Islam is a false doctrine or an imposture. Inaccuracies are used also to prove that the Qur'an is man-made, whereas the Old and New Testaments are revelations of the Word of God. Through this process of stripping Islam of any virtues and of any legitimate claim to divine inspiration, the logical conclusion is that it is better to go to the source of all religious truths. This method also includes an analysis of Muhammad's "scheme of religion" and of its emergence and subsequent development. Here a variety of proofs of the false character of Islam is presented. Either Jews or Nestorians, or both, are credited with the inception of the idea of a new religion. Muhammad, who may have started out as a reformer, is said to have adapted this idea, plus some relevant Christian and Judaic teachings, to the Arab mentality and environment. In the process, however, Muhammad is shown to have departed from original intentions and used his scheme and his followers to further his personal interests and ambitions.

The American reading public was familiar with this Western view of Islam through various available sources, especially the works of the English writers mentioned earlier. The predominant attitude in these works is that of "overcoming," defeating, and being "master of the controversy," to use terms familiar to the polemics. Sale, whose translation of the Qur'an remained by far the best English rendering until late in the nineteenth century, advises his readers that his aim is not the propagation of knowledge of Islam for its own sake. He explains that Christians should follow new methods of converting Muslems, and states his conviction that "protestants alone are able to attack the Koran with success; and for them, I trust, Providence has reserved the glory of its overthrow."[79] Ross' "Needful Caveat or Admonition..." had also explained that the translation of the Qur'an arrived for "what use may be made of it" and for the uncovering of its falsehoods. Most importantly, Ross indicates what kind of readers he has in mind. He says:

> ...they only may surely and without danger read the *Alcoran*, who are intelligent, judicious, learned, and thoroughly grounded in Piety, and principles of Christianity; but weak, ignorant, inconstant, and disaffected minds to the Truth, must not venture to meddle with this unhallowed piece, lest they be polluted with the touch thereof, as they were who came near to a leprous Body; and if we will not venture to go into an infected House without preservatives, much less should any dare to read the *Alcoran*, that is not sufficiently armed with Grace, Strength, and Knowledge, against all temptations.[80]

Henry Jessup and Royall Tyler

By a curious coincidence, both the beginning and end of the nineteenth century were marked by the publication of two important American works on Islam. These works, each in its own way, emulate the traditional pattern of Western polemics on Islam. *The Algerine Captive* (1797) by Royall Tyler includes a fictitious narrative (despite the author's protestations to the contrary) of the near-conversion to Islam of an American Christian, Dr. Updike Underhill, at the hand of a Muslim priest in Algiers. Henry Jessup's *The Setting of the Crescent and the Rising of the Cross; or Kamil Abdul Massiah* is the real story of his own conversion of a Syrian Muslim to Christianity in Beirut.[81]

Jessup's approach to the subject of Islam and the Arabs becomes clear in the theme of his various works: Muslems should be converted to Christianity because their beliefs are degrading and because of their state of backwardness, immorality and corruption. Jessup spent the better part of his life working toward this goal. The aforementioned work by Jessup is described in the "Introduction" (written by F. E. Ellingwood) as the "simple story of the brief Christian life of Kamil Aietany [which] furnishes a striking illustration of the power of the gospel over the human heart, even when intrenched in the most inveterate types of error."[82]

The basic premise on which Jessup builds his approach to Islam is twofold. First, Muslems are entrenched in error, and secondly, they can be saved and brought to the light of the Christian gospel. The form of the dialogue is also presented in the introduction: "a young Moslem visits the Jesuit school in Beirut," with the purpose of studying the Greek language, but "he there gains some partial views of the truth of the New Testament which had previously been withheld from him."[83] The experiences gained by Jessup in the Arab World, and indeed that of the hero of his book, prove that it is possible and worthwhile to convert Muslems because, according to Ellingwood, one of the reasons which make the story of Kamil "a valuable accession to the missionary literature of the day...[is that] it proves the utter falsity of the oracular assertion so often made by transient travellers, that no Moslem is ever converted to the Christian faith. We have never known clearer evidence of the genuineness of the work of the spirit of God in connection with this truth. The transformation in Paul's life was scarcely clearer or more impressive."[84]

Such a reference to transient travellers clearly points to a number of statements made by Americans who made the Holy Land tour and who advised against the efforts of missionaries among Muslems. One prominent American writer, Herman Melville, had stated that conversion of Muslems was an impossibility, and J.V.C. Smith was of the same opinion.[85] The anonymous writer of *Letters from Asia*, however, while agreeing that missionary work among Muslems was futile, based his opinion on a fairly sympathetic look at the faith of Muslems.[86]

Kamil follows the lines of argument drawn by De Cusa and emulated by George Sale and others who considered the conversion of Muslems a clear possibility, but insisted that this goal could 'not be achieved without a close study of the Qur'an and the religious beliefs of Islam. In the "Preface" to *Kamil*, Jessup indeed admits that "it is not easy for a Mohammedan to embrace Christianity...but when he is converted the Moslem becomes a strong and vigorous Christian."[87] This is because

> the element of divine truth which Mohammed derived from the Old
> and New Testaments, and which runs like a vein of gold through
> that extraordinary book, the Koran, teaching the existence and at-

tributes of God, the responsibility of man, and a final judgement, is a good foundation to build on.[88]

Ellingwood states that in the story of *Kamil* "an admirable example is afforded to missionaries in heathen and Moslem lands, and indeed to preachers and evangelists at home as well, of that alert and even wise tact which finds 'the line of least resistance' to the heart and conscience of one's adversary."[89] One other idea advanced here is the necessity of studying Islam to be able to argue with Muslims: "There are those," the writer goes on to say,

> who stoutly deny the necessity of learning anything whatever concerning the non-Christian religions, who deem it utter folly to study the Koran, even though one labors in Syria or Persia,...all that is needed is the story of the Cross. This young Syrian did not thus believe. If he had been a student of the Koran before, there was tenfold necessity now, for it was upon the teaching of the Koran and the entire cult of Islam that he proposed to move with an untiring and fearless conquest. He would have to deal with men of intelligence and intellectual training, and if he would show superiority of the gospel of Christ, he must know how to make an intelligent comparison.[90]

In the course of the narrative, and in the tradition of Western Christian polemics on Islam, Jessup enters into a "dialogue" with Kamil, armed with a long experience with the world of Islam and with the missionary enterprise in that world. Kamil is therefore convinced he should read the Bible and is provided with a number of aids, interpretations and books of catechism. All of this is necessary, in Jessup's view, for Kamil to get rid of the prejudices of twelve centuries. The young, impressionable man, a model of simplicity and innocence, immediately recognizes the virtues of Christianity and enters, in Jessup's narrative, into an inner "dialogue" reminiscent of the tradition of Christian "dialogues" with Islam. "I have heard this kind of prayer before," Kamil exclaims in a moment of discovery upon participating silently in Jessup's prayers. "It is talking with God. We Muslims repeat words five times a day, but we have no such prayers as yours."[91]

Jessup later confirms Kamil's statement in his *Mohammedan Missionary Problem* where he describes all acts of Muslim devotions as physical, outward gestures which do not reach the heart. Islam, says Jessup, is an intensely formal and ritual system, a religion of words—outward words, not affecting the heart or requiring transformation of life. Fasting, the pilgrimage to Mecca, praying five times a day, testifying "There is no God but God, and Mohammed is his apostle," almsgiving, genuflections, circumcision and repeating the one hundred names of God, are some of the rites and acts by which the believer purchases Paradise. Similarly, the life-time missionary, Dr. Eli Smith of Beirut, observes that

> the good works of Islam are of the lips, the hand and the outward
> bodily act, having no connection with holiness of life, honesty,
> veracity and integrity.[92]

This was a prevalent view of Islam in the West. For Jessup, as well as Kamil (represented by Jessup), the dialogue is concluded and the argument is decided then and there. Each side, after a fashion, has presented its case.

The rest of the dialogue is handled quite as easily and as successfully. To the ambiguous question of the Trinity and the three aspects of the Godhead, Jessup offers an explanation which even Kamil's childlike mind delights in. Says Jessup to Kamil: "God is a spirit, infinite, eternal, and unchangeable, in his being, wisdom, power, holiness, justice, goodness, and truth."[93] The explanation "charmed" Kamil, and, his teacher-priest continues, "there are three persons in the Godhead: The Father, the Son, and the Holy Ghost: and these three are one God, the same in substance, equal in power and glory." This, says Jessup, "set his mind at rest." Kamil then presents his now-disowned Muslim view: "We Mohammedans think that the Christians worship three Gods, but you do not; for there is one God in three persons: the Eternal Father, the Eternal Word, and the Eternal Spirit. That is all clear."[94]

Jessup then explains the doctrine of salvation and atonement to the young convert. He says:

> Then we read the Bible together for two hours and he listened with
> astonishment and delight. He seized upon the great doctrine of the
> atoning sacrifice of Christ with such eagerness and satisfaction that
> the seemed to be taught by the divine Spirit from the very outset.
> 'This,' he said 'is what we need. The Koran does not give us a way of
> salvation. It leaves us in doubt as to whether God will forgive our
> sins. It does not explain how he can do so and preserve his honor
> and justice. Here in the gospel it is plain. Christ bore our sins; he died
> in our stead; he died to save us from dying. This is beautiful; it is just
> what I want.'[95]

One by one, in the form of a dialogue, the arguments for Islam are articulated by Jessup and his young convert, and then refuted by the arguments for Christianity. Eventually Kamil becomes a Christian missionary and tours the Arabian peninsula teaching the word of the Gospel. His encounters with Muslims become an extension of the same form of dialogue and controversy in which American Protestant polemics is at its best. At one meeting with Muslim "fanatics" Kamil and his adversaries have an argument as to which of them was destined to go to hell. Kamil concludes, "God knows which of us will go to Jenneh [paradise] and which to Jehennam [hell]....I returned to my house, thanking God that I had escaped from them."[96]

The story of Kamil takes an ironic twist when on several occasions he has encounters with Roman Catholics whom he—the convert from Islam—tries to lead to the right path of Christ.

A more elaborate work by Jessup on the formula of missionary labor in Muslim countries is his *Mohammedan Missionary Problem* which purports to be an analysis of the relationships between Islam and Christianity. The purpose of the book appears in a statement in the "Preface":

> It is our earnest hope and prayer that this revival of interest in the historical, theological and ethical bearings of Islamism may result in a new practical interest in the spiritual welfare of the Mohammedan nations. It is high time for the Christian Church to ask seriously the question whether the last command of Christ, 'Preach the gospel to every creature,' concerns the one hundred and seventy-five millions of the Mohammedan world.[97]

The problem which seemed pressing to the American missionary establishment at the time was, in Jessup's words: "connected with its fulfillment of the great missionary commission of its divine Head for the world's salvation." How are we, he asks,

> to reach the one hundred and seventy-five millions of Mohammedans spread over one hundred and twenty degrees of longitude...embracing vast nations speaking thirty different languages, yet unified and compact by a common faith which has survived the shocks and conflicts of twelve hundred years?[98]

In this book, as in his other works on the subject, Jessup employs the formula of the polemics in his juxtaposition of Islam and Christianity, and in the basic assumption that Muslims need to be enlightened regardless of the outcome of the dialogue. Favorable and unfavorable features turn out to be virtues and vices, the former are common to Islam and Christianity, the latter peculiarly Islamic. For example, the list of the unfavorable features in Islam includes, among others:

> Islam suffers from "A divorce between morality and religion," and although the Koran has some "moral precepts...it can be said that whatever in the Koran is true" is taken from Christianity.[99]
>
> Islam is characterized by its "Ishmaelitic intolerance." For the Koran does not have any precept "enjoining love to enemies. It teaches kindness, charity and forgiveness of injuries, but only to Mohammedans. It knows nothing of universal benevolence."[100] Time and again Jessup describes Islam as "an Arab, an Ishmaelitic faith—its hand against every man." He places a great deal of emphasis on what he describes as the aggressive nature of Islam, not only for

using the sword to subdue others and bring them into its fold,[101] but also because Islam to him is a missionary religion employing even some of the Christian missionary methods such as the printed word.[102] "There still exists," he concludes, "not a little of the old Crescentade spirit of the seventh century."[103]

Islam also suffers from gross immorality[104] and untruthfulness[105] which, to Jessup, are inherent in the religion itself and in the nature of the people whom it addresses.

The positive features in Islam are analyzed by Jessup not as inherent virtues in the religion itself, but as borrowings from Christianity and Judaism. They include the Islamic belief in the unity of God.[106] This is a big step in the way of converting Muslems. In fact, Jessup wonders "whether Mohammad would not have led his followers directly into Christianity had he understood the meaning of the New Testament doctrine of the Trinity and the divinity of Christ."[107]

Muslems hold the Old and New Testaments in great reverence, as they do Christ and "they have especial *respect for Christians and Jews as the 'people of a book'—Ehel Kitab.*"[108] Other favorable features are the Muslem "*reverence for Law*" and their "*total abstinence from intoxicating drinks.*" But Jessup adds here that "one of the chief reasons which moved Mohammad to prohibit the use of wine was undoubedly to make them different from Christians, Jews and pagans, all of whom used wine."[109]

One final feature cited by Jessup is "the *doctrine of fate, and of absolute surrender to the decree and will of God* [which] are elements of strength in the Moslem character."[110] He says:

> This doctrine of fate may yet play an important part rt in restraining the fanatical passions of the Moslem multitude when great movements toward Christianity begin to take place among them. Were the Arab Moslems to hear to-morrow that the sultan himself had become a Christian, it is not unlikely that the only thought would be, "It is the decree of God;" "It is mukoddar, kismet;" "Let the will of God be done!"[111]

Jessup's total picture of Islam is a self-contained analysis through the form of a dialogue or comparison with Christianity. The ultimate goal was the defeat of Islam and the conversion of Muslems. In Jessup's view, that goal would be achieved.

When Royall Tyler wrote *The Algerine Captive* at the end of the eighteenth century he undoubtedly had in mind the popular reputation of the horrors of captivity in the Muslim countries of North Africa. Tyler's novel, however, is not exclusively the story of the captivity of Dr. Updike Underhill in Algiers; this occupies only a part of Book Two. The rest deals with Underhill's early life, education and experience at home in the North and South. Significantly, Tyler inserts within the story of the hero's captivity a number of chapters dealing with Islam, the Prophet Muhammad, and, more importantly, a dialogue between Dr. Underhill and a Muslem priest who tries to convert him. Yet these chapters and the accounts of the cruelty of his Muslem captors are not disconnected from the other parts of the novel and the hero's earlier experience. Instead, Muslem fanaticism serves as a satiric reflection on Underhill's early encounters with what he considers Puritan zeal and Southern bigotry—the cruel treatment suffered by negro slaves back home and on board a slave ship named "Sympathy," on which he himself was a passenger. Underhill's treatment of Islam is at one and the same time a critical view of bigotry and fanaticism wherever they exist, and of the traditional Western treatment of Islam. It might be said that Tyler offers one of the earliest Western tolerant attitudes to Islam in the West, as well as a prophetic satire of what was to become, during the subsequent century, an obsessive fanatic drive in some missionary quarters to convert the Muslem world to Christianity.

Tyler's presentation of Islam and the Prophet shows a considerable knowledge of Islam and its basic tenets and an awareness of some Western literature on the subject. In Chapter 22 Tyler, without departing from the prevailing view of Islam as an imposture, gives a rather favorable account of "the founder of the faith." "This fortunate impostor," he says, "like all other great characters in the drama of life, has been indignantly vilified by his opponents, and as ardently praised by his adherents." Tyler announces that he would "endeavour to steer the middle course of impartiality; neither influenced by the bigoted aversion of Sales and Prideaux, or the specious praise of the *philosophic* Boulainvilliers [sic]."[112] The hero expresses a similar sentiment earlier in the novel when he falls captive to the Algerians and is transported to their ship.

Tyler presents a fairly objective, though basically Christian, portrait of the Prophet of Islam. He answers the stigma attached to him as a cameldriver by simply stating that Muhammad "had the direction of camels it is true. The merchandize of Arabea was transported to different regions by caravans of those useful animals, a troop of which he was conductor."[113]

Like Ross and other Western writers, Tyler sends Muhammad on trips to Syria, Palestine and Egypt, and thinks that these travels gained him "the most useful knowledge of each country."[114] To this experience, according to Tyler, Muhammad brought some rudiments of education, contrary to the claims of the Turks that he was illiterate. For, says Tyler,

> his father Abdalla was a man of moderate fortune, and bestowed upon his son such an education as a parent in confined, if not impoverished, circumstances could confer. The Turks say he could not

> write, because they pride themselves in decrying letters, and be-
> cause the pious among them suppose his ignorance of letters a suffi-
> cient evidence of the divine original of the book he published, as
> received from and written by the Finger of Diety.[115]

Tyler maintains there can be little doubt that Muhammad "was possessed of all the literary acquirements necessary to accomplish him for
his business."[116]

As for Muhammad's personal merits, Tyler says,

> he is represented as a man of a beautiful person and commanding
> presence. By his engaging manners and remarkable attention to
> business, he became the factor of a rich Arabian merchant, after
> whose death he married his widow, the beautiful Cadija, and came
> into the lawful possession of immense wealth, which awakened in
> him the most unbounded ambition.[117]

The facts and motives presented here are not very different from those
presented by Sale, Hayward, the *Hand-Book* and others. Yet Tyler's tone
is less incriminating and more understanding.

Conditions, according to Tyler, were favorable for the introduction of
a new religion, and Muhammad availed himself of these conditions. "He
was surrounded by Arian Christians and Jews, both of whom had been
persecuted by the established church; by Pagans, whose belief in a
plurality of gods made them ready proselytes of any novel system; and
by the wise of them who were disgusted with the gross absurdities of
their own mythology."[118] Muhammad appealed to all these groups by
gratifying their principles and needs. As for the popular

> stories of Mahomet's having retired to a cave with a monk and a Jew
> to compile his book, and falling into fits of the epilepsy, persuading
> his disciples that these fits were trances, in order to propagate his
> system more effectually, so often related by geography com-
> pilers...[119]

These stories, says Tyler, "are fit only to amuse the vulgar. It is certain
he secluded himself from company, and assumed the austerity of manners becoming the reformer of a vicious world." Perhaps this was the
first such favorable presentation in published form to become popular in
the western world, certainly in the United States. Tyler's acquaintance
with previous literature on the subject is seen in his conclusion of his
short biography of the Prophet. He says:

> European writers, who have destroyed almost as many great per-
> sonages by poison as the French have with the guillotine, have at-
> tributed his death to a dose administered by a monk. But when we
> consider his advanced age and public energies, we need not recur to
> any but natural means for the cause of his death.[120]

Tyler's contribution to the subject of the Islamic faith is found not only in his presentation of the principal tenets of Islam but also in his differentiation between Islam as a creed and the state of the people who professed that creed. This is all the more striking because it ostensibly comes from the hero of the novel who has suffered from the most brutal treatment at the hands of these people. Of the Qur'an, Tyler is certain that "the portions which I [the hero] have heard chanted at funerals and quoted in conversation ever exhibited the purest morality and the sublimest conception of the Diety."[121]

Tyler then proceeds to treat the "fundamental doctrine of the Alcoran," which includes the unity of God, the divine messages of Abraham, Moses, Jesus and Muhammad, and the "belief in the eternal decrees of God, in a resurrection and final judgement to bliss or misery."[122] As to the practical duties enjoined upon Muslems, Tyler enumerates the daily prayers, frequent ablutions, acts of charity, and fasting. "The Alcoran also forbids games of chance and the use of strong liquors; inculcates a tenderness for idiots and a respect for age."[123]

Tyler's conclusion is also very striking, especially when compared with later writings by persons whose experience and observations, coupled perhaps with their predispositions, blinded them to the doctrine itself. "Upon the whole," Tyler concludes,

> there do not appear to be any articles in their faith which incite them to immorality, or can countenance the cruelties they commit. Neither their Alcoran nor their priests excite them to plunder, enslave, or torment. The former expressly recommends charity, justice, and mercy, towards their fellow men. I would not bring the sacred volume of our faith in any comparative view with the Alcoran of Mahomet; but I cannot help noticing it as extraordinary, that the Mahometan should abominate the Christian on account of his faith, and the Christian detest the Mussulman for his creed; when the Koran of the former acknowledges the divinity of the Christian Messias, and the Bible of the latter commands us to love our enemies. If either would follow the obvious dictates of his own scripture, he would cease to hate, abominate, and destroy the other.[124]

In *The Algerine Captive* (Book II, chapters 5, 6 and 7) Tyler provides what could be considered the first American contribution to the traditional Western polemics on Islam. The fictional situation of Tyler's hero, who is subjected to the Mollah's efforts of persuasion and conversion, is a prophetic anticipation in reverse of Kamil's situation. Nor is Tyler's story completely fictional; for there were many Western (some American) prisoners who were persuaded to "turn Turk" in exchange for freedom and a comfortable life.[125] What distinguishes Tyler's "dialogue" between Dr. Underhill and the Mollah is its candid presentation, in a contrastive form, of the principles of both Islam and Christianity—point counterpoint. And in spite of Underhill's final decision to resist the temptations of conversion and endure the physical bondage and sufferings of slavery, this does not diminish the balanced presentation of the arguments—sometimes the fanaticism—of both sides.

The dialogue presented by Tyler is clearly at one and the same time a critical view of the traditional Western attacks on the faith of Islam, if only because those traditional attacks as presented by Underhill are refuted by the Mollah; it is also a bitter criticism of Western, especially American, culture which condones cruelty to and enslavement of fellow human beings. The dialogue also indirectly repudiates the belligerent crusading spirit of Christian nations which caused bloodshed and persecution in the name of religion.

The argument condensed by the author into a "dialogue" is truly a summing-up of the traditional Western polemics on Islam. The Christian slave tells his adversary that he will "bring my religion to the test. Compare it with the—the—." The Mollah interrupts gently: "Speak out boldly. No advantage shall be taken. You would say 'with the Mahometan imposture.'"[126] The hero says that the "Bible was written by men divinely inspired." To which the Mollah replies that the Qur'an was divine revelation too. What proof can either of them offer? It is, for the first time, one Christian's word against one Muslim's. Each is speaking for himself.[127] Each party to the dialogue insists that his religion is genuine because of its humble beginnings and the miraculous force of its propagation. In fact, the Mollah uses Underhill's arguments in this respect to support his own, and Underhill's reaction is a wisely suppressed aside.

> My blood boiled to hear this infidel vaunt himself thus triumphantly against my faith; and, if it had not been for a prudence which in hours of zeal I have since had cause to lament, I should have taken vengeance of him upon the spot.[128]

Instead Underhill withholds his anger and continues the dialogue by citing miracles as proof and support of the divinity of Christianity. But the Mollah would not be silenced; Islam and the life of Muhammad, he claims, are full of miracles and manifestations of God's favor.

But, says Underhill, "our religion was disseminated in peace; yours was promulgated by the sword." To which the Mollah answers: "My friend, you surely have not read the writings of your own historians."[129] He then proceeds to remind Underhill of the "bloody massacres" which characterized the "history of the Christian church," of the "thundering legions under Constantine the Great," of the Inquisitions and presecutions of the Moors in Spain, and of "the dragooning of the Hugonots from France under Louis the Great."[130] In contrast, the Mollah claims that Muslems "never yet forced a man to adopt their faith," they revere the Christian and the Hebrew religions and sacred books, they "leave it to the Christians of the West Indies, and Christians of your southern plantations, to baptize the unfortunate African into your faith, and then use your brother Christians as brutes of the desert."[131] The hero's only comment on this is a silent remark, "here I was abashed for my country, I could not answer him."[132] Yet he still has some arguments, obviously drawn from traditional polemics. Underhill says to the Mollah: "But you hold a sensual paradise."[133] This draws from the Mollah a long speech in which he cites an equally sensuous paradise promised to Christians by their religion. He sums up the case for Islam by exhorting the Christian slave to read the Muslem's "spotless book," where he says,

> You will learn the necessity of being virtuous here, that you may be happy and not miserable herafter. You will learn resignation to the will of the Holy One; because you will know what all the events of your life were, in the embryo of time, forged on the anvils of Divine Wisdom. In a word, you will learn the unity of God, which, not-withstanding the cavil of your divines, your prophet, like ours, came into the world to establish, and every man of reason must believe. You need not renounce your prophet. Him we respect as a great apostle of God; but Mahomet is the seal of the prophets. Turn then my friend, from slavery to the delights of life.[134]

Underhill's final remarks show his faithful adherence to his religion in spite of the promise of freedom and a luxurious life: "After five days' conversation, disgusted with his fables, abashed by his assurance, and almost confounded by his sophistry, I resumed my slave's attire, and sought safety in my former servitude."[135]

The dialogue ends in a draw, so to speak, but only on the face of it. Neither one of the adversaries gains a convert, but both of them have been given a chance to present their views. Tyler was truly a pioneer of what was to become, by the second half of the nineteenth century, a more even-handed, but no less Christian, attitude towards other religions, Islam included. But that attitude was limited to certain universalist and free-religion circles, and, unfortunately the century was to end on the more forceful notes of Jessup's and similar voices.

Changes in the American Attitude

In the meantime, there were gradual developments in the reputation of Islam and of the Prophet Muhammad in the United States of America. Some of these developments came in the use of this subject in works of literature. But they were more direct and obvious in the treatment of Islam in essays and brief statements which were scattered in periodicals and other writings. This favorable change in the fortunes of Islam was very slow and gradual; it was also limited to a number of what could be called in modern terms "liberal-minded circles" and it did not noticeably affect the missionary and religious establishments in America.

The first signs of a more favorable attitude towards Islam and Muslems can be traced to two major works which were popular among the American reading public. These two works are George Sale's translation of the Qur'an, as mentioned earlier, and Thomas Carlyle's *Heroes and Hero-Worship*. Sale provided the English reading public with a fairly good translation of the Holy book of Islam. He also introduced his translation with an analysis of the religion and Prophet of Islam. Although he still considered Islam as imposture, Sale gave the Prophet Muhammad some credit for his sincere belief in the unity of the Diety and his search for religious truth.

In an attempt at understanding Muhammad's motives, and in reply to the charges of sensuality and self-advancement, Sale says of Muhammad that "his first views perhaps were not so self-interested. His original design of bringing the pagan Arabs to the knowledge of the true God were certainly noble, and highly to be commended." This was definitely a new idea for the general reading public. Sincerity also was a mark of Muhammad's efforts, for, according to Sale, he "was no doubt fully satisfied in his conscience of the truth of his grand point, the unity of God, which was what he chiefly attended to; all his other doctrines and institutions being accidental and unavoidable, rather than premeditated and designed."[136] Sale's statement seems to be a rebuttal of the then prevalent view of Muhammad as a cold-blooded schemer who aimed at advancing his own interest. Neither does the translator of the Qur'an agree with Dr. Prideaux and others that Muhammad made his nation "exchange their idolatory for another religion altogether as bad."[137] Sale finally concludes: "whether this was the effect of enthusiasm, or only a design to raise himself to the supreme government of his country, I will not pretend to determine."[138]

Sincerity and truth are also the two main attributes of Muhammad and his calling, according to Thomas Carlyle. For his *Heroes and Hero-Worship*, Carlyle chooses Muhammad as a model of the "hero as prophet," not, as Carlyle explains, because he considers him as the most eminent nor the truest of prophets. Carlyle justifies his choice on the basis of being able to speak freely of Muhammad without exposing anybody to the danger of becoming "Mohammetan." Yet Carlyle says: "I mean to say all the good of him I justly can. It is the way we get at his secret: let us try to understand what *he* means with the world; what the world meant and means with him will then be a more answerable question."[139]

Carlyle begins by refuting the "current hypothesis about Mohamet" which accused him as "a scheming Imposter, a Falsehood incarnate, that his religion is a mere mass of quackery and fatuity."[140] That hypothesis is no more tenable for Carlyle. "A man," he says, "must conform himself to Nature's laws, *be* verily in communion with Nature and the truth of things, or Nature will answer him not, No, not at all!"[141] And Nature has answered Muhammad, else how could his permanent influence on millions of people be explained? The essence of Muhammad's message, according to Carlyle, is sincerity. He is, he says, "what I call a sincere man. I should say sincerity, a deep, great, genuine sincerity, is the first characteristic of all men in any way heroic."[142] But the principal characteristic of sincerity, as possessed by Muhammad, is the lack of affectation and consciousness of his greatness. He is truly "an original man; he comes to us at first-hand."[143]

Carlyle's works were an immediate success in America and were especially popular in Transcendentalist circles. Emerson himself maintained close contact with Carlyle and was of invaluable help in getting Carlyle's works published in the States. Correspondence between the two shows Emerson working on the publication of Carlyle's *Heroes* while he was writing some of his own essays, including "Heroism," "Self-Reliance," "History," and later "Man the Reformer," and one cannot fail to see the influence of Carlyle's ideas on the young aspiring writer and his friends. This influence is in fact attested to by a prominent Trancendentalist, Margaret Fuller, who says of the British author's *Heroes and Hero-Worship* that "there is no living writer who is more sure of immediate attention from a large circle of readers, or who exercises a greater influence than he in these United States....thousands turn an eager ear to the most distant note of his clarion."[144]

Fuller recognizes the essential character of Carlyle's ideal heroes. "To *be* and not to *seem*," she says, "to know that nothing can become man which is not manlike...; that all conventions not founded on eternal law are valueless, and that the life of man, will he or no, must tally with the life of nature."[145] This basic transcendental creed, which is the essence of Emerson and Thoreau's philosophy, was re-enforced in Fuller's view "by Carlyle with that depth of 'truthful earnestness' he appreciates so fully in his chosen heroes,...in the delineation of examples, rarely equalled in any age of English literature."[146]

The immediate effect of Carlyle's "Hero As Prophet" can be seen in statements made by American writers which show signs of sympathy towards Islam and the Prophet Muhammad or, at least, less prejudiced opinions of them. Shortly after the publication of Carlyle's *Heroes* and the new edition of Sale's translation, two articles and one play were published in the States showing these signs. The *Dial* of October 1840 published a book review of *Sectarianism as Heresy* which included very novel remarks about the universality of religion. The review says: "For the dwellers in Truth are like the inhabitants of this earth...No matter what creed we house our heads under, we never touch the firm land of Truth." No matter with what religious description we call ourselves, continues the article, be it "Catholic or Baptist, Jew or Mahometan, so far as we dwell in the light of the principles of truth and goodness, and so far only, we are members of the true church."[147] The writer insists that although people claim the existence of many different religions, there is and can be but one Religion. All else is but diversity of form. The eternal principles, which lie at the bottom of all religious systems, are the same. "Religious truth is universal, uncontradictable. The religions of Adam, of Moses, of Mahomet, and of Christ are grounded on the same great principles of man's relation to God. The difference lies in the *degree* in which the truth is promulgated through these persons, and in the kind of truth presented. One system has greater *fullness* of truth than another. We speak of the fundamental ideas of such systems, and not of their subordinate parts."[148]

A more adulatory article on the Prophet Muhammad came from a reviewer of Sale's translation of the Qur'an in the *North American Review* in October 1846. The writer credits Carlyle, Sesmondi, and Sale with the new ideas about Islam and the Prophet Muhammad, which, he says "have done something, of late years, to make us believe that the old orthodox notion of Mahomet's, or Mohammed's, power and success is not as well founded as might be." The writer recognizes their efforts "to convince the world that naked, selfish, mean imposition never could have done what the spirit of the founder of Islam did." Yet the writer admits that

> the mass of those who write on the prophet still write in the tone of the Crusaders; they buckle on their armor to do battle with the false leader of the infidel host, in place of opening their eyes and purging their minds, to see and understand aright one of the great phenomena of history, that is to say, one of the great facts in God's government of the world.[149]

Not many facts, he continues, are known with certainty about the life of Muhammad, and neither "Saracens nor Christians are to be believed." Therefore the only way to judge the sincerity of the Prophet is to read the Qur'an with understanding and impartiality:

He that reads must read *as Neibuhr* did. He must question every statement, weigh every intimation, compare friend and enemy on every point of praise and dispraise. The Koran alone may be trusted, and to the study of that more than all else the inquirer should turn, and strive to find the needle which shall guide him through that vast stack of mingled weeds, flowers, and food.[150]

The Prophet is described as "calm, acute, quick, imaginative, and devout by nature, and devout also through suffering."[151] His observation of the social traditions, habits, and beliefs of Arabia, and his knowledge of Christianity and Judaism, made him aware of his nation's need for reform. Muhammad thus devoted himself entirely for the cause of reform. In quite an unprecedented statement, contrary even to Sale's opinion (whose translation of the Qur'an was the subject of the review) the writer places Muhammad on a par with Jesus and Moses. He traces the long intellectual and spiritual journey of Muhammad, his doubts and his desire to purify the evils of Arabian society, law, and religion. How he questioned his own mission, compared it to that of Moses and of Jesus, and finally synthesized his purpose, is dramatically told in this critique.[152]

The year 1850 saw the publication of a play which had won in the previous year "a prize of *one thousand dollars*...for the best original *tragedy, in five acts*."[153] The title of the play is *Mohammed: the Arabian Prophet*, and although it has no great merit as literature, it reveals the impact of works like Carlyle's and Sale's on the contemporary attitude towards the Prophet Muhammad, especially in the literary world. In an interesting introduction to the play, the playwright, George Miles, dramatizes the ambivalence which characterized that attitude at the time: an ambivalence which wavers between admiration for the integrity and nobility of the person of Muhammad on the one hand, and, on the other, the traditional rejection of the new religion and of the Qur'an. "The design of this play," Miles says, "is to explain the life of Mohammed from the age of forty to his death, a period of twenty years."[154]

Quite obviously, Miles tries in his play to reconcile Carlyle's complimentary picture of the Prophet to the prevalent Christian picture, without indulging in vitriolic attacks on Islam and the Prophet. In his view, "it is no compliment to Christianity, to make Mohammed a monster; it is rather a bitter sneer at human credulity."[155] Yet there is a lesson to be gained "by the life and death of the Arabian imposter [which is] the inability of the greatest man, starting with the purest motives, to counterfeit a mission from God, without becoming the slave of hell."[156] Thus, while recognizing the greatness of the Prophet of Islam, Miles tries to show how deceit is capable of corrupting the greatest of men. Miles' analysis of the character and motives of the hero of his play is an example of the attitude which swung back and forth between Carlyle's hero and Sale's imposter.

This ambivalence in the American attitude to the Prophet of Islam and the Qur'an was not uncommon in American literary circles. Washington Irving's popular work *Mahomet and His Successors* is indeed a good example of the shifting between admiration and condemnation. Irving has nothing but praise for the silent suffering and self-sacrifice of the Prophet in his quest for religious reform of his fellow Arabs. He also commends Muhammad's abstention from worldly ambition and glory. "His military triumphs," Irving explains, "awakened no pride nor vainglory, as they would have done had they been effected for selfish purposes."[157] Neither was he corrupted by the power he had attained from a greater following, for "in the time of his greatest power, he maintained the same simplicity of manners and appearance as in the days of his adversity."[158] And in spite of the enormous amount of riches acquired by the Islamic state under him, the Prophet Muhammad, Irving admits, exercised self-discipline and "did not leave a golden dinar nor a silver dirhem." It becomes obvious to Irving that there is something puzzling about the character and calling of this seemingly great man. But Irving attempts an answer anyway:

> It is this perfect abnegation of self, connected with this apparently heartfelt piety, running throughout the various phases of his fortune, which perplex one in forming a just estimate of Mahomet's character. However he betrayed the alloy of earth after he had worldly power at his command, the early aspirations of his spirit continually returned and bore him above all earthly things. Prayer, that vital duty of Islamism, and that infallible purifier of the soul, was his constant practice. 'Trust in God,' was his comfort and support in times of trial and despondency. On the clemency of God, we are told, he reposed all his hopes of supernal happiness....[159]

This puzzled look at Islam notwithstanding, by the second half of the nineteenth century there was a degree of tolerance among certain groups towards other religions, Islam included. In the year 1874, for example, Moncure Conway, a later Transcendentalist, edited a collection of religious texts he called *The Sacred Anthology*. For the first time in America, this *Anthology* presented selections from Christian, Hebrew, Muslim, Hindu, Chinese and other sacred writings side by side under athematic classification. No attempt is made to show the superiority of one text over another; in fact, the absence of comments on these texts is in itself an even-handed treatment. Conway's brief "Preface" shows the spirit with which the effort was undertaken. He says that "the purpose of the work is simply moral. The editor has believed that it would be useful for moral and religious culture if the sympathy of Religions could be more generally made known, and the converging testimonies of ages and races to great principles more widely appreciated." What Conway chooses to exclude from his selections is either of temporary and local interest, or marred by "the rust of superstition and the dross of ritual."[160] But much more is omitted,

> because unknown to him; but he would be much misunderstood if his suppressions should be regarded as intended to disparage the many cherished passages of sacred writings not to be found in this book. Each nation has its full scriptures, and it is among the hopes with which this selection is offered to the public that it may lead to a more general and reverent study of them.[161]

Certainly, presenting this more general and reverent view was a great advance over the more prevalent studies which sought to defeat Islam and the Prophet.

Another landmark in this development is James Freeman Clarke's *Ten Great Religions* (Part I, 1871, and Part II, 1883), which, in spite of its bias towards Christianity, looks tolerantly on all major world religions. The quotation on the title page of Part II indicates the thesis of Clarke's work: "He who only knows one religion can no more understand *that* religion than he who only knows one language can understand *that* language."[162] Clarke holds that old classifications of religion are false. Islam receives a particularly favorable treatment in his analysis of world religions when he claims that his comparative study would prove that "all great religions of the world, except Christianity and Mohammedanism, are ethnic religions, or religions limited to a single nation or race. Christianity alone (including Mohammedanism and Judaism, which are its temporary and local forms) is the religion of all races."[163]

Those who believed in a universal religion to which all true believers belonged, and those who subscribed to the concept of the God of Nature or the Oversoul, looked upon all men with benign tolerance and accepted them together with their beliefs. Islam and the Prophet of Islam were given a legitimate place in the scheme of religions by these groups. It is unfortunate that the nineteenth century should end on a note sounded by Jessup and not by Clarke or Conway. The obvious result of this in the twentieth century has been works like Salman Rushdie's, the disfigured media image of Islam and Muslims, and the false notions subtly disseminated in popular literature and school textbooks.[164]

4

THE SHORES OF TRIPOLI
America's First Encounter
with the Muslim World

See what dark prospect interrupts our joy!
What arm presumptuous dares our trade annoy?
Great God! The rovers who infest the waves,
Have seiz'd our ships, and made our freemen slaves.
David Humphreys, "Poem on the
Future Glory of America," 1805

It is an unfortunate fact of history that the young, aspiring nation of America should come into conflict with the world of Islam immediately after Independence, although many Americans at the time viewed this development as part of the overall Providential plan. The story of America's entanglement with what was called, at the time, the Barbary States of North Africa is long and complicated. American ships were seized, their goods confiscated and United States citizens captured and held for ransom. The actual events themselves, and the prolonged tortuous negotiations, are interesting and had a great impact on America's earliest images of Muslims and influenced its attitude towards them. This political and strategic involvement provided the first real person-to-person contact Americans had with representatives of Islam.

In fact, some American involvement with Muslim North Africa came well before the emergence of the United States of America as an independent state. In 1679 the British King's appointed Governor of Carolina (which at the time included North and South Carolina) was on his way to take up his post in the New World when the ship on which he was travelling was intercepted and captured by sea bandits who were known as the Barbary Pirates. Governor Seth Southell was taken as a captive to Algiers, where he petitioned the King to ransom him. The process of negotiations and deliberations took a few months, and on July 2, 1679, the King ordered "the peticoner to be redeemed in exchange for Hodge

Omar ["late Commander of the Tiger of Argier"] and Buffalo Ball two Turkish Prisoners aboard Vice Admiral Herbert in the Mediterranean or either of them."[1] After another interval of deliberations at the King's Council, Seth Southell was finally freed and proceeded to occupy the governor's seat in the British colony of Carolina. The matter did not end there, though, for one of Southell's unfortunate companions in captivity, one Robert Cole, complained to the British authorities that Southell had defrauded him of a sum of money given in return for a promise to obtain Cole's release. The Council considered Cole's complaint and a number of letters were exchanged with the Governor of Carolina. Finally the Council decided to acquit the Governor and not to insist on his recall to England to answer the charges.[2] Other similar incidents took place during the Colonial period; the records of the House of Lords show that in 1680 the Governor of Massachusetts complained of the dangers encountered by sailors on the high seas, a matter which, he said, "creates a backwardness in persons most suitable to be employed as agents, for we have already lost five or six of our vessels by Turkish pirates, and many of our inhabitants continue in miserable captivity among them."[3]

About a century later, when the U. S. was an independent nation, it came into conflict with the same Barbary States, once again over American captives. The engagement was very serious, because of its consequences on future relations with Muslem North Africa as well as on public preoccupation with the issue in the United States. The complex and urgent nature of this encounter with the Barbary States makes it necessary to present a brief description of the atmosphere which prevailed between European countries and North Africa during the eighteenth century.

The "Barbary States" is the term which was used to describe the Muslem countries which line the north African coast on the Mediterranean. They were—from East to West—Tripoli (modern Libya, including the Barca region), Tunis, Algiers, and Morocco. These states occupied a very strategic position in the attempts to control Mediterranean navigation. Morocco's position was especially powerful since it had extensive coastlines on the Mediterranean and Atlantic, in addition to its domination of the Straits of Gibralter.

These north African states were nominally provinces of the Ottoman Empire. Their rulers were supposedly selected by consensus of the ruling classes of officers and dignitaries, subject to the approval of the High Porte. But in practice these rulers were often soldiers of fortune who paid their subordinates, as well as the Ottoman authorities, in order to maintain their positions. They were (as a general rule) absolute governors who were often deposed by force rather than by popular consensus.

They carried the titles of Basha of Tripoli, Dey of Algiers, Bey of Tunis, and Emperor of Morocco.

Political instability, poverty and the plague were endemic in the Barbary States. Their rulers had to face these societal problems and still maintain a steady flow of revenue to satisfy the High Porte and to ensure the well-being and loyalty of their subjects and subordinates. A major source of income for the rulers of these states were the annual tributes and "presents" paid by European countries in return for allowing their ships free navigation in the Mediterranean in their commercial intercourse with the Levant and the Orient. In the absence of such negotiated "Treaties," the vessels of European countries were intercepted and seized, their goods confiscated, and their passengers taken captive. Ships and passengers were held for ransom, and the extent of payments depended on the values attached to them at the time.

It should be noted, that although the Barbary States became notorious for their piratical practices, they were not the only countries which sanctioned or benefitted by such practices. Centuries of these intrigues on the high seas by adventurers, buccaneers and government-sponsored privateers gave them an acceptable status, especially in times of war. As early as the sixteenth century, Queen Elizabeth I gave her royal sanction to certain privateers like Sir Francis Drake, who plundered Spanish ships of their valuable cargoes brought back from the American continent. More recently the French, British and Americans employed pirates and privateers in their wars and revolutions. The New World had its own brand of pirates who operated with impunity and even became men of distinction. In fact, as one authority states,

> for the first hundred years and more after the establishment of the colonies in the New World, the distinction between privateers, slavers, pirates, and even Government cruisers was vague, and at times obliterated altogether. It was a period in which, on the high seas, might was right; and when their home Governments were at war with each other—and sometimes when at peace—the colonial seaman seized whatever he could, whether he was a pirate, privateersman, or a king's officer. The astonishing growth of commerce in the New World made it a tempting field for depredations of every kind....[4]

In the case of North African piracy the lines between private and government involvement were blurred, and the treaties which were concluded from time to time between the Barbary States and European powers gave the Barbary corsairs a status of acceptance by both parties. Moreover, the Ottoman Empire (and its tributaries such as the Barbary States) had long assumed sovereignty over the Mediterranean. European (i.e., Christian) ships sailing the Mediterranean were expected to pay for the right of passage or face the consequences. Treaties of amity and friendship were the means agreed upon to regulate the amount of annual tribute and the manner of payment. In effect, the ancient Muslim-Christian rivalry over control of the Mediterranean was still at work here, and countries belonging to either side were considered in a state of war with those of the other, unless that state was regulated by treaty.

Negotiations with the North African States

This was the situation which the newly-independent United States of America found itself facing when it tried to conduct its own commerce in the Mediterranean. During the Colonial period American ships, goods and sailors had enjoyed the protection of the English flag, under the umbrella of the existing treaties between the mother country and the Barbary States. When the United States became independent, England withdrew its protection of American vessels in the Mediterranean and around the Western coast of Africa. Anticipating such a situation, and hoping to protect its extensive trade with the Barbary States, the new nation tried to substitute French protection for that of England. To this purpose the Continental Congress adopted, on September 17, 1776, an enabling statement for inclusion in an agreement with France. In 1778 France refused to give such formal protection to American ships, but promised to use its good offices with the Barbary States to secure the safety of American vessels and goods. From that point on, events moved too fast and matters became too complicated for a simple solution. The following is a bare outline of what happened, as extracted from the muddle of correspondence, negotiations, Congressional deliberations and international intrigue:

John Adams, Thomas Jefferson and Benjamin Franklin were the first American leaders to realize the importance of concluding treaties with the Barbary States; in September 1778 Adams and Jefferson asked Congress for permission to negotiate terms for treaties with these states and to appropriate money for this purpose. Congress did not respond quickly to the suggestion, so in September 1783 Adams, who was the American Peace Commissioner, again recommended such treaties with the Barbary States. In May 1784 Congress authorized Adams, Jefferson, and Franklin to negotiate the terms. By that time, the Emperor of Morocco, Sidi Mahomet, had made friendly overtures to the United States expressing the desire to establish peaceful relations. His ships had seized the *Betsy*, and he proceeded to release her as a gesture of good will. The Peace Commissioners were empowered to draw up a treaty and sign for the United States; David Humphreys was named secretary to the Commissioners, and a maximum amount of $80,000 was promised as a price for such a treaty. In 1786, Thomas Barclay conducted negotiations with the Emperor of Morocco, who showed a friendly attitude toward the United States, and the treaty was signed by Adams and Jefferson in January 1787. On July 18, 1787, Congress ratified the treaty stipulating that a few thousand dollars would be presented to Morocco, but no tribute would be approved. In May 1791 Thomas Barclay was again appointed by the President of the United States to go to the court of the new Emperor of Morocco to negotiate recognition of the treaty which the Emperor's late father had signed. Barclay was to take further instructions and the necessary funds from Colonel David Humphreys, United States resident representative at Lisbon.

The United States was also able to conclude a treaty with Tunis. This time another patriotic intellectual (and a poet), Joel Barlow, was involved in the negotiations. Barlow gained the help of a French merchant, Joseph Famin, by appointing him as the U.S. Charge d'affairs in Tunis. The treaty, which gave the U. S. a most favored nation status, was concluded in August 1797, at the cost of over $100,000. It was approved by Colonel Humphreys in November, and in 1799 it was ratified by the U. S. Congress.

The United States had more difficulty, however, in dealing with the other two North African Muslim states: Tripoli and Algiers. Eventually, and after wars waged against both of them, peace was reached in 1816 and the United States commenced thereafter to establish commercial as well as diplomatic relations with the Ottoman Empire and its tributaries—on an equal footing with the European powers. The negotiations and ensuing hostilities with these two countries involved Americans at the highest levels, occupied the United States Congress, and became a subject of popular interest and concern.

In March 1785, sensing the need for a treaty to regulate the relations between the United States and Tripoli, Adams and Jefferson each held a series of meetings with the Tripolitan Ambassador to England, Abdurrahman. But the sum which Tripoli demanded was not approved by American authorities, so nothing came out of negotiations at that time. Finally, by the end of 1796, a treaty was concluded between the Tripoli authorities and an American delegation. It was approved by Humphreys in February 1797 and ratified by Congress in June of the same year. This treaty cost the United States government $56,000 but no tribute was approved, and the Dey of Algiers, who was negotiating with the United States at the time, guaranteed peace between the Americans and

Tripolitans. Here again, the treaty gave the United States a most favored nation status.

In July 1785, while John Lamb, The American emissary, was preparing to leave for Algiers to negotiate a peace treaty, Algerian ships captured two American vessels. The *Maria*, out of Boston, was captured on July 25, and the *Dauphin*, out of Philadelphia, was captured on July 20, 1785. Adams and Jefferson immediately authorized Lamb to ransom the twenty-one passengers and crew for the amount of $1200 per person. The Dey of Algiers demanded $3000 per person and also a negotiated treaty. There was no immediate response from the United States despite a number of petitions sent by the prisoners. In 1787 Thomas Jefferson obtained permission of the Congress to use the good offices of the Order of the Mathurins of France to obtain the release of the American prisoners. This did not work. In 1790, when George Washington became President and Jefferson his Secretary of State, both men took the issue of the Algerian captives very seriously. Jefferson sent to Congress successive reports on the matter, urging immediate and decisive action and enclosing petitions sent by some of the prisoners. Jefferson's reports stressed the need for action and suggested either the payment of money or the use of force.[5] By May 1792, the Senate made it known that it would be willing to pay a total of $105,000—of which $40,000 would be the price of a peace treaty; $25,000, an annual tribute; and $40,000, ransom money for the captives. But in the same month Congress approved only $50,000 to be spent on the entire mission to be undertaken by John Paul Jones and Thomas Barclay to Algiers—seeking both a peace treaty and the release of prisoners.[6] The death of the two would-be emissaries delayed the process of negotiations, and when in September 1793 instructions were given to David Humphreys to go to Algiers, the Dey refused to give him audience.

It seems that Portugal found the time suitable to come to an agreement with the Dey of Algiers, thus advancing its own interests and impeding any progress in the American-Algerian negotiations. In the fall of 1793 a truce with Portugal was signed by the Dey, which made peace with the United States now a matter of secondary importance. In November of that year eleven American ships were captured, bringing the total of American prisoners to one hundred and nineteen. This eventuality was in fact predicted by one of the American prisoners in Algiers—Richard O'Brien—in one of his reports to Thomas Jefferson as early as June 1789. Jefferson sent Congress the following extract of that report:

> What dependence or faith could be given to a peace with the Algerines, considering their present haughtiness, and with what contempt and derision do they treat all nations; so that, in my opinion,

until the Algerines more strictly adhere to the treaties they have already made, it would be impolitic in any nation to try to make a peace here: for I see they take more from the nations they are at peace with, than they do from those they are at declared war with. The Portuguese, I hope, will keep the Algerines inside the straits: for only consider the bad consequence of the Algerines going into the Mar Grande. Should the Portuguese make a sudden peace with this regency, the Algerines would immediately go out of the straits, and, of course, take many an American.[7]

It was then that Jefferson urged, and Congress approved, the construction of an American naval force in preparation for war with Algiers. The Algerian ruler became suspicious of the intentions of the United States and called for a prompt response, so Humphreys authorized Joel Barlow to promise the Dey a gift of a frigate and resumption of the negotiations. In April 1795, Humphreys left for Paris and dispatched Thomas Donaldson to Algiers to conduct the negotiations. A treaty was concluded between the two teams in September, making provisions for setting the prisoners free. In March 1796, the Senate ratified the treaty with Algiers; it included the payment of $642,000 and an annual present of naval stores amounting to $21,000.

By that time, however, the United States government had decided not to follow the European practice of paying tribute for the right of passage and for trading with that part of the world. The humiliation of paying tribute and suffering the capture of American citizens was to be avenged whenever an opportunity presented itself. That opportunity came in 1800 when the American emissary to Tripoli was forced to go to Constantinople to meet with Ottoman authorities. The American navy went into action—blockading the ports of Tripoli and Tunis and seizing some vessels. Quarrels and in-house competition between American naval officers and diplomats prolonged the conflict and resulted in its being inconclusive. In 1804, William Eaton, with official American approval, led a group of men to Egypt with the aim of marching on Tripoli to topple the government of the ruling Pasha and to appoint one of his rivals. By the time Eaton arrived in Derna, however, a strong United States naval expedition had forced the Tripolitan government to sign a treaty in June 1805. There was to be no tribute or ransom payments and United States vessels were to navigate the Mediterranean unmolested.

In a similar course of action, the United States declared war against Algiers in 1815 and blockaded the port of Algiers while the Algerian fleet was at sea. The Algerian government was forced to sign a treaty of capitulation under the threat of bombardment of the city and the destruction of its fleet on return to port. The letter sent by the American

Consul at Algiers, William Shaler, and the fleet commander, Stephen Decatur, to James Monroe, the Secretary of State, shows the manner in which the signing of the treaty was conducted. After receiving American threats to bombard Algiers, and upon learning of the capture of Algerian war vessels, the Algerian delegates were forced to negotiate on board the *U. S. Guerriere* instead of in the city of Algiers. They were given the text of the treaty and told to return with a signed agreement immediately. The letter reports:

> They returned on shore, and, although the distance was full five miles, they came back within three hours, with the treaty signed as we had concluded it, and the prisoners.
> They now show every disposition to maintain a sincere peace with us, which is, doubtless, owing to the dread of our arms;...[the means to maintain] the peace just concluded with these people is, the presence in the Mediterannean of a respectable naval force.[8]

The two Americans concluded that this treaty had placed the United States "on higher grounds than any other nation." James Madison reported to the Senate on this treaty on December 6, 1815, explaining that it resulted in the freeing of "10, more or less, American citizens," and the delivery of "500, or more or less, Algerians now in possession of the United States."[9]

This, in bare outline, is the course of events which brought the United States for the first time, into contact with the Muslim World during those crucial years when Americans were in the process of formulating their policies towards other nations. The experience was novel and challenging, and the United States was obviously probing for a policy which would guarantee dignity and national pride, as well as the opportunity to extend American trade and ideas to the larger world. This was a difficult task, especially since America, during that period, was engaged in hostilities with France and Britain on its own borders and on the high seas. But the immediate difficulty actually came from European intrigues and covert action to block America's entry into Mediterranean trade on an equal footing. For these reasons, and because of the deep interest of the United States in that part of the world, these events in the "Barbary States" left a permanent mark on American policy and attitude towards the Orient.

Initiation into International Diplomacy

One of the significant aspects of this early history is that most of America's leading statesmen and intellectuals were either directly involved or had been introduced, to the Orient as a distinct area. The list of those who were active *dramatis personae* includes, among others: George Washington, Thomas Jefferson, James Madison, John Adams, John Jay, James Monroe, Benjamin Franklin, William Eaton, Stephen Decatur, Joel Barlow, David Humphreys and William Shaler.

An essential question for which these men had to find an answer stemmed from America's inexperience in the world of international politics. They asked, why would the great European powers allow this state of affairs to continue? Why, with their naval might, did they agree to pay tribute and suffer humiliation? The question came from various quarters. One of the Connecticut Wits, who (through his diplomatic assignments noted earlier) contributed directly to the efforts of dealing with the Barbary States, David Humphreys, put the question in rhyme:

> O Ye great powers, who passports basely crave
> From Afric's lords to sail the midland wave—
> Great fall'n powers, whose guns and golden bribes
> Buy paltry passports from these savage tribes—
> Ye, whose fine purples, silks, and stuffs of gold
> (An annual tribute) their dark limbs enfold—
> Ye, whose mean policy for them equips,
> To plague mankind, the predatory ships—
> Why will you buy your infamy so dear?[10]

Another man of letters, Royal Tyler, asked the same question through the fictitious hero of his novel of Algerian captivity. His "Argument" in Chapter 25 goes like this: "Why do not the Powers in Europe suppress the Algerine Depredations? is a Question frequently asked in the United States." Tyler's analysis of the situation is most perceptive and reveals knowledge of the intricacies of European-Muslim relations:

> I answer that this must be effected by a union of the European maritime powers with the grand seignior; by a combination among themselves; or by an individual exertion of some particular state. A union of the European powers with the grand seignior most probably would be attended with success; but this is not to be expected; as it never can be the interest of the Sublime Porte to suppress them, and the common faith of the Mussulman has more influence in uniting its professors than the creed of the Christian, to the disgrace of the *latter*: and, as the grand seignior's dominion over the Algerines is little more than nominal, he is anxious to conciliate their favour by affording them his protection; considering prudently, that, though intractable, they are still a branch of the Mussulman stock. Provoked by their insults he has sometimes withdrawn his protection, as was the case when he, by treaty with the Venentians, permitted their fleet to enter the Ottoman ports, for the express purpose of destroying the

Algerine galleys; but it is obvious the Sublime Porte meant merely to chastise not to ruin them.[11]

Tyler went on to relate how, during the siege of Gibraltar, the garrison received supplies from the Barbary states. However, the intervention of Louis XVI influenced the cessation of this support. He says it is apparent that Muslim potentates can reap advantages from favors received from European nations, and thus change the course of events. Both Benjamin Franklin (1783) and Thomas Jefferson wondered at the situation also, the latter actually suggesting a unified stand by the European powers against the Barbary States.[12]

Many answers were offered, but the most convincing was one which American statesmen were to discover through practical experience. It was the politics of intrigue and rivalry among the European countries themselves which maintained the situation. Again, Tyler supplied his contemporaries with a good picture of these intrigues:

Jealousy as often actuates mighty nations as weak individuals. Whoever turns over the pages of history attentively will there perceive that sordid passion is the impulse of action the greatest states. Commercial states are also actuated by avarice—a passion still more baneful in its effects. These excite war, and are the grand plenipotentiaries in the adjustment of the articles of peace. Hence it is that, while every European power is solicitous to enrich and aggrandise itself, it can never join in any common project, the result of which, it is fearful, may benefit its neighbour; and is content to suffer injury rather than its rival should share in a common good.[13]

David Humphreys found out the secret plot of European powers through practical experience.[14] The case of the Portuguese treaty with Algiers was one which opened the eyes of American politicians to the realities of European-Barbary relations. American negotiators also reported the receipt of an anonymous *Letters From Barbary*, presumably sent by an English official to his government, in which the writer advised the English authorities to support the Moroccan fleet in order to maintain a "proper check on your enemies."[15] More explicit was the advice given by Lord Sheffield, which laid out the policy to be followed by all European powers against the American newcomers:

It will not be in the interest of any of the great maritime powers to protect them [the Americans] there from the Barbary States. If they know their interests, they will not encourage the Americans to be carriers—that the Barbary States are advantageous to the Maritime powers is obvious. If they were suppressed, the little States of Italy, etc., would have much more of the carrying trade. The French never showed themselves worse politicians than in encouraging...armed neutrality...[which] would be as hurtful to the great maritime powers as the Barbary powers are useful. The Americans cannot protect themselves from the latter; they cannot pretend to a navy.[16]

It is quite possible that the points raised in Lord Sheffield's argument were at work in the negative stand taken by France and Britain toward America's request for protection in the Mediterranean after Independence. The unfolding of events in the Orient soon made these internal factors clear. Americans at the highest levels of the government became aware of European intentions. On May 29, 1786 John Jay sent to Congress the report written by Adams and Jefferson on their meeting with the Tripolitan ambassador in London, Abdurrahman, in which they made it clear that they saw through European intentions. Adams and Jefferson remarked that European powers would be pleased to see the United States at war with the Barbary States, and that "those nations to whom our war with the Barbary States is not disagreeable will be little inclined to lend us money to put an end to it."[17] And on December 9, 1791, Thomas Jefferson, Secretary of State, sent Congress an extract of a letter from William Short, United States Charge d'Affaires in Paris, dated August 24, 1791, in which the latter stated:

> I observed to M. Pujet, that such Powers as were at peace with these piratical States, would probably put as many obstacles as possible in the way of others obtaining it, and that the United States might perhaps meet with some difficulties on that account. He agreed that his policy did prevail. He thought, however, that France would, in the new order of things, abandon it; and would aid the United States in obtaining a peace....I have thought it well to communicate these things to you, that you might judge how far they deserve weight in an attempt to redeem our unhappy captives, or to secure a permanent peace.[18]

In fact, the first Algerian conflict with the United States came as a result of this kind of policy by Europeans. In the summer of 1785, while American negotiators were about to come to an agreement with the Algerian government, Spain suddenly concluded a peace treaty with Algiers. This treaty made it possible for Algerian ships to pass through the Straits of Gibralter, where they proceeded to seize the first two ships belonging to Americans with whom they considered themselves in a state of war. This new possibility could not have escaped the Spanish government when it signed the treaty with Algiers. Joel Barlow, who was then the American representative in Algiers knew of these European intrigues. He wrote home about the attempts of the former British consul at Algiers to ruin the chances of the United States of improving its relations with the Muslim states of north Africa. Barlow cited as evidence the story told him by a Mr. Sloan, a former American captive in Algiers who was employed in the Dey's household, of the time when he was present at an audience between the British emissary and the Dey. The British Consul, Sloan told Barlow, even went to the trouble of instructing the Algerians on how and where they could seize American ships.[19]

The Literature of Captivity

America's initiation into the Orient was thus shrouded by internation-al intrigue, shady diplomacy, capture of its ships and citizens, and a number of small wars and campaigns against the first representatives of Islam with whom it came in contact. Preoccupation with these issues was not limited to politicians and diplomatic representatives. During those three decades and the following few years, the reading public was introduced to a new kind of the literature of adventure—one which described the horrors of captivity in the Muslim states of north Africa. Even while some of the writers were still in captivity, their letters were published in America. This was the case of the letters of Captains Pen-rose and M'Shane which were included in Mathew Carey's *Short Account of Algiers*, published in 1794. Another contemporary account is that of the *Travels and Sufferings* by Daniel Saunders, was also published in 1794 and subsequently appearing into six editions. In 1798 the public also read John Foss's *A Journal, of Captivity and Sufferings of John Foss; Several Years A Prisoner in Algiers*, and in 1821 William Ray's *Poems on Various Subjects* included a "Sketch of the Author's Life" which related his experience in captivity in Algiers.

Popularity of this type of writing can be seen in the career of James Riley's account of his captivity. In 1817 Riley's *An Authentic Narrative of the Loss of the American Brig Commerce, wrecked on the Western Coast of Africa, in the Month of August, 1815* was published in New York, and a London edition was published simultaneously by Murray with the addi-tion of "an Account of Tombuctoo, and of the Hitherto undiscovered great City of Wassanah." In 1851 this book was popular enough for James Riley's son, W. Willshire Riley, to bring out a *Sequel to Riley's Nar-rative; Being a Sketch of Interesting Incidents in the Life, Voyages and Travels of Captain James Riley, from the Period of His Return to His Native Land, After His Shipwreck, Captivity and Sufferings Among the Arabs of the Desert, As Re-lated in His Narrative, Until His Death*. W. Willshire explained that he wrote the *Sequel* from the journal and manuscripts left by his father, and, although the *Sequel* was supposed to relate the part of Riley's life after his return home, it included the bulk of his experience in captivity. However, the original *Narrative* by James Riley had gone into three editions by

1818, the last one including another "narrative" of the shipwreck and capture of the *Oswego*.[20] Accounts of sufferings and captivity in north Africa found their way to popular periodicals and anthologies. In May 1817 the *North American Review* published a lengthy account of the captivity of Robert Adams, prefaced with an account of this self-same American sailor found wandering in the streets of London in a deplorable condition; it was his story of capture and mistreatment in "Tombuctoo" which had first been noted (but was unpublished) by an American correspondent in Cadiz. The London *Eminence* inquired about this story, which consequently excited a great deal of public attention in Great Britain.[21]

The same narrative was also included in a collection of "authentic adventures" which carried the curious title: *Robinson Crusoe's Own Book; or, The Voice of Adventure* by Charles Ellms "Author of the Tragedy of the Sea" (Boston: Joshua V. Pierce, 1846). *The Voice of Adventure* also included the *Perilous Life of Nathaniel Pearce*, who, according to the editor "after remaining in Abyssinia a long time, left that country for Egypt, where he died, at Alexandria, in 1820, at the age of 41 years."[22]

These popular accounts, together with the stories brought back by the captives themselves, must have made a strong impression on the American public, and consequently contributed to the popular concept of the Muslem, or Arab, at that early stage in the history of the young nation. Exaggeration was necessary as a means of attracting the attention of the reading public, so these accounts emphasized the sufferings and hardships of captivity and the pain inflicted on fellow-Americans by the "Muslem barbarians." John Foss's description of these aspects of the captivity narratives is a good example. In the address "to the Public," Foss explained his intentions. "The following narrative," he said "contains a simple statement of facts, which can be attested to by many living evidences this day in America." Yet Foss told "the Public" that

> In this work I have not attempted a full description of the many hellish tortures and punishments those piratical searovers invent and inflict on the unfortunate Christians who may by chance unhappily fall into their hands.
>
> Sincerely wishing that none of my fellow-citizens may ever be so unhappy as to experience the miseries of Algerine slavery, I commend the following to their candor and patronage.[23]

It must have brought anguish to many readers at the conclusion of the American-Algerian controversy to read Foss's "To the Public" wherein he predicted that "the tears of sympathy will flow from the humane and feeling, at the tale of the hardships and sufferings of their unfortunate fellow countrymen, who had the misfortune to fall into the hands of the

Algerines—whose tenderest mercies towards Christian captives are the most extreme cruelties."[24]

William Ray's poetic expressions of the cruelty of Muslems and the heroic exploits of American naval commanders also provided the reading public with certain aspects of the character of the Oriental. Tyranny, cruelty, despotism, inhumanity and barbarism stand out in Ray's lines in his "Description of Tripoli" which he wrote in 1803, using his poetic powers to describe the tortures meted out to Christians and the blood of the patriotic American Christians which was spilled, after "unspeakable tortures," by the "infidel". He called upon justice to awaken on behalf of the valiant Westerners, the descendants of "the immortal Washington," and to bring about victory over "Muslems despotism."[25]

Other eloquent expressions of patriotism in the context of the conflict with the Barbary States can be seen in Ray's elegies on the death of William Eaton and James Decatur. In reference to the latter, he described the noble cause for which Decatur sacrificed his life:

> He left, to free us from barbarian chains,
> His country's blooming groves and peaceful plains;...
> 'Twas heav'n's own cause—'twas freedom's injur'd name.[26]

The horrors of torture and death in the prisons of the Barbary States are also a common feature of these narratives. Ray's poem "Elegy on the Death of John Hillard, Who Died January 3d, 1804, in the Prison of Tripoli" was first published in *Port Folio,* then was included in his *Poems on Various Subjects.* In it these American leaders saw both the helplessness of the captive and the inhumanity of the captors:

> But foes, and of a barb'rous kind
> Surround him as he dies;
> A horror to this fainting mind,
> And to his closing eyes.[27]

In spite of the hardships and sufferings, the American determination to break European monopoly and intrigues and become an active partner in Mediterranean commerce never wavered. Even as Jefferson sent to Congress the captives' petitions, he reminded the legislators of the importance of that part of the world for their own nation. In December 1790, and after laying before Congress possible measures to be taken in order to free American captives in Algiers, Jefferson reminded Congress that "the liberation of our citizens has an intimate connexion with the liberation of our commerce in the Mediterrean, now under the consideration of Congress. The distresses of both proceed from the same cause, and the measures which shall be adopted for the relief of the one, may, very probably, involve the relief of the other."[28] In a very detailed report on "Mediterranean Trade," sent to the House of Representatives in December 1790, Jefferson listed the types of commodities the United States exported to the Mediterranean and the loss which would be suffered if agreements were not reached with the Barbary States. In this "Report" Jefferson told the House that

> The loss of the records of the custom houses in several of the States, which took place about the commencement and during the course of the late war, has deprived us of official information as to the extent of our commerce and navigation in the Mediterranean sea. According to the best which may be obtained from other sources meriting respect, it may be concluded; that about one-sixth of the wheat and flour exported from the United States, and about one-fourth in value of their dried and pickled fish, and some rice, found their best markets in the Mediterranean ports; that these articles constituted the principal part of what we sent into that sea; that, that commerce loaded outwards, from eighty to one hundred ships, annually, of twenty thousand tons, navigated by about twelve hundred seamen. It was abandoned early in the war. And after the peace which ensued, it was obvious to our merchants, that their adventures into the sea would be exposed to the depredations of the piratical States on the coast of Barbary.[29]

Jefferson's lengthy report continued with accounts of incidents involving friendly intervention of the Spanish throne in instances of seizures of an American vessel by Morocco; the importance of treaty with that country; the intransigience and cruelty of the Algerian Dey towards American captives, as well as demands for ransom, and similar incidents with Tunis and Tripoli. He projected a means of continuing trade in the Mediterranean by the establishment of a fixed tariff for ransom, but was fearful that such an arrangement would neither attract the best of seamen nor bring about the resumption of commerce in that part of the world. Finally, Jefferson proposed to "purchase peace," in the manner of other nations—a method, he suggested, may have to be weighed against the cost.

In his turn, George Washington was also mindful of the importance of the Orient to American trade and prestige. In his December 8, 1790 speech, he told Congress:

> Your attention seems to be not less due to that particular branch of our trade which belongs to the Mediterranean. So many circumstances unite in rendering the present state of it distressful to us, that you will not think any deliberations misemployed that may lead to its relief and protection.[30]

And later, in March 2, 1795, President Washington suggested to Congress the appointment of "3 consuls, in Morocco, Algiers, and Tunis or Tripoli for more successful conduct of our affairs on the coast of Barbary."[31]

But it was not only trade, or the American desire to navigate the Mediterranean freely, which prompted the United States to pursue this policy with such determination. Religious fervor and patriotic zeal were also powerful factors undergirding the American sense of Manifest Destiny that nourished a dogged determination to expand westward. At the same time, the Orient presented another challenge—a new frontier—which also invited the American sense of Manifest Destiny. Ray's poems reflect the desire to extend freedom and civilization to less fortunate nations, Barbary included. It was America's destiny to step in where European nations had failed. David Humphreys considered the freeing of the Mediterranean as part of the design of heaven and believed America was equipped for the task:

> Where lives the nation fraught with such
> Such fast materials for a naval force?
> Where grows so rife the iron, masts and spars,
> The hemp, the timber, and the daring tars?
> Where gallant youths, inur'd to heat & cold
> Thro' ev'ry zone, more hardy, strong & bold?
> Let other climes of other produce boast,
> Let gold, let diamonds grow on India's coast;
> Let flaming suns from arid plains exhale
> The spicy odours of Arabia's gale.[32]

It is quite significant that Foss ended the *Journal* of his "Captivity and Sufferings" with an "Extract from a Poem on the Happiness of America, by Col. Humphreys." After recounting the advantages of the new nation and its qualifications, the poet addressed his country:

> Then wake, Columbia! daughter of the skies!
> Awake to glory and to greatness rise!
> Arise and spread thy virgin charms abroad,
> Thou last, thou fairest offspring of a God!
> Extend thy view where future blessings lie,
> And ope new prospects for th'enraptur'd eye!
> See a new era on this globe begun.
> And circling years in brighter orbits run!
> See the fair dawn of universal peace,
> When hell-born discord thro' the world shall cease!
> Commence the task assign'd by Heav'ns decree,
> From pirate rage to vindicate the sea![33]

American interest and involvement in the Orient were taking a definite shape during the first few decades of Independence. A vision of Orientals had been introduced into the minds of the populace and its leaders and stereotypical attitude towards them was in the making. This attitude was to be more fully developed by missionaries and travellers in the course of the nineteenth century, but even in 1823 William Shaler, American Consul at Algiers, felt free to suggest to the French government the permanent annexation of the Muslim states of North Africa. He even instructed it on the exact manner of invading these states.[34] This was the first stage of active American involvement in the affairs of the Orient. It was Orientalism in its new Eastward direction.

5

THE GREAT COMMISSION
American Missionaries in the Muslim World

The time will have come, when the light of science and of
Christianity will have rendered obsolete the grossness of
idolatry, the imposture of Mahommed, the superstitions of
popery, and the impurity of infidelity."
Missionary Paper no. 4, 1823

Throughout the nineteenth century there was a surge of missionary activities by American societies and individuals in many parts of the
world. The Orient, and the Holy Land in particular, claimed a good deal
of these activities because of the special position they had for Americans.
By the second half of the nineteenth century, there were more Americans
in the Levant than any other foreign nationals except for the British.
Most of these Americans were directly or indirectly associated either
with the missionary enterprise. There have been a number of accounts
and studies of American missionary work in this area of the world;[1] the
present study will go beyond the activities themselves into the underlying assumptions and the attitude which prompted and gave force to
them and the consequent behavior of Americans towards the area and its
peoples. It should be noted here that the term "missionary" is also used
to describe individuals who, though not associated with a particular organized group or activity, express missionary sentiments and reveal missionary behavior and attitudes.

Basic Premises of the Missionary Enterprise

American as well as European Christian missionary activities and tendencies were Occidental in nature and cultural orientation. Geographically, this enterprise marked an Eastward movement—a movement from
West to East—and ideologically the missionary enterprise had definite
Western cultural assumptions. Western missionaries, especially Americans, did not consider Oriental Christians their equal coreligionists. At

best, Oriental Christians merely stood a better chance of being converted to true Christianity than their Muslim compatriots. A typical example of this tendency from the missionary literature of the time is the statement in the 1819 *Report of The Prudential Committee* that

> in Palestine, Syria, the Provinces of Asia Minor, Armenia, Georgia and Persia, though Mohammedan countries, there are many thousands of Jews, and many thousands of Christians, at least in name. But the whole mingled population is in a state of deplorable ignorance and degradation,—destitute of the means of divine knowledge, and bewildered with vain imaginations and strong delusions.[2]

The *Report* expresses the hope that some true and committed Christians might awaken to the necessity of extending the treasure of the Bible to the Jews, Mohammedans, and Pagans among whom they lived.

It becomes clear in the light of numerous statements of this kind that the Bible—Old and New Testament—which was carried by American missionaries and travellers to the Orient was part of the heritage of the West and that this is how it was viewed by both parties to the encounter.[3] American missionary activities in the Orient had cultural and ethnic undercurrents, and consequently Orientals, whether Muslim or Christian, were considered to be deluded, benighted, and in dire need of the saving hand of the West.

Contrary to a widespread belief, American missionaries, like their European counterparts, had specific political aims and sometimes exercised political and military pressures in the Orient. In his penetrating study of this American missionary enterprise in the region, A. L. Tibawi observes that "unlike Spanish, Dutch, and English missionaries, who often followed in the footsteps of soldiers, the American missionaries were preceded only by merchants and sailors." This is true. The rest of Tibawi's statement, however, should be subjected to closer scrutiny. He says: "European missionary work in foreign lands tended to assume, in addition to its essential spiritual character, some political colouring. By comparison, American missionary work derived no prestige from such colonial or political background. Hence its spiritual character was not in doubt."[4]

A close examination of American missionary literature and activities shows that there was, however, a continuous coordination between missionaries and officials of the United States. American missionaries had strong political opinions regarding the area and indeed some of them had proposed definite designs for its future; such aims were bound to influence missionary behavior and activities.

Although American missionary activities were closely associated with European, especially British and French, missionary organizations and individuals, the American missionary establishment developed an independent program of action, philosophy and character. American missionaries were moved by a sense of urgency and by a clear vision of the special duties which they shouldered and which Providence had assigned them. There was, moreover, an obvious, if not often explicit, association between the American concept of Manifest Destiny and the missionary tendency, both very strong influences in America during the nineteenth century. There were also vital factors proceeding from the cultural milieu of nineteenth century America: the frontier mentality, the concept of Manifest Destiny, patriotic feelings, and various religious movements including the Great Awakening, Revivals and millennial tendencies. To this overall picture we must now direct our attention.

At the basis of nineteenth century American missionary efforts there were a number of assumptions which were explicitly stated or were taken for granted. Although all of these played important roles in promoting missionary efforts, a few, in particular, contributed to the development of an American missionary character and attitude towards the rest of the world—especially towards the Arab-Muslim peoples. These assumptions were:

1. That Christianity is a missionary religious movement begun by Jesus Christ whose example was followed by his immediate disciples and sanctioned all missionary efforts thereafter.

2. That America is truly a divinely-commissioned missionary nation entrusted with the task of enlightening mankind. This commission resulted from the claim American clergy laid to the true Church of Christ, from the missionary example of the Pilgrim Fathers, and from the unique American experiment in political independence.

3. That there was a certain degree of urgency in the missionary enterprise which resulted from what were considered "the signs of the times" and, more practically, from the enormity of the task set by zealous missionaries for themselves. This sense of urgency gave special priority to missionary efforts in the Holy Land and led some missionaries to devise solutions to its problems which they then set out to apply. A number of such plans and solutions were envisioned and suggested in the writings of American missionaries.

For many religious divines the true nature of missions and of missionary obligations stemmed from the example set by Jesus Christ himself and by his disciples. "Jesus Christ stands at the head of the work," says a writer on the "Divinity of Missions" in the *American Theological Review* of

November, 1859. The writer goes on to say that Christ was "in a peculiar sense" the first missionary, and by his authority "the enterprise was inaugurated as the work of the church."[5] Members of the true Church of Christ—and American religious spokesmen constantly referred to themselves as the true church—were enjoined to take up the task of spreading the message which, according to the *American Theological Review,* "contains the element of remedial power for the guilty, lost race of man."[6] Christ had given the message: "Go ye into all the world, and preach the gospel to every creature." This, says the writer of the "Divinity of Missions," is "the charter of the enterprise, with Christ's own signature. This charter will not expire, till the earth shall be full of the knowledge of the Lord. We act under it to-day, unaltered, binding as ever, with the seal of the author."[7]

Thus Christ himself was the divine authority who sanctioned and sanctified the efforts of the missionaries in their zeal to spread the knowledge of the Lord. American religious quarters resounded with the call, and many church organizations devoted a great deal of time, effort and money to promoting missionary work. One of the first American missionaries to the Holy Land, Josiah Brewer, considered it his duty "to fulfill the farewell command of the Savior, 'Go ye into all the world and preach the gospel to every creature.' "[8]

American missionary advocates saw in this call both a command and a justification for their action. "We plant ourselves on this foundation," says the writer in the *American Theological Review.* And to dismiss any doubt from the minds of those who were not convinced of the benefits and necessity of missionary work, the writer adds: "let this fact stand out first, that the Son of God brought it into being." This is truly divine authority for the fulfillment of the task.

The American Protestant church considered itself the true Church of Christ, carrying the burden of the original Christian mission. Protestantism, as a movement, was seen to be a continuation of the tradition of the early Christian church, but it was left for Americans to fulfill the task. In an address to missionaries who were about to leave for the Eastern Mediterranean, Samuel Worcester explained the direct link between the Covenant given by God to Abraham and his seed and the American church.[9] The "great and interesting doctrine," Worcester told his congregation, could be illustrated in the following manner: "In God's covenant of promise with Abraham, provision was made for the transmission of the privileges and blessings contained in it, from generation to generation, down to the close of time."[10] The promise was given to Abraham who is father of all nations of believers, and the American church had carried on the principal element of Abraham's doctrine:

faith. God's covenant with Abraham ensured "justification of all true believers by faith."[11] It was confirmed by God in Christ, and it was by the authority of this covenant that Americans were qualified to answer the call: "go, and from the heights of Calvary and of Zion proclaim to the long lost tribes of Israel, to the followers of the Pseudoprophet, and to the bewildered people of different lands, tongues, and religions, the *foundations* there opened, for the cleansing of all nations—the banner there displayed, for the gathering of all people."[12]

America's Traditional Missionary Character

American missionary enthusiasts of the early nineteenth century also saw in their immediate continental history the origins of the enterprise they were about to launch throughout the world. Had not the Pilgrim Fathers and early Puritan settlers come to the New World as missionaries in the wilderness? This also had been a divine calling which their forefathers had answered. "Many things conspire to show that God has raised us up and commissioned us to become a Missionary Nation." This is the opening sentence of the long essay entitled "The United States a Commissioned Missionary Nation," published in 1859 in the *American Theological Review*.[13] Recognizing the historical basis of the commission, the writer says: "The character of our origin indicated this. Our forefathers were missionaries of precisely this character. They were not sent out to this land by an organized association. But the providence of God placed them in such circumstances as to make them all self-constituted missionaries."[14]

From the beginning the settlers did indeed show missionary tendencies in their concern for the souls of the "savage" Red Indians. Missions to neighboring Indian groups were invoked by the earliest settlers. But succeeding American missionary efforts were not to be restricted to the immediate backyard. As early as May 1700, Cotton Mather was involved with the Danish missionary activities in Malabar. In a sermon, *A Pillar of Gratitude*, Mather explained the virtues of missionary work among the unbelievers; and later, when preparing the sermon for print, he added "an account of the fate and great Success of the Gospel in the East Indies."[15] Mather's diary shows frequent contact with these missionaries and prayers for their success. The entry of May 26, 1716, says: "I forsee an Opportunity for me to do some notable Service in my Correspondence with the Danish Missionaries at Malabar." And in another entry Mather offers prayers and a "humble Memorial" to His Kingdom, and particularly to "some Servants of His, industriously at work for His Kingdom in the world. Among these, I particularly mentioned those of the Malabarian Mission." On the 6th of March, Mather mentions that he planned to "send several pieces of Gold, for the Support of the Charity Schole at Malabar."[16]

An obvious sense of divine mission informed the thinking of both the early Puritan immigrants and their nineteenth century American descendants. William Bradford, for example, expressed the hope to lay "some good foundation, or at least to make some way thereunto, for propagating and advancing the gospell of the kingdom of Christ in those remote parts of the world."[17] In his turn, the *American Theological Review* writer of May, 1859, reports with total conviction that there were many indications, "all conspiring to prove that Providence has put in our hands the facilities for doing a great work for this wretched world."[18] This "sense of mission to redeem the Old World," according to the American historian Frederick Merk, which had been possessed by the Pilgrim Fathers, "appeared thereafter in successive generations of Americans" and remained unaltered throughout.[19] It was a sacred duty shouldered by a people who were in covenant with God.

By the early nineteenth century, Americans were no longer satisfied with a minor role in Christian missionary efforts throughout the world. The first quarter of the century was to witness a surge of zeal on a national scale, and an unwavering commitment to fulfill the command of the Lord. The United States was by then an independent country, in the prime of its youth, with every reason to look forward to a prosperous future. The country's natural resources seemed limitless, the population was increasing daily, expansion on the Western frontiers was a continuously challenging process and, most important of all, the nation was experiencing a religious awakening matched only by its patriotic fervor. Moreover, the young nation had just launched itself successfully on the international scene through a war against the strongest of maritime powers and thereby had taught a number of small states to respect its right to navigate oceans thousands of miles away from its own shores.

The connection between the historic missionary tendency and the religious zeal of the Great Awakening and the Revivals cannot be overemphasized. Although the missionaries saw in the conduct of their Puritan ancestors an example to be followed, practically speaking, they were children of the strong religious revival of their immediate American past and present. Sidney E. Ahlstrom has rightly stated that "no 'school' of American thought...has been graced by so many men of originality and intellectual power as the New England Theology founded or set in motion by Jonathan Edwards."[20] Edwards' successors established and maintained three theological seminaries devoted to the orthodox cause (Andover, Yale and Hartford). Seminarians from these institutions were to launch the first organized missionary campaigns directed to the Holy Land. It was, in fact, the proposition of three graduates of the Andover Seminary which precipitated a series of events leading to the expanding activities of the American Board of Commissioners for Foreign Missions (ABCFM) and making of the Board an organization of international dimensions.[21]

The Second Awakening, with its popular revivals and camp meetings, was the setting which gave birth to the missionary enterprise and which supplied it with nourishment and continued sustenance. Indeed it was Edwards' grandson, the patriot and missionary Timothy Dwight, who according to Ahlstrom "is credited (though not with complete justice) with precipitating an awakening which far outshone that associated with his grandfather."[22] The fabric of American culture in the nineteenth century was permeated by evangelical Christianity, and this aspect of nineteenth century America gave rise to the missionary spirit which essayed to reach "lost souls" throughout the world.

There was, it would seem, a slight alteration in the basic dogma of the strictly Calvinistic Puritan Church. The American church establishment was becoming more open to converts and new members, and consequently there developed an urge to work for the salvation of non-Christians. In the words of the American historian William Lee Miller, "out of this free church idea of the nineteenth century came the great energy of revivals, of the missionary enterprise spreading Christianity over the nation and the world."[23] One of the important factors which gave force to the missionary enterprise was the communal nature of American religious life. In nineteenth century America, religion, as Ahlstrom observes, was not "the product of solitary activity."[24] Religious devotion mainly took the form of a corporate church life which can be seen in church services, Sunday schools, family Bible reading, camp meetings, revivals and other similar activities.

Missionary Interests in the Holy Land

Although American missionary agents sought to spread the light of the Gospel throughout the world, the region of the Holy Land lay special claim on their efforts; Western Asia was associated with the rise of Christianity and with the first efforts to spread the religion of Christ. Thus it seemed appropriate that during the first two decades of its life, the American Board of Commissioners for Foreign Missions (ABCFM) made strong efforts to establish a permanent and central station in Jerusalem and to keep up its interest in the Holy Land. This region was accorded unique importance in the annual report submitted by the Prudential Committee to the tenth meeting of the Board in 1819:

> if the countries of Southern Asia are highly interesting to Christian benevolence, and have strong claims upon Christian commiseration, on account of the hundreds of millions of human beings immersed in the deepest corruption and wretchedness; the countries of Western Asia, though less populous, are in other respects not less interesting; nor do they present less powerful claims.[25]

The report concludes its section on the Orient with an address to the Board, stating that "by these, and other kindred considerations, your committee have long had their mind and heart drawn towards Western Asia, and particularly towards the *Land of ancient Promise*, and of *present Hope*."[26] Words were backed with action, and the Holy Land, especially Jerusalem, assumed a central position in American missionary efforts. In Missionary paper no. 8 (mistakenly numbered 7 in the first edition), the Board claims with a certain degree of pride that

> Mr. Parsons was the first protestant missionary who visited the holy land with a view to a permanent establishment; but, owing to the disturbed state of the country, he remained there only a few months. Eight years have not yet elapsed since his visit was made, and he soon after died. Messrs. Fisk and King, accompanied by Mr. Wolff, a Jewish missionary, arrived in Judea in the spring of 1823.[27]

The same paper quotes another American missionary, Isaac Bird, who says in "his journal" that "it is about four years and a half...since those of us who have been particularly connected with this station, came to anchor in this port. We had then no intention of staying at Beyroot, except long enough to obtain animals or a boat to carry us on toward Jerusalem."[28] The goal of many missionaries was to direct their paths toward Jerusalem; the feeling was overwhelming and often drew support from the public. Thus when Plinny Fisk and Levi Parsons were preparing for their journey to the Holy Land to establish a missionary station there, Fisk preached a sermon in the Old South Church in Boston on October 31, 1819, appropriately quoting from Scripture: "And now, behold, I go bound in the spirit into Jerusalem, not knowing the things that shall befall me there."[29] His speech caused an emotional scene among the congregation; Jerusalem remained the spiritual center for all true believers, whether they thought of it as a geographical locality or a symbol. Another missionary who was sent by the Board to the Far East also drew the Board's attention to the priority which should be given to the Holy Land, saying, "When I think of these things, I long to be on my way towards Jerusalem."[30]

The missionary pilgrim to Palestine, J.V.C. Smith, who aimed, among other matters, to inspect "the prospects of the Missionary enterprises" there, expresses a strong, if also vague, spiritual feeling that came over him "on entering Palestine."[31] As he puts it, "the traveller at once feels an uncontrollable desire to reach the Holy City; and till that desire is gratified, all other objects however important in themselves, fail to receive an appropriate share of his attention."[32]

The land of spiritual metaphor and the physical geographical location sometimes come together in a descriptive picture of the region as that given by William Thomson:

> God so made this land of Canaan that its physical conformation should furnish appropriate types and emblems through which invisible realities should be so pictured to the eye and imagination as to affect the heart. These mountains point to heaven; this sunken sea of death to still lower depths. The valleys, the plains, the brooks and fountains, from the swellings of Jordan to the waters of Siloah, that go softly from under the altar of God, all were so made as to shadow forth, dimly but impressively, divine revelations.[33]

But the actual conditions in the Holy Land were a disappointment to the missionaries who sought to reestablish there a center for Christian enlightenment. Not only was the land sitting in utter darkness and wretchedness, its Christians only Christian in name;[34] it was also populated by another race with different religious beliefs. Many times travellers and missionaries cried "shame that the Turk is permitted to keep and desecrate the Holy Land."[35] The missionary—more than the traveller—who left his home and family in the United States was discouraged by the "wretched state" of the Holy Land. "In a word," said the experienced missionary Eli Smith to his fellow-countrymen who were preparing for the journey, "the misery of the present scene will deminish, and perhaps ultimately destroy the charms of classical and sacred associations." Drawing on his own experience in the area, Smith warned the prospective missionaries, "the nearer you approach to Jerusalem, the less will be your desire to visit it; from the expectation of more pain from views of its present wickedness, than of pleasure from reflections upon its ancient glory."[36]

Yet, in spite of the disappointing state of the Holy Land, especially Jerusalem, and in spite of the domination of an "alien" culture, American divines had a way of looking at the positive side of the situation and making the best of it. For was it not prophesied that there would come a time when "the cup of wrath and desolation from the Almighty has been poured out upon her to the dregs, and she sits sad and solitary in darkness and in dust"? The situation in the Holy Land was seen by the

American author of a popular textbook of geography as the fulfillment of prophecy. Jerusalem, said the Rev. F. G. Hibbard, "retains not the shadow of its departed glory..., though its exterior appearance is still imposing in most parts, within its walls poverty and even squalid wretchedness prevail."[37]

Even in the details of everyday life in and around Jerusalem, signs were seen of God's will and of Scriptural prophecy. The ploughing and cultivation of Mount Zion overlooking Jerusalem, a process which had gone on for centuries, are seen by the writer of an article in *The Ladies' Companion* as fulfillment of prophecy. The magazine quotes a Dr. Richardson who visited Mount Zion in 1818:

> one part of it supported a crop of barley: another was undergoing the labor of the plough, and the soil turned up consisted of stone and lime mixed with earth, such as is usually met with in the foundations of ruined cities....We have here another remarkable instance of the special fulfilment of prophecy:—'Therefore shall Zion, for your sakes, be ploughed as a field, and Jerusalem shall become heaps.'[38]

The situation in the Holy Land, and the Levant in general, presented the missionary ideologists with problems which required urgent answers and solutions. In this, as in other situations, American visionaries easily transcended geographical boundaries and national political sovereignty and drew up plans and dreams on political as well as spiritual bases.

American Efforts to Convert Muslems

The starting point of the missionary enterprise then was that the missionaries, and the United States, were both divinely commissioned to go forth to all nations and spread the light of the Gospel among the heathens. Instructions given by the missionary societies are clear on this point; one such statement by the Prudential Committee tells the missionary agents that "the great object of your Mission is to impart to those who sit in darkness and in the region and shadow of death, the saving knowledge of Christ....The deplorable ignorance of the poor heathen will constantly be in your minds, and deeply affect your hearts."[39] Although the home organization gave priority to bringing the light to the Christian element of the population,[40] the missionaries concentrated their efforts, overt or covert, to winning the lost souls of Muslems. All of this was done in spite of the strict policy of the Sublime Porte and the local authorities throughout the region—a policy which prohibited any attempts by missionaries to convert members of the Muslim religion or any other faith which enjoyed the status of a *millet* (sect). An expression of joy appears in missionary literature whenever success is achieved in converting the Muslems, and a feeling of frustration is obvious because of the slow process which leads to the final goal. In February 1860 The *American Theological Review* reported with satisfaction the details of a conversion of Muslems through the efforts of American missionary agents. In part, the text says:

> The impression of the American missionary operations in Turkey upon the Mohammedan mind is becoming deeper and more widespread. Dr. Schauffler has recently baptized four converts from Mohammedanism—one of them a near relative of one of the highest grandees of the empire. Great numbers of Turks, in all the walks of life, are found to have become well acquainted with the Christian Scriptures and to have lost, altogether or in good part, their confidence in Islamism. Mr. Williams (the converted Turk and preacher) is increasingly abundant and aggressive in his labors, and is unmolested. In an interesting scene described by Dr. Hamlin, he recently avowed boldly his faith in Christ to the Pasha, Chief Kadi, and "Defterdar" of Broosa, and was treated with marked consideration.[41]

And in the same issue the *Review* brought "news from Mesopotamia" giving little comfort because of the slow progress of the evangelizing process:

> In the field of the "Assyrian Mission" of the American Board, popular violence, and the inefficiency and corruption of the civil authorities, occasion much suffering and hinder the progress of evangelical truth. This is especially the case at Mardin, the ecclesiastical capital of the Syrian Church, and also the stronghold of Rome, which is newly occupied as a station....Mr. March says: The great enemy of evangelical truth in our entire field is the Papacy. Other influences are either unorganized or decrepit.[42]

In May 1880, the *Review* reported more cheering news because the Turks "are giving ear to the Gospel," especially as a result of the official recognition by the Ottoman authorities of Protestantism as a *Millet*.[43]

The same period saw the conversion of still more persons from Islam. "A report for the *Independent*, writing from Constantinople, February 13th," according to the *Review*, "gives a cheering picture of the progress of the Gospel among the Turks." Not only did the authorities recognize Protestantism as "a distinct sect, by order of the Sultan," but also the converts were getting bold enough to openly profess their newly-adopted faith. The *Review* describes a meeting where

> ten native born Turks, or rather Mohammedans (two being Persians) were present. Of this ten, one was a colonel in the Turkish army, and whose sister is wife of the Shah of Persia. One was a Persian Sheik of great wealth and influence in his own country. One was

an officer in the royal palace, a member of the Sultan's household. One was a nephew of a Pasha, who had been disowned and cast off by his relatives because he had become a Christian. And one was, a few months ago, an Imam (priest) in one of the mosques of the city, an old man, seventy years old, and who was baptized four weeks since. With eyes fixed on the speaker, they listened with breathless attention to the end of the lecture. It was a sight worth coming six thousand miles to see.[44]

The *Review* ends its news of the missions for the month with the prayer: "May God bless the movement, the first of the kind in the history of Islamism."

There is a certain degree of ambivalence in the attitude of mission-minded Americans towards Islam as a religion and the way they choose to deal with it in the context of their missionary efforts. Their basic position is that the followers of the "false prophet" are deluded and, as is clear from the passages quoted above, there is a self-congratulatory note on the success of efforts to convert Muslims to Christianity. There is also an equally clear imputation of backwardness and bigotry to Islam itself. "Mohammedan feeling," as seen by the *American Theological Review* report, was "outraged by the reform policy, which is rapidly undermining faith in the Koran."[45] Some missionaries like Henry Jessup, on the other hand, in spite of hatred and contempt of Islam, indirectly recognized some good qualities in the religion. Jessup described the bedouins as "Moslem in name only; they break every rule of the faith."[46] He was at the same time very jealous of the efforts of the local authorities who sent teachers to the Bedouins in order to educate them in their faith and "make them Mohammedan."[47] This, he feared, would forestall his missionary efforts among them.

There are other interesting cases of this negative attitude towards Islam and Muslims whenever Americans travelling among Arabs recognized a degree of devotion and sincerity in Islamic practice, but this did not diminish the zeal to convert the practitioners. The Arab Muslim guide of Charles Wesley Andrews, replacing a tricky and unreliable Arab Christian, performed his prayers with complete devotion and abandon. This only elicited from Andrews the wish that "God might hasten the day" when he would see the light of the Gospel and accept the Savior.[48]

If, in some cases, Muslims were thought worthy of conversion, some Americans declared it was futile to attempt to spread the knowledge of the Gospel among them. One of the most forceful statements made on the impossibility of converting Muslims was by Herman Melville, following his sojourn in the Levant. In an entry in his *Journal* he says: "Might as well attempt to convert bricks into brick-cakes as the Orientals into Christians. It is against the will of God that the East should be Christianized."[49]

For those who saw in Islam the reason for the wretchedness and seeming debasement of Muslims, some more radical solutions were occasionally suggested. J.V.C. Smith commented on the generally low moral standards he observed in the Orient ascribing that to Islam, and despaired of bringing about the conversion of Muslims:

> Morals are certainly at low-water mark in every country where Mohammedanism is in the ascendant; consequently in Palestine and throughout Syria, the sins most abhorrent and abominable are as common as the instincts of its followers are depraved and beastly....No hope or expectation should for a moment be indulged, that they are to be reached through conscience or heart, and that they are yet to become Christians.[50]

There were numerous similar statements revealing a negative attitude towards Islam as a religion and ascribing to it the encouragement of ignorance, cruelty, and injustice among its followers. An article published in the *New York Herald* on August 3, 1840, remarked that Muhammad, the Prophet of Islam, intentionally tried to keep his followers ignorant.[51] Moreover, the vast amount of literature relating accounts of Americans held in captivity, and the treatment they received at the hands of the "Barbary Corsairs" and African tribes, resulted in the association of Islam with cruelty and barbarism. Descriptions of such experiences in captivity gave a general impression of Muslims as cruel. One such story, told by Robert Adams, was published orginally in England, but immediately related in America by the *North American Review* in 1817. Adams described his experience with a particular African group of "wandering and savage Moors," a tribe which

> consisted of about two hundred persons, men, women, and children, inhabiting thirty or forty tents. They are Mahometans, and as strict in their religious duties as at Tangier and elsewhere. Their faces are nearly black, their hair long and of the same colour, their persons squalid and dirty, and in the manners and customs they are brutal and cruel....They speak the Arabic language, and are governed by a shiek from their own numbers. They are much more wretched and uncivilized than the negroes.[52]

This association of Islam with habits and stereotyped behavior which travellers were likely to encounter on their journey in the Levant influenced the attitudes of missionaries and the way they approached their task among Muslims. J.V.C. Smith presents a good example of this direct association of Islam with fierceness and ignorance in his treatment of the "influence of the American missionaries," where he says (in part):

> In Beyroot it is evident that the American Missionaries have modified the character of the place by the force of their example. The fierce moslem expression is not so marked there as in many other towns where their mild efforts are hereafter to be exerted. Such has been and such no doubt will be the future influence of the Missionary enterprise, in connection with the civilizing tendency of the consuls and merchants from Europe and America, that the inhabitants of Beyroot will become distinguished for their civilization, courtesy and good manners.[53]

Converting Christians

Naturally, such a harsh attitude towards Islam was not only shaped by American background and experiences; the prejudice of European heritage, as Chapter III, "The Prophet's Progress" shows, was an influential factor in the process. Nonetheless, the overall attitude towards Islam and Muslims which American missionaries took with them to the Orient while on their sacred task of evangelizing the world reflected their own sense of "Muslim barbarity." And the mission had to be carried out whether Muslims were capable of conversion or not, and whether or not they were worth saving. Work had to go on to achieve fulfillment of the divine mission. Even Christians of the Holy Land constituted an obstacle, but one which could be surmounted. There were objections back home to the efforts and financial resources devoted to "converting Christians," but the missionary argument was that apart from Protestants, who were American and English, most other Christians were deluded and had to be returned to the fold. Furthermore, there was in the Orient a sharp competition presented by Roman Catholic and other missionaries whose efforts would lead to "possession of the land for the Pope," not for Christ. This challenge had to be met and matched by more energetic efforts from American missionary societies. In many cases both Catholics and Muslims were seen as dangerous obstacles to Protestant missionary efforts. In "Missionary Paper no. 4," missionaries are warned against these seemingly competitive religions:

> Turning our eyes now to that interesting region, which was anciently the dwelling place of the church of God, what do we behold? The inhabitants of Mount Lebanon, comparatively a hardy, courageous, and intelligent people, become so sensitive to the approaches of truth, that the missionaries at Beyroot are obliged to restrain themselves from travelling, lest the country be thrown into uproar—as Ephesus was, by the apostle Paul; and yet, in their houses, they find full occupation in conversing with such as brave the terrors of spiritual excommunication to call upon them. —We al-

most tremble to hear again from that land, lest some of the messengers of our churches may have fallen beneath the scimetar of the
Turk, or the dagger of the vengeful papist of the mountain.[54a]

In fact, sometimes Muslims did not represent as big an obstacle as
Papists; some missionaries were happy to see "that Infidel, but impartial,
Turk" squat and smoke his pipe while guarding Christian places of wor-
ship and bring "his soldiers to keep order" among the Catholics and
Greeks.[54b]

Many American travellers and missionaries expressed feelings of
resentment at the presence and practices of local Christians in the Holy
Land. They regarded this Christian Community as not truly Christian;
its rituals and behavior caused Americans to be bitterly disappointed.
The regaining of these souls became a high priority. One prominent
American churchman, the president of Wesleyan University, Stephen
Olin, was shocked at the state of resident Christians and did not wonder
that Muslims treated them with contempt.[55] Similar views are expressed
by a number of American travelers. James Brooks, the editor of the *New
York Express*, describes the fanatical practice of "the Priests of all the
religions...who show up every thing spoken of in the Scriptures," including "a fragment of prophyry column, called the column of
Flageliaba, being a piece of that to which the Savior was bound when
scourged by order of Pilate"; the prison where Christ was confined; and
"the very column of grey marble on which the Jews made our Savior sit
while they crowned him with thorns, and mocked him." These priests
are not satisfied with giving a name and "local habitation" to every historical point of the New Testament in Jerusalem.[56]

Brooks observes, moreover, that although the dome over the Holy
Sepulchre

> is leaky and broken, and rain creeps through and in upon it, but it
> cannot be repaired, for such is the jealousy that Greek will not let
> Latin or Armenian do it, and *vice versa*. Well is it, I repeat, then, that
> Infidel but impartial, Turk squats and smokes his pipe by the door as
> doorkeeper, and brings in his soldiers to keep order. But what can
> Turk think of such Christianity, and all this gewgaw—cool, calm,
> simple-minded, unimpassioned Turk who, in plain simplicity
> spreads his mantle upon the bare earth, and with his face to Mecca,
> offers up, humbly on his knees, with forehead bent to the earth, his
> prayers to the Prophet alone—no image of him, no painting, no
> sculptured form, no Virgin—no—nothing but the Prophet himself—
> and, through him, to Allah his God![57]

A more down-to-earth description of the rituals of local Christians is
that given by McI. Robertson who watches them at prayer, then states
emphatically that one minute at a camp meeting back home is much

more rewarding than all of this "curious humbug."[58] And the renowned traveller John Lloyd Stephens gives an interesting account of the celebration held by the Greek Church of Syria on the Saturday preceding Easter. He describes in great detail the Holy Easter Vigil of the Greek church, noting that the service consisted of hours of a "monotonous and unintelligible routine of prayers," discordant screams, waving torches, inordinate solicitation of money, and lack of solemnity. He says:

> I do not wonder that the Turks look with contempt upon Christians, for they have constantly under their eyes the disgusting mummeries of the Greek church, and see nothing of the pure and sublime principles our religion inculcates.[59]

A more severe and penetrating criticism comes from the pen of J.V.C. Smith, a pilgrim in search of the ideal missionary operation in the Holy Land. In Jerusalem, Smith visits the Church of the Holy Sepulchre where, he says, he would not go into details in describing the "disgraceful unchristian conduct" of the various sects worshiping there. He does, however, single out the Greek monks who "have the reputation of being as scandalous a set of fellows as ever went unhung. Stories are related of their vileness, and the corrupt, demoralizing transactions permitted through their connivance, in the very abodes of holiness."[60]

Finally, there is Charles Wesley Andrews, whose political insight made him realize how local Christians and Muslems played into the hands of foreign powers, who fanned the flames of discord among them to realize their own goals. Andrews wrote to the *Episcopal Recorder* from Alexandria on November 17, 1841, that

> By a letter received here by the last packet from Beyroot, Mr. Thompson of the American Board, writes that the Maronites (Roman Catholics) had attacked the Druses of Mount Lebanon, & that there had been a most destructive war between the parties wh: the Druses are said to be victorious. Mr. T writes that while he was writing fifty villages c^d be seen on fire, & that many years c^d not repair the losses sustained, & that many must perish in the ensuing winter unless assistance is procured from Europe. It is believed that the Maronites were stimulated to this attack by Jesuit Missionaries, who it is not unlikely were encouraged by the French party who is ambitious of authority in Syria.[61]

The efforts of American missionaries to reclaim the souls of Eastern Christians often resulted in friction with local church authorities and increased the ongoing wrangling among local Christian sects. The reaction of the local church authorities varied from inducing the Ottoman administration to ban the distribution of Protestant material printed abroad, to calling for a Papal bull excommunicating anyone who maintained contact with Protestant missionary groups. The best example of this aspect of missionary activities can be seen in the conversion of a local Maronite Christian, Asaad Shidiak, and the "Brief Memoir" which he wrote in collaboration with "his friend and patron the Reverend Isaac Bird, missionary to Syria."

Shidiak relates how he "was very fond of engaging Mr. King [Jonas King, the American missionary] in disputatious conversations, to prove him to be in error," but this led Shidiak to apply himself "to reading the world of God with intense interest." This in turn brought about the discovery of "many of the doctrines of the Roman Catholic church which I could not believe, and which I found opposed to the truths of the Gospel; and I wished much to find some of her best teachers to explain them to me, that I might see how they proved them from the holy Scriptures." He found this to be impossible and, to make matters worse, he was made aware of the Catholic doctrine "that whoever does not believe that the pope is infallible, is a heretic" who should be "destroyed."[62]

Shidiak was subsequently referred to letters of censure from the Maronite Patriarch, warning him, under threat of excommunication, to abstain from converse with "the English." Unless he obeyed those commands, the Patriarch could not assure him of a situation. Unable to tear himself away from his new religious probings, he returned eventually to Beirut and his new missionary friends.

American Officialdom and the Missionary Establishment

The official American stand regarding the missionary establishment and its efforts abroad had evolved over a long period of time, becoming clearer and more aggressive during the nineteenth century. This stand was originally based on the missionary nature of the first few settlements in America. But the earliest explicit official statement was made by the administration of John Quincy Adams in a letter sent by his Secretary of the Navy to the King of the Sandwich Islands, emphasizing the President's position that the efforts undertaken by American missionaries are a means of diffusing "the knowledge of letters and of true religion." This, the letter went on to explain, was "the best and the only means, by which the prosperity and happiness of nations can be advanced and continued." It was made clear that the missionaries had Adams' wholehearted support in their efforts for "the cause of religion and learning."[63] Thus, when in May 1850 the Commander of the American Mediterranean Squadron, Commodore Morgan, dispatched the *Cumberland* to visit ports of the Ottoman Empire, he gave its captain a letter to the American missionaries in Syria informing them that the show of force was intended to insure their safety and success. He also assured them that they could count on the support of the President of the United States and the Secretary of the Navy. The missionaries, for their part, expressed gratitude for the visit of the *U.S.S. Cumberland* and requested more frequent visits because, as they said, this would impress the local authorities and population with "the strength and resources of our country" much more than "it is possible for any description verbal or written."[64]

In the Holy Land and the Ottoman Empire there were many indications of coordination between the U.S. representatives and the missionary community. One has only to read accounts such as those by David Porter, William Lynch and others to realize that American missionaries and other Americans formed a close-knit community. Lynch, who headed a U.S. scientific expedition, carried with him a package of books to Mr. Goodell, the missionary resident in Constantinople.[65] Mr. Goodell, "the gentleman appointed by the missionary society of America," furnished Porter with some religious books to distribute.[66] Lynch's expedition made extensive use of the services of the missionary establishment and individuals. While preparing for his trip, he received help from Edward Robinson, the biblical scholar, and carried letters from him to the mission in Syria. In the Orient the missionaries gave him all the support he needed—material and moral.[67]

Cooperation between the missionaries and the various branches of the U.S. government was not limited to the exchange of logistic support, hospitality and distribution of missionary literature. Official records and missionary reports and correspondence show a gradual, but very definite, unfolding of official American concern not only for the safety, but also for the success, of missionary efforts in the Orient. To this end, the successive administrations responded favorably to what was to become a fairly habitual missionary practice of "calling on the navy." This aspect of governmental involvement in missionary activities should be noted here because it reveals a definite stand towards the area and its people in the context of the wider policy of "spreading the light of education, liberty and religion." This aspect of official activities in the Orient is all the more important to the present study because, although naval warships were sent to the area at the request of missionaries or diplomatic representatives, they were often an expression of official policy regarding the missionary enterprise itself and not merely the result of concern for the safety of U.S. subjects.

The dispatch of the *U.S.S. Cumberland* to Ottoman Ports was not the first such measure taken by the United States, nor was it to be the last. As early as 1834 Commodore Patterson, Commander of the *U.S.S. Delaware*, visited Beirut, where he told his hostess, Mrs. Sarah Smith, and the rest of the missionary society that "he had come to Beirut mainly as a demonstration of their government's support for them, and Sarah Smith found this very gratifying."[68] Patterson had already made a similar visit to Alexandria before going to Beirut.

The missionaries were more than happy to see the American flag waving over American warships at Ottoman ports. In 1835, Eli Smith, ordinarily of a meek and gentle spirit, requested United States official action against what he considered infringement on the rights of the missionaries, adding that local authorities in Syria should be taught "that we are a powerful nation. And there is no other way to teach them this but to make them *feel* it."[69]

By far the most serious incident leading to the direct intervention of the Secretary of State, Daniel Webster, was David Porter's handling of the conflict between the Maronite Patriarch of Mount Lebanon and a group of American missionaries. The missionaries attempted to establish their right to work in Mount Lebanon. Asking for their expulsion, the Patriarch complained to the Ottoman Sublime Porte of what he described as the efforts of the American missionaries to convert the local population. The Ottoman Foreign Minister thereupon wrote a friendly, but firm, letter to David Porter asking him "to adopt measures for their removal" from Mount Lebanon. In a similarly friendly reply, Porter informed the Ottoman Minister that "the Constitution of the United States allows to all its citizens the right of free exercise of their religious opinions." Porter conceded, however, that

> no article of the Treaty of Commerce and Navigation between the United States and Turkey gives them authority to interfere in any way with the rites and religion of any person living under the authority of Turkey; therefore after this correspondence has been made known to the American citizens residing in the vicinity of Mount Lebanon, any attempt to excite the minds of the inhabitants to change their rites and religion must be done at their own risk, and on their responsibility.[70]

The missionaries, however, were not so happy with the idea of being left on their own, with no protection from their government's diplomatic representative. They immediately took their case to Washington via the Prudential Committee of the American Board of Commissioners for Foreign Missions (ABCFM), and soon after that the Secretary of State wrote Porter an admonishing letter. Nevertheless, Porter's position and behavior was reasonable, and in accordance with the terms of the Treaty of Friendship between the United States and the Ottoman Empire. Anticipating complaints by the missionaries, Porter had written the Secretary of State informing him that although his behavior may have

angered some zealous American individuals, the alternative was violating the treaty between the two countries. He could do that, he said, only
upon instructions to that effect. His argument did not help. The Secretary
replied:

> It has been represented to this Department, that the American Mis-
> sionaries, and other citizens of the United States not engaged in com-
> mercial pursuits, residing and traveling in the Ottoman Dominions,
> do not receive from your Legation that aid and protection to which,
> as citizens of the United States, they feel themselves entitled, and I
> have been directed by the President, who is profoundly interested in
> the matter, to call your immediate attention to the subject, and to in-
> struct you to omit no occasion, where your interference in behalf of
> such persons may become necessary or useful, to extend to them all
> proper succor and attentions of which they may stand in need, in the
> same manner that you would to other citizens of the United States,
> who as merchants visit or dwell in Turkey.[71]

Porter was undeniably sympathetic to the cause of the missionary
enterprise, as seen in his cooperation with them on several occasions. He
did, however, have extensive experience in dealing with the authorities
and people of the Ottoman Empire, and was conscious of the consequences of missionary interference in people's beliefs and way of life. Perhaps
it was this which prompted his reluctance to go all the way in supporting
the American missionaries in 1841. In one of his *Letters from Constantinople,* in which there is implicit criticism of the impatience and lack of
understanding on the part of the advocates of change. He said:

> I am not the apologist of Turkish prejudices, but it cannot be
> denied, that the barbarous invasion and excesses of the mad
> crusaders; the persecutions and final expulsion of the Mahometans
> from Spain; the uniform language of all Christian writers, as well as
> the uniform conduct of Christian states towards the Ottomites,
> having all combined to furnish no slight justification of their feelings
> towards the nations of Europe....Religion instead of being a bond of
> peace, has proved to them but a firebrand of bloody discord, and the
> unity of belief in one God, nothing more than the signal of eternal
> disunion. It is my firm belief that nothing is wanting to the final ex-
> tinction of this bloody feud of ages, than a reciprocity of friendly
> policy; and that under Sultan Mahmoud, the Great, for so he deser-
> ves so to be called, there will be little difficulty in establishing friend-
> ly relations.[72]

Porter's successor, Dabney Carr, was more of a missionary enthusiast—one who was ready to come to the help of the missionary establishment. If need be, as he said on one occasion, he would call on the
whole American fleet in the Mediterranean to come to their aid in

Beirut.[73] In fact, in April 1845 he asked for the largest naval force available to visit the Syrian coast during the conflict between the Maronites and the Druze of Mount Lebanon. The object of the measure was support for the Maronite Christians against the Druze Muslims, although these same Maronites were still objecting to the proselytizing efforts of the American missionaries among their ranks! In 1848 Carr even jeopardized relations between the United States and the Ottoman Empire by sending the Ottoman government a memorandum whose threatening tone and interference in Ottoman internal affairs could not but offend the host country.

This official intervention with local authorities to further the missionary cause, including extension of support to those who were working for that cause and of using frigates and warships for purposes of intimidating the authorities and people of the area, was undertaken with the knowledge and approval of the United States government, sometimes by official instruction. It was clear that the American stand toward missionary activities was that which had been formulated by the administration of John Quincy Adams: support for the missionaries who were diffusing "the knowledge of letters and of true religion, ...the best and the only means" to ensure the prosperity and happiness of nations. In addition to its political implications, this policy reveals a cultural attitude towards others which is part of that original American Puritan doctrine of the "covenant people" who were given a commission to enlighten the rest of mankind. The inner drive which propelled ordinary American citizens and government representatives beyond the call of duty (indeed, against immediate national interests at times) in order to ensure "the prosperity and happiness of nations" was an essential part of a messianic obligation they felt towards the rest of the world. Such an attitude implies on the one hand the spiritual, political, and social superiority of one part of mankind and the inferiority of a larger segment, while, on the other hand, emphasizing the duty of the former towards the latter.

At the turn of the century an objective critic of the missionary establishment, and an advocate of universal religion, Moncure Conway, gave a candid description of the extreme practices of missionaries and their official supporters. In *My Pilgrimage to the Wise Men of the East,* Conway said:

> It is no joke when the youngest of nations, whose constitution ignores religion, strains itself morally with precisely that criminal complexion which was once attributed to Mohammedanism. Fifty years ago Protestant preachers were never weary of accusing Mohammed of propagating his religion by the sword; but in the

opening twentieth century, our government sends warships to the chief Moslem nation and says in effect, 'Pay for the American missionary property damaged by a mob or we will murder your people and burn your capital.' And I heard a missionary, lecturing in our Century Club, New York, boast that by this menace the American mission was the only one that got its money![74]

The ultimate goal of the missionaries was to convert the entire world to their religion. This tendency was based, as the missionaries saw it, on the examples set by the conduct of Christ and the Apostles. One of the active missionaries in the Orient, Eli Smith, put this idea succinctly when he told his congregation in America that the missionary's task was to strive "to complete what the Savior bled on the Cross and now sits upon the throne of the universe to accomplish, the subjection of the whole world to his will."[75] It was taken for granted by American missionaries that theirs was the task to execute that will.

American Missionaries and Manifest Destiny

In the middle of the nineteenth century, when missionary enthusiasm was gaining national support, there was in America a simultaneous movement of national dimensions which was given the name "Manifest Destiny." In 1845 John L. O'Sullivan used that term to describe the highly charged Texas issue.[76] A closer look, however, at the subsequent development of that issue will show that the term "Manifest Destiny" was a description of a movement whose nature, polemics and goals were not different from those of the missionary enterprise. "Manifest Destiny" was actually as deep-rooted in American thought as the missionary tendency. Both the missionary zeal of nineteenth century America and the enthusiasm for westward expansion stemmed from the Puritan origins of the American religious wellspring and from an awakening to that religious and political evangelism which was a distinguishing mark of the American nation at the time. This tendency is partially recognized by S. E. Ahlstrom who describes the nineteenth century religious awakening as the "the heyday of a young republic's 'Manifest Destiny'."[77]

In spite of its political and territorial expansionist overtones, the movement known as "Manifest Destiny" was an expression of a self-righteous attitude on the part of those Puritan forefathers who had regarded territorial expansion as a sacred mission to save souls and "possess the land." In a statement characteristic of this attitude, John Cotton instructed the prospective Puritan immigrants not to offend "the poor Natives, but as you partake in their land, so make then partakers of your precious faith: as you reape their temporalls, so feede them with your spiritualls: winne them to the love of Christ, for whom Christ died....Who knoweth whether God have reared this whole Plantation for such an end."[78] The final rhetorical question notwithstanding, Cotton was certain that the plantation was designed by God as part of a plan, and, furthermore, that the Puritan settlers had an important part to play in the plan. This, after all, was "God's Promise to His Plantation," and was the root of the concept of "Manifest Destiny."

Contemporary advocates of Manifest Destiny used a similar language to describe their efforts. One of them believed that the "superintendence of a directing Providence" directed the steps of Americans and willed that their continent "should be but one nation, under one system of free institutions."[79] Another enthusiastic writer explained away the "subjugation and occupation of Mexico" by stating that this occupation would bring peace and would institute the reign of law, and provide "for the education and elevation of the great mass of the people, who have, for a period of 300 years been the helots of an overbearing foreign face." It would also cause "religious liberty, and full freedom of mind to prevail where a priesthood has long been enabled to prevent all religion save that of its worship,—such a 'conquest,' stigmatize it as you please, must necessarily be a great blessing to the conquered. It is a work worthy of a great people, of a people who are about to regenerate the world by asserting the supremacy of humanity over the accidents of birth and fortune."[80] Our mission, said the same writer, is "to liberate and enoble." This mission was described by Buchanan in a letter to the *Pennsylvanian* on December 20, 1847, as the fulfillment of "the destiny which Providence may have in store for" the United States and Mexico.[81]

The sense of Manifest Destiny, which evolved out of the early Puritan belief in the Providential plan, was at work in the development of the patriotic *plexus* of the young republic. Many spokesmen for the independent nation also expressed the early Puritan belief, that the U.S. was guided by Providence to fulfil a sacred mission. Such was the sentiment proclaimed by Joel Barlow when he advised his countrymen to "be sensible of the greatness of the charge that has devolved upon us. We have duties to posterity as well as to ourselves."[82] And in spite of the limited experience of the United States, Barlow called upon citizens of the new nation to "contemplate the height we have to climb, and the commanding station we must gain, in order to fulfill the destinies to which we are called, and perform the duties that the cause of human happiness requires at our hands."

These typically American factors in American thought were at work in both the concept of Manifest Destiny and the missionary enterprise. Both processes were seen as inherent in the sacred mission delegated to

America by Providence. Nineteenth century politicians and evangelists looked to the frontiers—Western and Oriental—within the context of that sacred mission. The former called their effort "Manifest Destiny",[83] the latter, the "Great Commission."[84] Both politicians and missionaries offered realistic justifications for their expansion—on economic as well as geographical grounds. The ultimate aim was to appropriate more territory. In the case of advocates of Manifest Destiny, the desire was to extend the geographical area of the American republic towards the West; in the case of the missionary establishment, it was to extend the American "Kingdom of God" throughout the entire world, although the process was variously called "reclaiming souls," "possessing the land" or "occupying new stations."

The American historian Frederick Merk gives some recognition to this point in his treatment of Manifest Destiny. He points out that in the middle of the nineteenth century Manifest Destiny was understood to mean "expansion, prearranged by Heaven, over an area not clearly defined."[85] Obviously the key words in this definition are "expansion" and "prearranged by Heaven." What needs to be emphasized here is the certain belief that the American people were chosen to fulfill a prearranged Heavenly plan. This assumption is reminiscent of the Puritan concept of being chosen to establish the Kingdom of God in America. It is contemporary with the belief of nineteenth century millenialists that theirs was the sacred task of rebuilding the City of the Great King, be it in Salt Lake City or in the Holy Land.

Frederick Merk describes one of the themes of Manifest Destiny as "the desire of some imaginative elements in American society to see the boundaries of the nation coincide with the rim of the North American continent."[86] How similar to the desire of some other imaginative elements to see the boundaries of the American Kingdom of God include perhaps the entire world, and certainly the Holy Land! One imaginative missionary, Moses Stuart, called on his fellow-laborers to extend the Kingdom of God to all the nations, including the American West: "be not weary in well doing....The cause is the most important in which men can be engaged. The public eye is fixed on you, for example of patience and perseverance in it. Asia, Africa, and our western wilderness are crying to you for help. You will not abandon their cause."[87] And in "an Address to the Christian Public on the Subject of Missions to the Heathen... ," the Board of Commissioners for Foreign Missions said in November 10, 1812, that "it is not only practicable for multitudes to unite in the great purpose of evangelizing the world; but such a union is absolutely necessary in order to bring about this event in the shortest time. All the power and influence of the whole Christian world must be in requisition during the course of those beneficient labors, which will precede the mil-lenium."[88]

That the concept of Manifest Destiny is expansionist by nature is al-lowed by Merk when he analyzes expansionism in general, but "expan-sionism," he says, "is usually associated with crusading ideologies. In the case of Arab expansionism it was Islam; in Spanish expansionism, Catholicism..."[89] The equivalent of these ideologies in the case of United States expansionism, according to Merk, was Manifest Destiny, "a mix-ture of republicanism, democracy, freedom of religion, Anglo-Saxonism, and a number of other ingredients. It was harnessed to the cause of con-tinentalism in the 1840's."[90] What Merk fails to see is that in varying proportions, these ingredients were also harnessed to the cause of the American missionary enterprise. In this field, furthermore, the in-gredients of republicanism, democracy, and Anglo-Saxonism, when ad-ministered to far-off lands and peoples, were often not too dissimilar to racism and bigotry.

To the task of spreading the word of God the missionary mustered all the arguments at his command to prove that he (as an American) was qualified for the job. In this respect also, the missionary idiom is similar to that of Manifest Destiny.

Geographically, the United States might be regarded as well-suited for missionary work throughout the world; politically, the new nation has devised an ideal system of democracy and social equality; and religious-ly, the diffusion of the Bible among the population and their societal membership in the Church of Christ makes then eminently qualified for the missionary task. The missionary advocate of the *American Theological Review* gave expression to this idea when he asked:

> We have only to open our eyes, and every American can see the finger of Providence pointing out a world enveloped in sin and ig-norance as his field of labor; and, if not deafened by the din of the world, he would hear the voice of Providence, saying, 'Go up and possess the land! Have I not commanded thee? Be strong, and of a good courage! be not afraid, neither be thou dismayed, for the Lord thy God is with thee, whithersoever thou goest.'[91]

The Missionary Polemics

By its very nature the missionary tendency is based on the premise that the missionary is a superior being, and the object of his efforts is an inferior being. This is the *raison d'etre* for missionary work and for the missionary establishment. In missionary thinking there are usually two sides to the encounter: one is the missionary, who is the first person in the missionary address or sermon; the second side is the other—usually the person who is described, analyzed and, it is to be hoped, brought closer to the position which the speaker represents. The "others" are always mute subjects waiting to be dealt with, i.e. saved, by the speaker. Missionary literature is replete with descriptions of the perfect state of the missionaries and their society, and of the "others" as people in a state of degradation and loss. The catalogue of epithets bestowed on the others is very long; it also includes descriptions of their situation, spiritual, moral, social and political.

The "Report of the Prudential Committee" of 1819 describes the "hundreds of millions" of the population of Southern Asia as "immersed in the deepest corruption and wretchedness."[92] In the Holy Land "the whole mingled population is in a state of deplorable ignorance and degradation."[93] The Instructions given by the Prudential Committee to its missionaries in 1812 describes the "superstitions and abominations of the heathens" which await them in the field of their work."[94] The native population, according to the Instructions, "sit in darkness, and in the region and shadow of death," and they suffer "deplorable ignorance."[95]

The whole population of the world was the constant concern of missionaries; thus Missionary paper No. 4, 1828, gives a detailed list of all religions of the world followed by the remark that "it is an appalling and heart-stirring fact, that the population of the earth should, in the nineteenth century, from the death of the Saviour of mankind, remain still victims, to so vast an extent, of superstition, delusion, and idolatory."[96] Another enemy "to the march of holiness" is the Imposture of Muhammad—sensuality, deception and the sword are the weapons used by him. There are, says the Paper, "one hundred and forty millions [who] have been grouped together under the most ferocious and horrid despotism that ever warred against heaven, or tormented man."[97] Christian missionaries from America had to contend with these enemies and with Papal superstition.

Facing this tremendous task with optimism and perseverance was the mark of the true missionary. There was no turning away from the sacred mission appointed by the Governor of the universe. America, which had accepted Christ and become partaker in the covenant of faith, was the nation chosen to fulfill the commands of the Lord "to reform and save the degenerate and perishing."[98] What made the task very urgent was that those millions who sat in darkness and sin, and who normally were pictured as passive recipients of the missionary efforts and judgements, were at times presented as eagerly awaiting the helping hand of the missionaries. One missionary, in fact, says that the wretched population of the whole world has been "struggling and sighing for thousands of years" for the American system which is meant to answer their needs.[99] Another American missionary informs his congregation that the whole world is "crying to you for help. You will not abandon them."[100] Peoples neighboring on the United States, more intimately the object of the Manifest Destiny controversy, were also pictured as in need of help from the United States. Like the heathens and Muslems of the Orient, they, too, were considered to be benighted and oppressed.

It was thus up to the American missionaries, citizens of the Kingdom of God, to take action. This sense of duty can be seen in such statements as the following verses printed on the title page of Josiah Brewer's missionary work,

> Shall we, whose souls are lighted
> With wisdom from on high,
> Shall we to man benighted,
> The lamp of life deny?[101]

The most impressive intermingling of national and religious tendencies is that offered by William Ray in his poem "The Star of the West," included with a collection of his work in an account of his captivity and adventure in Muslim lands. It is in a context like this that the United States becomes the spiritual hope of the world, the Star of the West, exactly as the Star of the East had been at the birth of Christ:

SPREADING OF THE GOSPEL

Star In the West

And I will give him the Morning Star.—Rev.

> T'ILLUME the earth's benighted face,
> With beams of all-redeeming grace—
> To give that face, in tears erewhile,
> A placid, heav'nly joyous smile—
> To light the weary world to rest,
> A star is rising in the west.
>
> With lustre mild and look serene,
> The fair phenomenon is seen;
> A lamp, to guide the darksome way
> Of infidelity astray,
> Back to the regions of the blest—
> A star is rising in the west!
>
> Has nature, then, revers'd her scheme?
> Does from the west a day-star beam?
> Yes—But it is not nature's light

A star more heav'nly, pure and bright,
Shines from the Great Immanuel's breast,
To light the nations in the west.

When stars of night and suns of day,
Extinguish'd shall have pass'd away;
And this vast universe decay'd—
Dissolv'd to nothing but a shade,
Of that supernal gem possess'd,
The star that's rising in the west.

What joyful millions shall behold
And feel, its mysteries unfold—
A sun of glory, brighter grown,
Blazing around JEHOVAH'S throne!
By all the ransom'd throng confess'd
The star that now illumes the west![102]

American Missionaries and the "Others"

The American missionary establishment based its course of action on the perceived needs of the "others." There is in the polemics of the missionary enterprise a set of terms, and idiom, which indicates the general direction of the process of evangelizing the world. The ultimate, and principal goal, is to change the others and to make them "like us," or as close to that as possible. Missionaries were very clear on that point. "The missionary goes to raise the standard of revolt," says one missionary, and to "change," or to "undermine" the beliefs of the local population.[103] The missionary was expected to "stand up there to proclaim all out of the way, and to exhort them to renounce their hereditary veneration of the Koran and Councils."[104] In missionary literature there are frequent statements calling on agents to "endeavor to change their [others] social, literary, and religious conditions."[105] In more general biblical statements they are to "beseige the citadels of the beast and of the false prophet, and whose conquest is to complete the triumph of the Lamb."[106]

If these instructions and statements were too vague for practical application, other advocates put the idea in more concrete terms. In 1823 the American missionary agent Jonas King said that the best approach "for the free preaching of the Gospel to the followers of the False Prophet" was through a total political revolution which should take place in the lands dominated by the Ottoman Empire.[107] In 1882, American missionary circles in Beirut were jubilant over British bombardment of Alexandria, which they thought was one of the methods of defeating Islam and spreading the light of the Gospel.[108] When Britain occupied Egypt, American missionaries believed this was a superb opportunity for the African continent to "be penetrated and absorbed by European control. Those northern borderlands along the Mediterranean that have been for a thousand years under the control of the Moslem shall revert again to the Christian. The present English occupation of Egypt is a typical and prophetic incident."[109]

The best and most practical scheme.; for the introduction of Christianity to Muslim lands were offered by a life-long missionary, Henry Jessup, and a missionary supporter and admirer, Sarah Haight. Jessup considered everything that was happening in the Orient to be a conflict between Islam and Christianity and his conclusion was that "*in the conflict between civilization and barbarism Islam must be the loser.*"[110] Islam, he said, is "in direct conflict with" modern civilization.[111]

"Geography," said Jessup, "will teach them that there are quarters of the globe where the observance of the fast of Ramadan would be impossible, and the growth of Christian political power will convince them that the *Jehad*, or religious war for the faith, has been fought for the last time."[112] But the final solution was to come as a result "*of the British Protectorate over Asiatic Turkey.*"[113] Muslim confidence in the English-speaking races, Jessup said, "involves us, who represent the Anglo-Saxon race among the people of the East, in great responsibility."[114]

In spite of the political overtones of Jessups' scheme, he insisted that he was not writing "from the political standpoint, but only from the position of students of the divine providence. The question has already passed from the domain of mere politics to that of a great and momentous providential fact, to which we do well to take heed."[115] With the power of the Anglo-Saxon race, i.e. Britain, surrounding the domains of Islam, and with the new British policy which renounced the principle of non-intervention in the internal affairs of Turkey, Jessup asked: "What are the moral and religious obligations arising from this state of things which rest upon the Christians of Great Britain and America?"[116] His answer to the problem is a blend of religious and political elements:

> The Christian Church cannot regard with indifference the welfare of one hundred and seventy-five millions of our race. The moral degradation, the spiritual blindness, the deep religious needs of so many men, the pitiful condition of Moslem women, the want of all that we hold dear and sacred in the Christian home, and the utter lack of anything like a provision for human redemption,—should awaken our deepest sympathies and enkindle new zeal in every Christian breast.[117]

In *Fifty-Three Years in Syria*, Jessup's final assessment of missionary work in Muslim lands, the author gloats over the occupation of Muslim countries by Britain and other European powers" "two-thirds of the

Mohammedans in the world are under Christian rule, one-seventh under non-Christian rulers (33,976,500) and only 37,928,800, or a little more than one-seventh, under purely Moslem rulers. This remarkable fact renders any political solidarity of Islam impossible. It also insures liberty of conscience to honest-minded Moslems who wish to read the Bible and even to profess Christianity."[118]

Sarah Haight's scheme of evangelizing the Muslim world was even more political; she proposed the removal of Muslims to the area beyond the Euphrates.[119] So did J.V.C. Smith and others.[120] Often these schemes included provisions which, in addition to spreading the light among the population, aimed at the extension of the domains of the Western—particularly the Anglo-Saxon—world. To "possess the land," in effect, becomes a literal, rather than a spiritual, command.

Here again some advocates of Manifest Destiny were thinking along the same lines as those of the missionary enterprise. The goal, they said, was to prepare other territories for a confederacy, and one of the methods was to "Anglo-Saxonize" them by intermarriages between "our Yankee young fellows and the pretty senoritas" of New Mexico.[121] The *American Theological Review* echoed this idea in 1859 when one of its writers saw in Anglo-Saxon colonization the means of spreading Christianity throughout the world. It is quite significant that in his efforts to "spread the light," to "possess the land," or "to colonize," the missionary transcended all concepts of national boundaries and international treaties and thought only of his "right to be there" so as to carry out his Christian duty. Conquest, possession, encroachment and similar terms such as those used in the context of Manifest Destiny are transferred from their scriptural context to an actual and legitimate operation in missionary literature. The *American Theological Review* writer tells the story in most eloquent words:

> The migratory and colonizing character of the Anglo-Saxon peculiarly adapt them for the work of missionaries. This trait belongs to the inhabitants of Great Britain, as well as to Americans...[who] have ever manifested a disposition to wander into every part of the earth, for gratifying a boundless curiosity, making discoveries in art and science, and eminently for purposes of traffic. Nor do they manifest so much of a desire to return home as other nations, with perhaps one one or two exceptions. The consequence is, colonization on a wide scale....Indeed, how feeble a barrier do right and justice, and solemn treaties even, now interpose to arrest that wave of population which sweeps on southwesterly with overwhelming might! How perfectly resistless will it become when two or three hundred millions shall be found on our soil! It will not stop

with Mexico and South America, but find its way across the Pacific and Atlantic to Asiatic and African shores.[122]

Missionary idiom derives a great deal from the basic encounter between the "saved" and the "lost," "we" and "they." For if the American system had come close to perfection spiritually, morally, culturally, politically and socially, then the process of evangelization had to include such adjectival elements as "enlightening," "liberating," "advancing," "educating" and so on. The American nation was urged, within the context of missionary work, "to send abroad the heralds of civilization, freedom, and salvation" and "to diffuse among the benighted the blessings of knowledge, liberty, and religion."[123]

In the idiom of missionary literature there was a constant overlapping and intermingling of the spiritual and the mundane, the biblical and the temporal. Light and darkness, fertility and barrenness, freedom and despotism—these were some of the favorite concepts used by missionary writers and they were useful on the metaphorical as well as the literal levels. One of the best examples of the repetition of this idiomatic language is a sermon by Heyman Humphrey, 1819, delivered at the ordination of a group of missionaries bound for the Sandwich Islands. The sermon carried the significant title: "The Promised Land," and the preacher impressed on his congregation the enormity of the task by reminding them "how large a part of the land of promise remains yet to be possessed! How vast and powerful and populous are the empires of Pagan darkness and Mahometan delusion! How much ground has the church even *lost*, both in Asia and Africa."[124] The whole of Asia, Humphrey said, "remaineth yet to be possessed," and extensive regions there "are still in the hands of the enemy."[125] The preacher continued:

> The great continent of Africa, also, remaineth yet to be possessed. The interior has not to this day been explored by civilized man; while those parts most accessible to Europeans, instead of receiving from them the light and freedom of the Gospel, have for ages resounded with the stripes and wailings of a most accursed traffic in human blood. Once, indeed, Abyssinia and the region round about, were blessed with Churches and Pastors, walking together in faith and love; but it is long since the glory departed. The true light has ceased to shine, and centuries have rolled away since the prince of darkness re-established his empire....Nor must it be forgotten, that most of the Mediterranean Isles, together with trackless deserts of ice and snow in the north of Europe, and other considerable portions of the globe, which have not been particularly mentioned, remain yet to be possessed.[126]

The goal of converting the world to Christ arose from the "great commission" which American missionaries believed they had received. The enterprise resulting from this belief was seemingly noble, seeking to reform the rest of mankind with Christian commiseration and bene- volence.[127] Education, economic aid, and other methods were used to advance the cause of the missionaries. There was, however, a frequent intermingling of religion and politics and an unmistakable attitude of racial and cultural superiority in the behavior and operations of many missionary efforts. It is an unfortunate, but perhaps an inevitable, fact that American missionary endeavor often became involved in the politi- cal wranglings among nations, in the territorial aspirations of the colonizing powers, and in the internal affairs of the host countries. The missionary establishment, moreover, shared in the American myth of Zion, of re-establishing the Kingdom of Israel.[128] The Oriental field of American missions therefore provides special insights into a complex religious landscape.

6

EASTWARD HO
American Travellers in the Muslim World

"In the wondering footsteps of the children of Israel."
John Lloyd Stephens, *Incidents of
Travel in Egypt, Arabia Petrea,
and the Holy Land,* 1837

On May 4, 1840 the correspondent of the *New York Herald* reported from Alexandria that the number of American visitors to Egypt and the Holy Land was noticeably increasing. Observing that he had seen Americans in Alexandria during that year more than he could "ever recollect to have heard of before," he adds that "upwards of twenty are now on their way to Mount Sinai, Petra, and Jerusalem." In fact, the *Herald* correspondent decides, that "should the Turco-Egyptian question be amicably settled, it is likely we shall have more visitors to Egypt next year than we have had this."[1]

Many remarks made by travellers to the Orient indicate that by the 1830's the number of Americans making the journey was on the increase. The famous American traveller John Lloyd Stephens, while in Smyrna, decided to give only a brief description of the city because "I need not attempt to interest you in Smyrna; it is too everyday a place; every Cape Cod sailor knows it better than I do."[2]

Americans contemplating a trip to the Orient did not lack company. There were regular trips from Europe which took travellers to Constantinople, Smyrna, Alexandria or Beirut, and Americans exercised their options depending on which European port they wanted to leave from and what route they wanted to take.[3] A letter from an American named Charles Edwin Bergh, for example, informed his father that he would have no trouble finding a fellow-traveller for his visit to the Orient despite having been abandoned by his first companion.[4] There are no complete official records of the names and numbers of Americans who visited the Orient during the nineteenth century although many contemporary sources indicate that the tour was becoming increasingly

115

popular among Americans. A list of those Americans who made the Oriental journey would include persons from all walks of life: it would include David Dorr, a black slave from Tennessee; Ulysses Grant, President of the United States; an uneducated farmer, [McI] Robertson; the renowned educator-statesman Henry Adams; Commodores Read and Patterson of the United States Navy, and Navy Chaplain George Jones; and some drunken tourists whom Robertson met in Cairo.

Others who made the popular pilgrimage were William Cullen Bryant, the poet and arbiter of cultural taste; newspaper editors like George William Curtis, and writers in the best tradition of American humor; Sarah Haight, the sophisticated "lady from New York", and the devout down-to-earth wife of a missionary, Sarah Smith; Stephen Olin, theologian and President of Wesleyan University, and William Thomson and Edward Robinson, biblical scholars and researchers. Finally, the list would include a long line of men of letters such as Emerson, Taylor, Melville, Twain, DeForest, Stoddard and Warner.[5] The impact on the American public of their writings and of the impressions communicated by them (and by a thousand others) must have been significant. What is remarkably striking to the modern reader is the relatively similar attitudes and conduct displayed by this heterogeneous group of persons, both in their tours of the Orient and in the impressions brought back home.

For a number of reasons the principal source of information on American travel to the Orient remains those accounts, both published and unpublished, which were written by some of the persons who made the journey. Travel accounts were very popular with the reading public; they revealed the travellers' reasons for undertaking the trip and for recording their experiences. These Travelogues are an invaluable source of information because of the numerous references to other Americans encountered along the way. In addition they show the extent of active involvement of ordinary American citizens in the Orient—the degree of which might otherwise have been unknown to the modern researcher. Most important is the realization that these travel accounts reveal some kind of collective logic—a pattern—which, perhaps consciously, attaches itself to the itinerary or general route traversed by many of the travelers to the Orient and to their all-but-common feelings. For these compelling reasons, travel accounts will be used extensively in the course of this chapter.

Popularity of Travel Literature

There is clear evidence that travel literature, especially that which dealt with the Orient, enjoyed tremendous popularity. Publication dates and the numbers of editions of these books indicate immediate success and continuing demand. Stephen Olin's *Travels in Egypt, Arabia Petraea, and the Holy Land,* for example, came out in 1843, but by 1844 a fourth edition became necessary. William Lynch's *Narrative of the United States' Expedition to the River Jordan and the Dead Sea,* which was published in May 1849, was issued in a second edition in November of the same year. By 1853 Lynch's *Narrative* ran into a ninth edition.

Among other books which gained immediate renown and netted their authors considerable profits are those by John Lloyd Stephens, George William Curtis and Mark Twain. Stephen's *Incidents of Travel in Egypt, Arabia Petraea, and the Holy Land,* originally published in October 1837, was issued in six consecutive editions by the next year. Stephens acknowledges popular favor in the sixth edition by stating that "the preface of a book is seldom read, or the author would express his acknowledgements to the public for having so soon demanded a sixth edition of his work."[6] A contemporary of Stephens, William Lynch, who made the Oriental trip in 1847–49, expresses his gratitude for a letter of advice and information he received from "Mr. Stephens of New York, the author of one of the most interesting books of travel which our language can produce."[7] The modern editor of the *Incidents* shows that Lynch's opinion was well founded. "*Arabia Petraea,*" Victor Wolfgang von Hagen says, "was widely reviewed, and without exception it was widely praised."[8]

Even the British, in spite of their lack of admiration for American writings, praised Stephens' work and continued to print it until 1866. But the *Incidents'* sales in America were phenomenal. "Within two years," says Stephens' editor, "*Arabia Petraea* had sold 21,000 copies," and the book continued in print until 1882. Stephens' royalties amounted to $25,000 in the first two years.[9] Mark Twain's book of travel, *The Innocents Abroad* (1869), sold more than 30,000 copies within five months and about 67,000 copies during the first year.[10]

Authors and publishers repeatedly show their awareness of this popularity and often reveal a sense of frenzied competition and fear of piracy. Sarah Haight's *Letters from the Old World* is prefaced by a "Publishers' Notice" and an "Author's Notice to the Reader," both of which offer reasons for rushing to press soon after the *Letters* were published serially in periodicals. The publishers say that portions of the letters were published "within the present year in columns of the New-York

American, and have been copied thence into several other journals." The "Notice" goes on to say that "the publishers confidently anticipate for the letters in their present form a reception from the public not less cordial than that which was bestowed upon a portion of them when they appeared weekly in the columns of a newspaper."[11] The author herself states that she was reluctant to allow her letters to be published, but she ultimately had to agree.[12]

Competition led Narrative of the United States' ExpeditionWilliam Lynch to hurry to the press with his *Narrative*, "induced," as he says, "by hearing of the proposed publication of a Narrative of the Expedition, said to be by a member of the party."[13] Lynch made sure to get the approval and blessing of Secretary of the Navy John Mason who had commissioned the Expedition and to whom the *Narrative* was dedicated. He also expresses confidence in a favorable reception of the book by the public in spite of the wealth of material on the Orient. The same confidence is seen in George William Curtis' playful "letter to the Pasha" with which he opens his second "Hawadji" book. "My Dear Pasha," Curtis says to his imaginary companion,

> In making you the Pasha of two tales, I confess with the Syrians, that a friend is fairer than the roses of Damascus, and more costly than the pearls of Omman.
>
> You of all men, will not be surprised by these pages, for you shared with me the fascination of novelty in those eldest lands,—which interpreted to us both that pleasant story of Raphael. When his friend, Marc Antonio, discovered him engaged upon the Sistene picture exclaimed,
> —"Cospetto! another Madona?"
> Raphael gravely answered,
> —"*Amico mio*, my friend, were all the artists to paint her portrait forever, they could never exhaust her beauty.[14]

This inexhaustible beauty of the Orient is often anticipated before the journey. Haight expresses such anticipation in her letter from Alexandria, upon leaving for Cairo, when in expectation of a rich field ahead of her, she tells her correspondent that "however often it may have been reaped by others who have preceded me, there is, doubtless, an abundance of rich gleanings which I may be able to gather into my garner."[15]

The field was open, and the public was very receptive. There were, in addition to the travel books, scores of articles in periodicals describing travel experiences. Mark Twain's trip was commissioned by the *Alta California*, and William Cullen Bryant and George William Curtis did a great deal to popularize this form of daily reading among the American public. In the manuscript letters of Charles Wesley Andrews and Charles Edwin Bergh we see the curious phenomenon of letters sent by travelers and subsequently published in periodicals under the signature of the paper's "correspondent."[16] Many of the travelers, moreover, upon their return home, went on lecture tours fascinating their audiences with tales of their experiences in the exotic Orient. Bayard Taylor, a traveler-poet of note, is said to have delivered his lectures wearing a full outfit of Arabian clothes. He earned an average of $5,000 per lecture season.[17]

American Presence in the Muslem World

Travel accounts by Americans tell the story of frequent crossings of paths and curious meetings in Oriental localities. Some Americans were in the service of the Ottoman authorities in Constantinople and its surrounding area or of the local authorities in various provinces of the Ottoman Empires. The most obvious examples are Henry Eckford and Foster Rhodes, who successively were in charge of building Ottoman naval vessels in the thirties and forties. Another conspicuous group of Americans are the soldiers of fortune who left the States after the Civil War and rendered services to the Egyptian armed forces, especially to train and rebuild these forces.[18]

There are many contemporary references to Eckford and Rhodes by Americans who visited Constantinople, but one very proud reference is by a United States diplomat at the High Porte. David Porter records with pride in his *Constantinople and its Environs* that one of the ships ordered by the Sultan, "a despatch boat, which was to beat every thing on the Bosphorus in sailing," was built by Henry Eckford. When the boat was ready for the Sultan's review, Porter says, "I went on board of her, on her first trial, and we beat up to the truely magnificient palace of Beglerbeg, just finished, and the present residence of the Sultan." In a typically Oriental scene, the Ottoman Emperor stood at the window, to watch the parading ship; following a Lear-like scene of jesting Foster records that the Sultan, "cast his eyes around among us, and immediately asked who I was? They told him. He then inquired who my nephew was, and on being informed called Mr. Eckford to him, and gave him a snuff-box set with diamonds." The scene ends with the Sultan showering the group of Americans who accompanied Porter with "individual gifts of money."[19]

Another traveller in the Orient, Mrs. Sarah Haight, confirms the efforts made by Eckford and Rhodes, and their great reputation in Constantinople. On one occasion she observes that the port of Constantinople was full of ships of all nationalities, but that the Sultan's navy has the best ship in the harbor, "the proudest of them all,...a Yankee frigate [which] rides here a proud monument of the skill of our lamented fellow-citizen, Henry Eckford."[20] Haight, however, takes consolation in the fact that Eckford's successor, Foster Rhodes, was also an American who distinguished himself in building ships for the Sultan.[21]

There were other American nationals, althought not so distinguished, who worked for the Ottomans. We learn from William Lynch, commander of the official American expedition to the Dead Sea and the River Jordan in 1847-1848, that while in Constantinople, he met a Dr. Davis from South Carolina who was there with his family, his brother, and a number of slaves. Dr. Davis was part of a United States official agricultural cooperation program and worked as superintendent of a farm and agricultural school in nearby San Stephano. Besides Dr. Davis, his slaves, and his family, "including his intelligent brother," Lynch also met "Dr. Smith, who holds the important office of geologist to the Ottoman government to whom we are indepted for many scientific suggestions."[22]

Other American expatriates impressing Lynch, Haight and most other travellers to the Orient were those belonging to the missionary establishments. Missionaries often operated "hospitality houses" to which travelers came for help and advice. In Constantinople, for example, Lynch records that "from Bishop Southgate, of the American Episcopal Mission, we received many kind offices, including a present of his work on Armenia, Persia, and Mesopotamia. By the gentlemen of the Evangelical Mission and their families, we were also welcomed with cordial hospitality."[23] The nature of David Porter's position as a government representative made it necessary for him to have a good deal of association and cooperation with the missionary establishment. Regarding the wide-ranging activities of the missionaries in the Ottoman Empire and his involvement with it, Porter states in a letter written on December 25, 133, that

> Mr. Goodell has established everywhere schools on the Lancastrian plan for the Greeks and Armenians, with the approbation of the patriarchs and bishops; and two Turkish schools of the same kind, have been established by him at the desire of the Sultan; one, at the barracks of Scutary, containing one hundred young soldiers; and the other at the barraks near Dalma Bashi, with four hundred and fifty scholars of the same kind. I visited both these schools three months after they were established, and saw the young soldiers first go through the exercise of their arms, with all the precision of veteran troops; after which they took their places in their classes in

the school room....It was a college for soldiers, what West Point is for our officers.[24]

Many other Americans had occasion to visit these schools, and they had every praise for their work. Sarah Haight comments on the excellent work done by "the veteran labourer in the good cause, the Rev. Mr. Goodell, and his coadjutor, the Rev. Mr. Dwight." Their admirable schools and establishments, she adds, "fully persuaded [me] of its immense utility, and firmly convinced [me] that they have adopted the right and only course to penetrate the darkness that overshadows this heathen land."[25] In Jerusalem, Haight is visited by "two American gentlemen, connected with the missionary establishment in this city. One was the Rev. Mr. Whiting, from the State of New York, and the other the Rev. Mr. Lannean, of Charleston, South Carolina."[26] And in Beirut Haight comments on the excellent house of the resident missionaries, adding:

> We dined with them and visited their school. Mr. Smith is, no doubt, one of the best qualified persons for this important service throughout the East; his amiable and indefatigable companion is making herself extremely useful by teaching a school of small children. All her books and exercises are in the Arabic language.[27]

American missionaries and residents in the Orient were active in many circles, including the military and agricultural communities and young children's schools. They seemed also to be present everywhere, even in the least expected places. In Damascus William Lynch "dined with Dr. Paulding, who with his brother-in-law, the Rev. Mr. Barnet, belong to the American Evangelic Mission in Syria."[28] While Lynch and his party were on their way from Damascus to Beirut, some of his companions became very ill: "at eleven, Beirut and the sea in sight, but the sick scarce able to keep their saddles, when fortunately we met our countryman, Dr. De Forest, of the Evangelical Mission, who prescribed some medicine to be administered as soon as possible."[29] The matter-of-fact manner in which the author records meeting "our countryman" in an unlikely place as the road to Damascus indicates the frequent presence of Americans in the area. On arriving at Beirut, one of Lynch's party, a Mr. Dale, died at the house of the Rev. Eli Smith "of the American Presbyterian Mission." Lynch records with gratitude "the kindest attention" received from Smith, his wife, Dr. DeForest, Dr. Vandike, the Rev. Mr. Thompson and many others.[30]

Dale was not the first American to be buried in the Orient. That was also the fate of John Ledyard, a young adventurer from Connecticut who died in Cairo in early 1788. He was remembered by Mrs. Haight who, while in Cairo, met a Mr. Bota, "son of the historian," and when she "looked upon him," she says, "I thought of the tomb of our own enterprising young Ledyard, who lies buried in the desert."[31] Two other Americans travelling in the Orient record memories of such sad events. Charles Edwin Bergh of New York writes to his mother on February 13, 1842, telling her that he visited the American cemetery in Jerusalem and that on Mount Zion he visited the Tomb of David and "prayed by the graves of W. Costigan who lost his life at the Dead Sea in 1830, and a young American who also died here the same year."[32] Charles Wesley Andrews of Virginia also mentions in a letter to his wife that the Rev. Mr. Gober died in Cairo "on Friday from Typhus fever…at a time when a stranger might well expect such a result."[33] Of the missionary establishment, a number of persons died in the Orient during their service there. Eli Smith's wife died in Beirut, working for the missionary cause to the last minute.

Perhaps because of its sacred associations, the Orient was sought by many Americans for what was believed to be its healing power, both physical and spiritual. In the Orient, a *New York Morning Herald* correspondent decided, "an invalid has every thing he can desire or wish for."[34] At about the same time, Charles Wesley Andrews, the Episcopal minister from Virginia, was convinced of this beneficial effect on his health when he wrote his wife from Paris to tell her of his plan to visit the Holy Land. His letter written September 6, 1841, shows a man torn between the duty of going back to his wife and children and the promise of spiritual as well as physical healing which would result from the intended journey. He finally decided to "comit my way unto the Lord that he may direct my path," and to go to Marseille, where he would wait for his wife's reply. He suggested gently that "the atmosphere of the holy land may invigorate my decayed constitution and give strength to preach again the unsearchable riches of Christ."[35] Andrews' health did improve during his Oriental journey, especially on his trip through the Holy Land.

The same fate was not to be the lot of two prominent Americans, Herman Melville and Ralph Waldo Emerson, both of whom made the journey to regain their physical and mental health. We learn from the editor of Melville's *Journal* that by the end of 1856 he was "severely ill physically (and evidently not a little mentally)."[36] His father-in-law, Lemuel Shaw, attested to this in a letter to his son explaining that the author's state of mind and body made the trip necessary.[37] With this resolve, the editor says, "the voyage through the Levant and Europe was projected in the hope of recuperating his failing health, and, perhaps, of restoring his spirits from a mood of profound skepticism, disillusion, and gloom."[38] Judging from the prevailing mood of his *Journal* and *Clarel*, the two works which directly resulted from the trip, Melville must not have received the salutary effect expected. Emerson's trip to the Orient in 1872 was a present from his friends and disciples, and was meant to raise the spirits of the aging Concord philosopher following a series of calamities which had culminated in the destruction by fire of his house and library. Emerson did not seem to have been inspired by Egypt, where "he did not find the Nile of his imagination,"[39] and although he temporarily recovered his health and spirits, he finally succumbed to illness and old age in 1882.

Travellers' Expectations of the Orient

For the majority of Americans, however, the Orient presented a prospect that was quite thrilling and very different from what they expected to see on a European tour. There was something about that part of the world—quite apart from its religious associations—which promised an experience which was as novel as it was exciting. Expectations were high even before the beginning of the journey, and were to a certain degree preconditioned by an accumulation of cultural as well as personal memories. We listen, for example, to Melville's enthusiasm as he records his reaction to an earlier plan to visit the Orient: "This afternoon Dr. Taylor and I sketched a plan for going down the Danube from Vienna to Constantinople; thence to Athens on the steamer; to Beyrouth and Jerusalem—Alexandria and the Pyramids....I am full (just now) of this glorious Eastern jaunt. Think of it! Jerusalem and the Pyramids—Constantinople...!"[40] There was a uniqueness to the very prospect of that first visit to the Orient.

And if Melville combined both Europe and the Orient in his joyous vision, many other travelers made a clear distinction between the European world and the Orient. The rapture of excitement was reserved for the latter, if only because Europe was more familiar. Yet there was also something familiar about the Orient—a preconceived notion of what was awaiting the traveller.

Such is the expression in Sarah Haight's first letter from Constantinople in which she apologizes for the dull letters she had sent from Europe. She tells her correspondent that her impatience at receiving more compelling descriptions of the Orient could not have exceeded Haight's impatience. But, she says, she hoped that the letters she had imposed on her correspondent from Europe "may have served to stay your craving appetite for sketches of Oriental wanderings." Continuing the gustatory metaphor, Haight says "I only hope that, like *caviare* before the feast, they may have been the means of whetting it to a keener edge. It will be impossible for my imperfect descriptive powers to mete out to you such a portion as you may expect, of the mental feast which I now begin to realize is before me." The "feast" is so sumptuous that Haight can only send "fragments, crumbs which fall from the table." Her aim, she says to her correspondent, is "to captivate your fancy, and subdue your judgement with the weapons of enthusiasm."[41] All of this anticipation, and she has been in Istanbul for a mere two days!

But Haight's expectations are justified, for the novelty and uniqueness of the experience are nothing like what the United States or Europe could offer. The catalog of opposites is long, as one look at the "Queen of the Orient" demonstrates to her. Departing, she says "from a modern European city (Odessa)...in two days I found myself in Turkey, with everything differing so materially from what I had ever before seen. The turban in lieu of the hat, flowing robes and wide trousers in place of short coats and pantaloons, red and yellow slippers instead of boots, long beards and curled mustaches instead of shorn faces, and veiled heads in lieu of the female face divine...minarets in the place of towers and steeples, and the cry of the Muezzin [sic.] instead of bells..."[42] A hundred other opposites are listed which transport the traveller to a world which has existed only in the imagination. The mood is one of joyous expectation and a craving for more of the same.

Such contrast is made all the more striking on the return trip to Europe, and the traveller feels the let-down which results from returning to his familiar European life. Charles Edwin Bergh recognizes this contrast on arriving in Vienna from Smyrna and in his travel account warns his readers of the change which is inevitable.[43]

The first serious modern attempt at a detailed study of the archeology of Palestine was made by an American, Edward Robinson, who prefaced the published results of his labors in the Holy Land with the statement that the journey "had been the object of my ardent wishes, and had entered into my plans of life for more than fifteen years."[44] The Holy Land, in fact, was part of the plan of life, dreams and ardent wishes of many Americans in the nineteenth century. And the desire to make the journey was not limited only to religious scholars and missionaries. The naval officer William Lynch, who headed what was ostensibly a scientific expedition commissioned by the United States government, admits in his account that he had entertained the trip for a long time. "The yearnings of twenty years," he says at the start of his journey,

> were about to be gratified. When a young midshipmen, almost the very least in the escort of the good Lafayette across the ocean, my heart was prepared for its subsequent aspirations....

Twice, since, at distant intervals, I contemplated making the desired visit. But the imperative calls of duty in the first instance, and a domestic calamity in the second, prevented me. As I have before said, in the spring of the present year I asked permission to visit the lands of the Bible, with the special purpose of thoroughly exploring the Dead Sea; the extent, configuration, and depression of which, are as much desiderata to science, as its miraculous formation, its mysterious existence, and the wondrous traditions respecting it, are of thrilling interest to the Christian.[45]

The lands of the Bible were, in a sense, considered to be the sacred spiritual property of church-going and devout Christians. They saw these lands graphically presented in every chapter of the Bible, in religious hymns, in Sunday school instruction, at revival meetings, and in the stories of the early Christian community in Palestine. The mental picture of Palestine was deeply impressed on their thoughts. These sentiments are expressed by Edward Robinson in his work on the Holy Land:

As in the case of most of my countrymen, especially in New England, the scenes of the Bible had made a deep impression upon my mind from the earliest childhood....Indeed in no country in the world, perhaps, is such a feeling more widely diffused than in New England; in no country are the Scriptures better known, or more highly prized. From his earliest years the child is there accustomed not only to read the Bible for himself, but he reads or listens to it in the morning and evening devotions of the family, in the daily village school, in the Sunday school and Bible class, and in the weekly ministrations of the sanctuary.[46]

This shared communal interest gave added incentive to explore the actual geographical area. When Lynch, for example, planned his expedition, he kept his plans secret (with official approval, especially that of the Secretary of the Navy) for fear that not enough financial support could be mustered. Nonetheless, Lynch himself had no doubt that support would be forthcoming. In the preface to his *Narrative* he says:

I had an abiding faith in the ultimate issue, which cheered me on; for I felt that a liberal and enlightened community would not long condemn an attempt to explore a distant river, and its wondrous reservior,—the first, teeming with sacred associations, and the last, enveloped in mystery, which had defied all previous attempts to penetrate it.[47]

These sacred associations in the minds of Americans were what led many to seek to verification on the spot. In one brief statement, a devout American, David Millard, sums up the attraction the Orient held for Westerners, particularly Americans. He introduces his *Journal*:

> In later years, my profession led me to study and contemplate every-
> thing connected with sacred history. The reading of the Sacred Scrip-
> tures often awakened in me an ardent desire to visit the principal
> places of their historical scenery....By too much study and intense
> labor, my health had been seriously impaired. Suffering greatly
> under an affected state of the nervous system, I was advised by
> physicians to take a voyage to sea. I chose the direction of the
> Mediterranean, with the intention, should my health permit, of visit-
> ing Egypt and the Holy Land.[48]

A more emotional expression of the opportunity to visit the land of
Scriptures comes from the pen of Charles Wesley Andrews in a letter to
his ailing wife. Torn between the sense of duty to return to her bedside
and the temptation of a visit to the Holy Land, the Episcopalian minister
writes from Paris:

> Tuesday morning, September 7, I have been thinking more and
> more about my journey and trying to commit my way unto the Lord
> that he may direct my paths. I think I will at last go to Marseilles and
> wait for yr: next letter. There I shall know again of yr: state and hope
> if you really wish me to come back this fall, that letter may contain
> an expression of your wish and you will see me by the 25th of Oc-
> tober,: but in the workings of my mind upon the subject I sometimes
> think I hear you advising me to go on, that you will wait very cheer-
> fully until I come home and wd rather that I wd see Thebes and
> home and Jerusalem and that you might hear of those wonderful
> cities from my mouth.[49]

A less personal, but no less emotional, response upon actually reaching on the land of Scriptures is made by George Jones, Chaplain U. S.
Navy, in his *Excursions to Cairo, Jerusalem, Damascus and Balbec*. In Jones'
apostrophe on the Holy Land we have a rare combination of the land of
childhood memories and the wanderings of the imagination, together
with discovery of the physical location itself. While approaching the
coast of Palestine, Jones says:

> Early on the morning of the 12th we had the pleasure of seeing the
> hills of Palestine emerging from the waters. What a thrill was oc-
> casioned by the sight!
> The birth-place of a wide-spread and wonderful religion—the land
> of a thousand miracles—the original home of a people now spread
> every where, and every where a miracle; and every where, from
> Lapland to India, still yearning towards their fatherland—the moun-
> tains, the plains of Judea were before us. In our earliest infancy we
> had tried to picture them—they were mingled with the deepest and
> warmest feelings of our maturer years; in imagination how often
> had we wandered over the hallowed ground, and here before us was
> now the reality itself.[50]

The feeling of joy which came over the traveler as he set foot in the Holy Land made the journey more of a pilgrimage than a pleasure trip. The idiom and imagery which inform accounts of these pilgrimages are reminiscent of the symbolic Christian final journey to the Kingdom of Heaven, as well as those of the first migrations of English immigrants to the New World. One of the first Americans to undertake a religious mission to the Holy Land, Josiah Brewer, uses language similar to that of the Pilgrim Fathers:

> The Atlantic I have expected to find like Israel's 'waste howling wilderness,' spread out as a trial of patience, before entering the promised land. Short be our passage, is the prayer of the voyager, and shorter still, you may add, be the story of it. Yet, since you have requested to share in the benefits of my pilgrimage, think not to stand with me on Mount Zion, without first learning something of the inconveniences and trials encountered by the way.[51]

The Journey As Pilgrimage

A number of dominant factors in American travel idiom can be seen in this statement, especially in the context of travel to the Orient. The journey, from the traveller's viewpoint, is a pilgrimage to the Promised Land, the earthly Canaan; and crossing the howling wilderness is an essential requirement for the pilgrimage. Time has run full cycle: the Pilgrims first journeyed west across the expanse of the Atlantic in search of the land of promise; their descendants were now on a journey east—crossing other distances to reach the Promised Land. "In all thy ways acknowledge him, and he shall direct thy paths (Proverb iii, 6)." This was Thomson's "travelling motto, roving or at rest, ever since I left the banks of our bright Ohio for this 'Land of Promise'."[52]

The Pilgrim fathers sought to establish the Kingdom of God, an earthly Canaan, in the New World—perhaps in Boston or New Mexico. That was the Canaan of spiritual geography which colored the speeches of so many of the settlers and inspired them to give their settlements names like New Jerusalem, New Lebanon, and Bethlehem. Thomson and his generation, in their turn, made the journey to the Promised Land "with the cheerful hope and fervent prayer that our pleasant pilgrimage through the earthly Canaan may hereafter be resumed and perpetuated in the heavenly."[53] When he actually arrives in the Holy Land, Thomson exclaims:

> Our first walk in the Land of Promise! To me a land of promises more numerous and not less interesting than those given to the Father of the Faithful, when the Lord said, 'Arise, walk through the

land in the length of it and the breadth of it; for I will give it unto thee.' It is given to me also, and I mean to make it mine from Dan to Beersheba before I leave it.[54]

This was the *Pilgrim's Progress* of every ardent Christian. The American Canaan was a prelude to another earthly Canaan, itself representing for most American Christians the real Second Kingdom. It was not out of keeping with the setting that Charles Andrews took along *Pilgrim's Progress* on his journey to the Holy Land,[55] or that Charles Edwin Bergh, a less devout Christian, reached for "the little Bible," which his mother had packed in his luggage, and read passages from Exodus while at the Convent of St. Catherine on Mount Sinai.[56]

In the accounts of travellers to the Orient they demonstrate a sense of *deja-vu*—a shock of recognition—a rediscovery of previously-explored regions. It is as though these pilgrims were renewing an acquaintance with the land of their spiritual birth and nativity.[57] This is the ecstatic high that we hear in Stephen Olin's words upon approaching the city of Jerusalem and the Mount of Olives, a site, he says, which

yielded up my mind to recollections and emotions which rushed upon me with irresistible force. I had trodden the ground, and in all probability the very path most frequented by the blessed Redeemer and his apostles. The Garden of Gethsemane, through which I had passed in my way from the city, and which lay in the deep valley below me in full view, the declivity of the mountain which I had just ascended—its elevated summit, upon which I was now standing, were the favourite haunts of the Savior of the world...

With the exception of Calvary, no spot on earth is so historical and so rich in holy associations as the Mount of Olives.[58]

It becomes very difficult for the American divine to leave the city:

It was indeed painful to tear myself away from the sacred objects to whose power I had for several weeks so unreservedly yielded my imagination and my heart, and my thoughts still lingered upon Calvary and Olivet, and in the Garden of Gethsemane. Happy and swift were the hours spent in communion with these hallowed scenes, and deep and enduring the lineaments in which they have impressed their images and subduing associations upon my mind.[59]

Less eloquent, though sincere, are the words of a Tennessee farmer travelling in the Holy Land, showing that these emotions emanated from the less-educated masses as well as from the sophisticated clergy. In fact, the shock in the case of [McI] Robertson results from his inability to recognize in the actual locations the hallowed images of his religious imagination. "On our way to Jerusalem shortaly after we had lost sight of Hebron," Robertson says, "we observed the tree under which Abraham is supposed to have communed with the Angels; it is called...by the

Arabs Oak." Furthermore, Robertson is disappointed by the barrenness, and marvels at the great change that "must have taken place since it was the land flowing with milk and honey."[60] However, he is in awe of the realization that he actually is standing in that most sacred land which saw the birth of the Savior and is revered by Christians all over the world.

These ecstatic outbursts were the result of a host of sacred memories which rushed to the mind of the pilgrims as they travelled through the Holy Land. There is the sense of a fulfilled vision, a realization of a cultural historical past. The expression at times becomes a derivative of biblical experience, as when Sarah Haight writes:

> While I was returning to our tent, the impression made on my mind when I first landed on the coast of Syria returned to me with increased interest, now that I felt myself actually treading in the soil of Palestine, the theatre of so many mighty events. All my historical recollections, sacred and profane, came fresh to my memory; and I fancied I saw in every face a patriarch, and in every warrier chieftain an apostle.[61]

Every stop on the way was the scene of some biblical or early Christian event: while sailing from Smyrna to Constantinople, Josiah Brewer recalls the journey of St. Paul, conscious that he is in a sense, another apostle on a mission, even though he "reversed the order of the Apostle Paul's last voyage to Jerusalem."[62]

The land and the book came together with intensity and clarity in the experiences of travellers in the Orient. This was partly a result of their memories of childhood Bible-reading exercises, but they were made more vivid because many a traveller brought his Bible along on these journeys and spent hours reading the textual explications of sacred geographical locations. In fact, William Thomson, in his work *The Land and the Book,* stated in the preface that his aim was, "to illustrate the Word of God [which] is in itself commendable. On this fundamental fact the author rests his apology for obtruding the present work upon the notice of the public."[63] Thomson sought to guide his readers in the "good land" of Scriptures where they could read his words as a supplementary illustration to the Bible and thereby relive the "adventures and life of Christ and his disciples in the Holy Land."[64] Even those who might be reading the Bible in the comfort of their American homes could relive its events by viewing Thomson's illustrations which identify the sacred scenes where "in this identical land, amid the same scenes, the author of this work earnestly cultivated communion and intimate correspondence with this divine Teacher, and with the internal and external life of the Book of God."[65]

A contemporary review of *The Land and the Book* emphasizes the important position occupied by the Bible in the life of Christians in America. Thomson's writings are praised because, by describing the sacred stage on which the events of the Bible took place, he helped Christians understand the Word of God. On the other hand, for travellers in the Holy Land, including Thomson himself, the Bible acted as a guide to the land. The Bible was used to verify the authenticity of some places or to disprove others. If there was a doubt regarding any site, the Bible offered the higher proof; thus places were recognized by their Scriptural rather than by their current names.

As Sarah Haight toured the suburbs of Cairo, she paused at the site of Heliopolis and recalled that this was "the *On* of Scriptures." Although nothing was left but the remains of a ruined wall which had enclosed the temple, she states that the visit to the site aroused in her "feelings no other place in the world did." Even she could not explain the reason of that enchantment by a ruined place. But then her memory was aided by her "eye of imagination" and some passages from the Bible.[66] As she read "chapter after chapter" from the Scriptures, she realized that the attraction of the place was the result of her feeling that it "identifies with the earliest history of our sacred scriptures."[67]

The Bible was also useful on these voyages as a suitable source of topical materials for sermons and preaching. For example, when in Sidon, in Travellers, American;in Lebanon[Lebanon]South Lebanon, Haight cut short a letter she was writing, saying,

> The above must suffice for this evening, for the hour has come for our *scriptural* lecture. Mr. R's text tonight is in Genesis xlix, verse 13. 'Zebulon shall dwell at the haven of the sea; and he shall be for a haven of ships; and his border shall be unto Zidon,'... tomorrow our journey from Beyrout to this place, and our visit this day to Sidon.[68]

One of the biblical sites most celebrated by travellers in the Levant was Idumea of Scriptures, and Americans made every effort to identify the area, to find out its religious significance, and to be among the first to "walk through" it. Stephens in his *Incidence of Travels in Egypt* mentions that he decided to strike "directly through the heart of the desert from Mount Sinai to the frontier of the Holy Land." And in spite of the dangers and difficulties of this route, it would spare him the quarantine and would present "another consideration...which, in the end, I found it impossible to resist."[69]

When Edgar Allan Poe reviewed Stephens' book in the *New York Review* (October, 1837), he found it "of more than ordinary interest— written with freshness of manner, and evincing a manliness of feeling, both worthy of high consideration." But in spite of Poe's high praise, he finds reason to quarrel with Stephens' and Keith's interpretations of the scriptural prophesy concerning Idumea. In fact, Poe concludes, after a tortuous analysis of the text, that the Hebrew words of Scripture meant that the curse will fall on "he that passeth and repasseth therein," not those who pass *through* the land. Poe says that,

> The prophet means that there shall be no marks of life in the land, no living being there, no one moving up and down in it: and are, of course, to be taken with the usual allowance for that hyperbole which is a main feature, and indeed the genius of the language.[70]

So important was this subject that when in August, 1841, Poe reviewed Stephen's *Incidents of Travel in Central America*, the bulk of that review was devoted again to Stephens' passage through Idumea. Poe again concludes that the reference in prophesy is "to the inhabitants. The prophet speaks only of the general abandonment and desolation of the land."[71] Perhaps because of that "error" in interpreting the Scriptures, Poe changed his mind about Stephen's earlier book, and considered its high "reputation not altogether well deserved."[72]

Not all Americans, however, shared Poe's opinion of Dr. Keith's *Evidence of Prophesy*. In fact, this book was a constant companion for some travellers in the Holy Land and was their chosen guide through the sacred sites of the Bible. Sarah Haight, for example, says that,

> The Rev. Doctor Keith, in his *Evidence of the Truth of the Christian Religion*, derived from the literal fulfillment of PROPHECY has been invaluable to me in my travel, and was born out in the details of my experience.[73]

Millard may not have cared for the literal interpretation of the references in the Bible to certain places in the Holy Land. He did however, carry with him Dr. Robinson's *Researches*, for which he had the greatest respect. Millard also used Thomson's *The Land and the Book* and Keith's *Evidence*. Another traveller in the Levant, Stephen Olin, himself a man of the church, paid attention to these references and to the truth of the geographical locations of biblical places and events.[74] Even the liberal and politically-minded Charles Edwin Bergh read the 20th Chapter of Exodus at the Convent of St. Catherine on Mount Sinai, "especially the ten commandments." He also remembered to break "a piece of the granite rock on which I stood" and took it home as a souvernir.[75]

This literal interpretation of biblical texts in identifying certain sites is carried to such absurd extremes that at one point William Lynch admonishes those who spoil the moment by quibbling over the text. Overlooking the Sea of Galilee, and recalling its sacred associations, he says:

> I neither put implicit faith in, nor yet, in a cavilling spirit, question
> the localities of these traditions. Unhappy is that man, who instead
> of being impressed with awe, or exultant with the thought that he is
> permitted to look upon such scenes, withholds his homage, and
> stifles every grateful aspiration with querulous questioning of exact
> identities. Away with such hard-hearted scepticism—so nearly al-
> lied to infidelity.[76]

There were many unpleasant experiences encountered on the journey,
ranging from the scorching heat of the desert to the lack of bare neces-
sities. These conditions spoiled the religious delight of travelers as they
trod in Moses' footsteps or roamed among the sacred places of the Holy
Land. But the most unpleasant experience—one which evoked almost
universal repugnance—was the discovery that the area was actually
populated, indeed dominated, by people whose culture and beliefs dif-
fered from those of the traveler. There was a sense of injured pride, of
molested personal property, when the Western Christian traveler arrived
in Hebron, Jerusalem, or Constantinople after a long journey, with great
expectations, only to find that the guardians of "his" holy places were
either Muslims, or, at best, Eastern Christians and Catholics. These alien
natives, "occupiers" in the eyes of the travellers, were deluded intruders
in a land which the American traveller considered his own possession.
For some of them the Muslim presence in the Holy Land, indeed in the
whole surrounding area, evoked bitter historical memories of the spread
of Islam and raised the persistent hope of evicting these Muslims from
the land which "belonged" to the Christian West. Reflections like these,
superimposed on current realities in the Ottoman Empire, urged the
repossession by the West of the Holy Land and the speedy demise of
Islam.

Even as the traveler sets foot on the first port of entry to the Orient, his
mind becomes preoccupied by these reflections. Constantinople, the
European gateway to the Orient, capital of the Ottoman Empire, provides a rich source of Christian associations. Standing by the old wall of
the city, Josiah Brewer forgets everything around him and sees only "the
cannon gate, by which Muhamet entered the city in 1453."[77] Peacefully,
but certainly, Brewer predicts that "a holier cross than that borne by the
crusaders, shall take the place of the crescent which we now see around
us, on the top of the minarets; and instead of the blood-red flag, with its
drawn sword in the midst, there shall float on these walls, the white banner and branch of peace."[78]

And at that same spot, Sarah Haight imagines a weak point in the wall
of the city which reminds her that "in that breach perished the last of the
emperors, bravely defending the remnant of this once great empire.

Through that breach first poured into the beautiful city those Tartar hords, who, thirsting for the blood of Christians, bade the cimeter do its worst, and over the bodies of the prostrate Greeks was raised the standard of Islam."[79] In fact, the entirety of Haight's historical, political and religious knowledge is evoked as she sails across the Bosphorus towards the Eastern part of Constantinople. "At that point," she says, "where hostile Asia approaches nearest to Europe, two more castles mark the spot, where, when the Christian forces were worn out by constant watching, and weakened by dissensions, the proud Osmanlies descended like a torrent upon Christian Europe, never to be driven back until their empire of repine shall have consumed itself, and its weak residium be trampled under foot by indignant Christendom."[80] Until then, however, "St. Sophia and her sisters churches," will wear "the degrading chains of the triumphant crescent."[81]

The anguish expressed by Haight at the sight of Constantinople suggests be the feelings of a former owner. The first great dome she sees is the mosque of St. Sophia, "once the magnificent temple of Constantine, and dedicated to the worship of the religion of Christ."[82] But many of these "splended structures," says Haight, have been "converted into mosques."[83] Constantinople has been desecrated by Muslems, and "every hill is covered with them [mosques], and the tortuous skyline of this beautiful panorama is everywhere broken by their swelling domes and lofty minarets."[84] The changes which had befallen the city of Constantinople could be seen only through the eyes of one who had had preconceptions and personal feelings toward it. The "Lady of New York," who had never before set eyes on the city, lets go a cry of pain at her first sight.

> Is not this the land by Nature blessed beyond her pale, and where "all save the spirit of man is divine?" and yet is it not here that those blessings are least appreciated, and left to run fallow through the sheer neglect and inanity of the lazy and stupid possessors of the soil? Is not this oncesplendid capital of a Roman empire now the mere rendezvous of a horde of beastly Tartars?...
>
> ...At that perhaps not distant epoch the crescent will fall from each proud minaret, and the emblem of the Christian faith resume its former place, and these swelling domes shall again resound with loud *Hosannas* to the Lord *of Hosts*.[85]

Stronger feelings of dismay and antagonism are expressed by American travellers in the "Bible Land proper" when they see Muslems, Arabs or Turks, hold sway over the land and exercise authority over Christian sacred places. The black American, David Dorr, for example, exclaims on arriving in Hebron: "after thirty-five days in the Desert, we came to Hebron, the burial ground of Abraham, Isaac, and Jacob. Here we were quarantined for three days. After travelling all these thousands of miles, the Arabs would not let us enter the Mosque built over these distinguished men's bodies."[86] Here is an insult that could not be tolerated! And in Jerusalem, the mere size and height of a mosque in the Holy City offends him: "The mosque of Omar's dome glittered in the sun beam, and this Mohammedan sanctum towered above all the other buildings in this city, that was once the 'glory of the world,' because of its godliness. Yes, the mosque of the Turk looked down upon our glorious sepulchre, as it were with contempt."[87]

Another fellow American traveller suffers the hardships of the desert route of the Israelites only to arrive at Hebron and find that the "walk through its dirty streets did not make a very favorable impression on me. The most prominent point as seen from the distance is the large mosque—a large building which covers the cave of Macphelah but into the building no "christian dog" is allowed to enter. The people of the town are the most bigoted musselmen in the world and scorn the Christian with a most disdainly smile."[88] Robertson, nonetheless, supplies his readers with a list of references to these holy places in Scripture, "as it would occupy too much time and space to quote."[89] And when Robertson and his party arrive at a spot which overlooks Jerusalem, they pause to admire "the most beautiful city in the world...[the] city of God's chosen people on whose temple he consented to visit his Divine Presence." But alas! the temple was not clearly visible, "its place was filled with a Mohammedan mosque and instead of the [illegible] of the glorious temple the dome and minarets have [illegible] their copious heads."[90]

In Jerusalem many American travellers were turned away from the Mosque of Omar, especially during prayers. This aroused feelings of resentment and called forth expressions of hatred against the Muslim population. Almost identical statements come from the pens of such different persons as Robertson, J.V.C. Smith, William Millard, Charles E. Bergh, Charles W. Andrews and many others, who protest against this Muslim "intrusion" on "their" rights. Smith calls on the "Pasha, the Turkish military governor in command" whose residence, according to Smith, adjoins "the wall surrounding the square prepared by Solomon for the temple, now desecrated by a mosque and a college of dervishes." Smith then describes the interesting interview with the Pasha:

> On a low bench against the ceiling, cushioned very indifferently, sat the great man, a mild, pleasant-looking personage, who may have been sixty years of age. He was sitting cross-legged, and smoking. An interpreter stated that we were Americans, and that the object of the call was to look into the holy enclosure. His pashaship

salamed gracefully, spun out a long wiry stream of tobacco smoke, remarked with becoming solemnity, "God is great," and readily gave permission.[91]

Smith proceeds to give a description of the mosque and of the religious treasures which the Western travellers could expect to find. (At the risk of being caught, Smith broke off a piece of the corner of a stone of the mosque to take back home as a souvenir.[92]) The same experience evokes a burst of anger from Millard against Muslims. When he is prevented from entering the mosque which, he says, occupies the site of the ancient temple, he shouts: "Shame on Mahommedanism!"[93]

Bergh and Andrews, two Americans with different turns of mind, react similarly to the experience. Bergh, the enlighted man of the world, follows the religious sites accurately and suggests that "the Moslem wretches" should be driven away from the land.[94] Andrews, the zealous missionary, is pained to see the sacred sites dominated by Muslims and ascribes their attitude to the teachings of "the false prophet."[95]

In the Footsteps of the Children of Israel

The most important part of the pilgrimage to the land of the Bible was the trip across the Sinai desert from Egypt to Palestine. This was a long stretch of desert track which the travelers took on camelback, following "the route of the tribes of Israel." A gruelling trip even with a convenient means of travel, it was very trying and dangerous in the nineteenth century. Yet most American travelers considered the trip an essential part of their pilgrimage and insisted upon taking it. In February 1842 Charles Edwin Bergh wrote to his mother from Jerusalem describing his feelings about that part of the journey. Despite the dangers encountered in the desert from Cairo to Akaba, Bergh says that he and his companions were anxious to be the first Americans to cross the Sinai desert and go through the "land of Edom" after a two-year interval during which no traveler dared make the trip:

> I was aware that this journey had not been made for the last two years by any traveller in consequence of the disturbed state of the country—but concluded that I had come almost too far to be disappointed. Notwithstanding the discouraging accounts we received from all quarters, we determined that Americans should be a second time the pioneers through the land of Edom.[96]

Bergh, like Olin, Stephens and others, was meticulous discriminating in following the exact track of the Israelites. In a letter to his father written on March 6 from Beirut, he describes how the dromedaries were "sent around the head of the gulf of Suez" while he and his party made sure to "cross the sea in a boat that was poled across the whole distance where it was a half a mile wide." After reaching the Asiatic shore, the party had difficulty meeting up with the rest of the caravan, and by the time they did, it was too dark to continue. They pitched tents and spent the night where, says Bergh,

> having consulted the various opinions of our writers relative to the miraculous exodus of the Israelites, the next morning we walked down to the sea and continued several miles along shore until we came to a point of land opposite to the valley between two mountains and which is generally supposed to be the place where the Hebrews crossed and the armies of Pharaoh were overwhelmed— although some fix the passage at Suez where our boat was *pooled* over.[97]

At about the same time, in December 1841, David Millard was in Cairo preparing to make the journey to Palestine, where he "providentially met two American gentlemen who had recently returned from the cataracts of the Nile, and had been making some arrangements to go to Palestine by the way of Suez, Mount Sinai, Akabah, and the ruins of Petra," and then to Hebron and Jerusalem. The news from Palestine and Syria, however, indicated that a "civil war" was raging, and "not a Frank traveller had ventured through the proposed route for about two years." Even the "American consul spake of such a journey in rather discouraging terms."[98] The two Americans were willing to take any risk rather than lose the opportunity of crossing Sinai and following the route of the Israelites. Millard also

> was indeed anxious to pass over that interesting route. It would lead through a country which, aside from the Holy Land, I considered from its sacred historical and prophetic scenery, the most interesting portion of our globe. Our route would embrace a very large part of the road travelled by the Israelites in their journey from Egypt to the promised land....Finally, I encouraged the enterprise, and said, 'I *will go.'*[99]

This "most interesting portion of the globe" was punctuated with sacred sites: Idumea, the land of Esau, the inheritance of Ishmael, the passage across the Red Sea, the Holy Mount—the list was quite extensive, and throughout the journey travelers drew on scriptural evidence to guide them to these sites. Bergh consulted various writers on the subject; Haight loaded her camels with a complete library of related materials; and Millard, attempting to ascertain the exact route carried with him the findings of meticulous American researchers. In fact, Millard did so much reading on the subject that he felt qualified to agree with Dr. Robinson on some points such as "the miraculous passage of the Israelites through the Red Sea [which] must have taken place but a few miles at farthest south of Suez." In a remarkably authoritative note, Millard states that

> Professor Robinson, in his 'Biblical Researches,' fixes the of Goshen from whence the Israelites fled, on the Pelusiac arm of the Nile, directly east of the Delta, constituting the part of Egypt nearest to Palestine. Having carefully examined his reasons for fixing that land where he does, I consider his arguments entitled to, at least, a good degree of credit....[100]

Robinson's attempts to explain the miraculous crossing in rational scientific terms, however, do not serve or strengthen Millard's devout faith. This, he thinks, is a futile exercise which does not lead to any satisfactory results, and, in spite of his admiration for the *Researches* of Robinson, he expresses the opinion that

> All that kind of reasoning which has for its object the means of dispensing with a direct miracle in causing the waters of the Red Sea to divide for Israel to pass over, I regard as savoring too much of direct scepticism. Nor is it without regret that I see so much of this kind of argument in Dr. Robinson's valuable 'Researches.' It has been contended that 'a strong east wind' caused the entire water at the north end of the gulf to recede southerly for miles, thus offering a way for the Israelites to pass over. 1. An east wind would not naturally drive the water in the gulf south, as the gulf itself leads off in nearly a south direction. 2. If this were possible, it would not agree with the sacred account of the event....In whatever way, therefore, 'the Lord caused the sea to go back' by 'a strong east wind,' it was in no other way than to leave the waters a wall on either hand. Nothing but a direct miracle could have affected this.[101]

The text of the Bible, not the process of scientific rational research, remains the only true guide. That text says: "for Pharoah will say of the children of Israel, that they are entangled in the land, the wilderness hath shut them in." So, Millard reasons while on his journey, the logical conclusion regarding the geographical location of the crossing goes like this:

> Had the children of Israel marched in any other direction than along the narrow stretch of shore between the present Gibbel Ataka and the sea, I cannot see how it could, with any propriety, have been said they were 'entangled in the land,' or that the wilderness had shut them in. But here the entanglement was complete.[102]

The pilgrim goes on tracking the miraculous route, visiting various sites along the way with the aid of the sacred text. At one point Millard observes with great satisfaction that "Mount Hor, with Aron's tomb on its top, had been in sight nearly the whole day. Late in the day we turned east into a valley called Waddy Mequrader, which divides the range of Mount Seir." There they pitched their tents and spent the night outside the city of Petra "in sight of Mount Hor."[103] At night, Millard and his company watched the wild Arabs sitting around the campfire and thought of their plans for the next day. In the morning they went up the mountain to inspect the tomb. This was an exhausting, dangerous adventure but one which had to be included in the pilgrim's itinerary, and the only fitting statement he could think of to crown the achievement of the day was the quotation from Scripture:

> 'And the children of Israel, even the whole congregation, journeyed from Kadesh and came unto Mount Hor. And the Lord spake unto Moses and Aaron in Mount Hor, by the coast of the land of Edom, saying, Aaron shall be gathered unto his people; for he shall not enter into the land which I have given unto the children of Israel, because ye rebelled against my word at the water of Meribah...'
> NUMBERS, XX.[104]

Then, and only then, could Millard conclude with certainty: "that this is the true Mount Hor of the Scriptures, I believe is not disputed by any traveller who has visited it. Its peculiar adaptation to the display of such an event 'in the sight of all the congregation,' is conspicuous to the observer."[105]

For Millard, and for most American pilgrims to the Holy Land, there was no disputing scriptural geography as evidence of geographical research, especially when the matter concerned the route taken by the tribes of Israel. In fact, even for those who could not exactly be described as reverent pilgrims, the very context of their journey was scriptural. George Lloyd Stephens, for example, illustrates not only the total acceptance of the scriptural text as his guide, but also a willingness to relive the text in every step he takes. So, having crossed the borders of Edom, Stephens stands on the shore of the Red Sea and contemplates "the doomed and accursed land" which stretches out before him:

> The theatre of awful visitations and their more awful fulfillment; given to Esau as being the fatness of the earth, but now a barren waste, a picture of death, an eternal monument of the wrath of an offended God, and a fearful witness to the truth of the words spoken by his prophets.[106]

And as he stands there, Stephens looks at the emptiness and barrenness of the land as a test of scriptural truth and recites the words of the prophets:

> 'For my sword shall be bathed in heaven: behold, it shall come down upon Idumea, and upon the people of my curse, to judgment.' 'From generation to generation it shall lie waste; none shall pass through it for ever and ever. But the cormorant and the bittern shall possess it;

the owl also and the raven shall dwell in it; and he shall stretch out upon it the line of confusion and the stones of emptiness.'[107]

I read," says Stephens,

in the sacred book prophecy upon prophecy and curse upon curse against the very land on which I stood. I was about to journey through this land, and to see with my own eyes whether the Almighty had stayed his uplifted arm, or whether his sword had indeed come down 'upon Idumea, and the people of his curse, to judgment.'[108]

He quotes further from the Scripture and then witnesses that a work by Keith proves beyond a doubt that the great trade routes to Mecca are laid waste and that no traveler has ever traversed the land upon which the Almighty's judgement was called down by the prophets.

Sacred history becomes a personal experience for Stephens when he embarks on his journey in the land of Idumea where, he says, the Bedouins have roamed and terrified pilgrims and travelers. Quoting a number of historians and travelers, he establishes the fact the "opposition and obstruction" of the Bedouins resembles "the case of the Israelites under Moses, when Edom refused to give them passage through his country. None of these [travellers] had passed through it, and…when I pitched my tent on the borders of Edom no traveller had ever done so."[109] It is now time for him to put to practical and hazardous test the words of the prophets. Stephens mounts his horse and gazes from the shore of the northern extremity of the Red Sea at "an immense sandy valley, which, without the aid of geological science, to the age of common observation and reason, had once been the bottom of a sea or the bed of a river." Without the aid of science, Stephens comes to the conclusion that

it was manifest, by landmarks of Nature's own providing, that over that sandy plain those seas had once mingled their waters, or, perhaps more probably, that before the cities of the plain had been consumed by brimstone and fire, and Sodom and Gomorrah covered by a pestilential lake, the Jordan had here rolled its waters….The land of Idumea lay before me, in barrenness and desolation; no trees grew in the valley, and no verdure on the mountain-tops. All was bare, dreary, and desolate.[110]

Scriptural idiom and prophecy overwhelm the narrative of personal experience, and the two become inseparable. The "extraordinary fit of enthusiasm" exhibited by Stephens and his companion, Paul, at the beautiful sight of the temple of Petra and its great theatre was soon replaced by a sombre reflection on the great city which had once stood there "in the earliest periods of recorded time, long before this theatre was built, and long before the tragic muse was known." At that time, "when Esau, having sold his birthright for a mess of pottage, came to his portion among the mountains of Sier; and Edom; growing in power and strength, became presumptuous and haughty, until, in her pride, when Israel prayed a passage through her country, Edom said unto Israel, 'Thou shald not pass by me, lest I come out against thee with the sword.' "[111]

Stephens documents his narrative with quotations and notes from Jeremiah xlix and Isaiah xxxiv as he observes the results of the Lord's terrible denunciations against the land of Idumia, "her cities and the inhabitants thereof."[112] After personally witnessing the fulfillment of prophecy in the perpetual waste, the absence of the city's nobels, Stephens bursts out in an angry cry:

> I would that the skeptic could stand as I did among the ruins of this
> city among the rocks, and there open the sacred book and read the
> words of the inspired penman, written when this desolate place was
> one of the greatest cities in the world. I see the scoff arrested, his
> cheek pale, his lip quivering, and his heart quaking with fear, as the
> ruined city cries out to him a voice loud and powerful as that of one
> risen from the dead; though he would not believe Moses and the
> prophets, he believes the handwriting of God himself in the desola-
> tion and eternal ruin around him.[113]

A concluding serene note—"Paul and myself were alone,"—comes as a quiet confirmation of his belief set against the doubts of the imaginary skeptic. After all, Stephens was there.

THE VISION OF ZION
The American Myth of the City on a Hill

With sacred lore, this traveller beguiles
His weary way, while o'er him Fancy smiles
Whether he kneels in venerable groves,
Or through the wide and green savanna roves,
His heart leaps lightly on each breaze, that bears
The faintest cadence of Idumea's airs.
John Pierpont, "Airs of Palestine," 1816

John Pierpont recounts in his long poem, "Airs of Palestine," a dream-like epic journey in the style of classical poetry. But instead of looking to Parnassus or Olympus for inspiration, the poet invokes a different muse:

No, no—a lonelier, lovelier path be mine:
Greece and her charms I leave, for Palestine.—
....
I love to walk on Jordan's banks of palm;
I love to wet my foot in Hermon's dews;
I love the promptings of Isaiah's muse:
In Carmel's holy grots, I'll court repose,
And deck my mossy couch, with Sharon's deathless rose.[1]

Pierpont's progress takes him on an imaginary pilgrimage to the Holy Land where he, "Religion's child," revels in the countless sacred associations, especially those connected with the woes of Zion. These verses, however, represent only one of the early American poetic attempts at articulating its first and most lasting myth: that of a vision of America as the city on a hill.[2]

The Pilgrim Fathers and Zion Hill

Pierpont's poetic memory unfolds the nation's cultural "childhood"—one nourished by a vision of Zion in America. Dreamlike, and difficult to grasp at first, the vision remained nonetheless an aspiration which teased the imagination of its spokesmen. The pervasiveness of this myth is revealed in what R.W.B. Lewis calls "peculiar and distinctive dialogues."[3] Ralph Waldo Emerson, the spokesman for an America which is divorced from the past, gives a lecture on the vices of slavery in which he invokes a biblical analogy of his nation as "a last effort of the Divine Providence in behalf of the human race."[4] This, however, should be placed in the context of the theme of America as "the Israel of our time" for a full understanding of its past and future implications. Herman Melville, the American novelist, and another prophet of American destiny, states the same theme in no ambiguous words. For him, just as Israel escaped the corrupt ways of the Egyptians and was given special dispensations, so

> we Americans are the peculiar, chosen people—the Israel of our time; we bear the ark of the liberties of the world. Seventy years ago we escaped from thrall; and, besides our first birthright—embracing one continent of earth—God has given to us, for a future inheritance, the broad domains of the political pagans, that shall yet come and lie down under the shade of our ark, without bloody hands being lifted. God has predestinated, mankind expects, great things from our race; and great things we feel in our souls. The rest of the nations must soon be in our rear. We are the pioneers of the world; the advance guard, sent on through the wilderness of untried things to break a new path in the New World that is ours.[5]

In this statement Melville recognizes America's attachment to its past and its future commitment, both seen in the framework of Scripture. In the idiom of the cultural discourse of Melville's generation terms such as "the peculiar, chosen people," the "first birthright," the "future inheritance," the "shade of our ark" were all too familiar, and they reached back to the source and origin of his national cultural heritage. Similarly, in the enthusiastic, optimistic language of the "great things we feel in our souls" and "the pioneers of the world," Melville gives utterance to the prospect of establishing the ideal state, which very often was the socio-political form of the Kingdom of God.

In a different medium of cultural discourse, but within the context of the same mythology, Pierpont' memory, "fancy's smile," takes him back and forth between the banks of Ohio and those of the Jordan. The first river had been part of the poet's experience with geographical reality; the second he had inherited, along with the rest of his countrymen, as part of the national mythology. And this same poetic vision which sends Pierpont walking "on Jordan's banks of palm" had fired the Pilgrim's imagination to seek what Vernon Parrington so aptly describes as "the Canaan of their hopes"[6]; it is also the same vision evoked by Timothy Dwight, Joel Barlow and their fellow Connecticut Wits for expressions of the heroic exploits of the "American Joshuas and Davids". Still alluring in the nineteenth century, it sends thousands of Americans to the real "banks of Palm."

There were various expressions of this first American mythology to embrace Zion. What follows will be an attempt to reconstruct the pattern and development of the myth as it grew from a vision of America as a symbolic city on a hill, to a national commitment to rebuild the New Jerusalem, i.e., *the* City on a Hill. It will be seen that this externalizing of the myth was often a determining factor which influenced the attitude and behavior of Americans through the various stages of national development.

As early as 1636, John Cotton searched the pages of the Scriptures for a model constitution to be adopted by one of the new American commonwealths. He finally came up with what he described as a "Model of Moses his judicials." The process is related by a contemporary American historian:

> It was then requested of Mr. *Cotton* that he would, from the laws wherewith God governed his ancient people, form an *abstract* of such as were of a moral and a lasting equity; which he performed as acceptably as judiciously. But inasmuch as very much of an *Athenian democracy* was in the mould of the government, by the royal charter....Mr. Cotton effectually recommended it unto them that none should be *electors*, nor *elected* therein, except such as were *visible subjects* of our Lord Jesus Christ, personally *confederated* in our churches. In these, and many other ways, he propounded unto them an endeavour after a theocracy, as near as might be, to that which was the glory of Israel, the 'peculiar people'."[7]

John Cotton, according to Mather, preferred the theocracy of God's "peculiar people" to the "Athenian democracy," thus providing a precedent in political science for Pierpont and Dwight's rejection of the Parnassus Seven in favor of Isaiah's muse.[8]

Citizens of the New World considered themselves subject of Jehovah and governed by principles of the Mosaic Law. And the Puritan immigrants to the New World had been prepared for this shift of emphasis in their everyday life by what Parrington describes as a "conscious discipline in ascetic Hebraism which was to change the Jacobean gentleman into a militant Puritan."[9] There are many examples of this process of change, but the one which stands out is the case of John Winthrop who, to use Parrington's words, "had gone to school to the English Bible, and the noble Hebrew poetry stirred the poetic imagination that was his Elizabethan birthright. Like so many of his fellow Puritans he delighted in the Book of Canticles."[10]

Winthrop, as well as his fellow immigrants, was aware of the special task placed in their hands and of the unique providential relations they had with God. When Winthrop left his country of birth—the kingdom of Laud—for his adopted new home, the kingdom of God, he bade a friend a pilgrim's farewell, saying with absolute faith: "I know not how to leave you, yet since I must, I will put my beloved into his arms, who loves him best, and is a faithful keeper of all that is committed to him. Now, thou, the hope of Israel, and the sure help of all that come to thee, knit the hearts of thy servants to thyself in faith and purity."[11] True to his Puritan heritage, Winthrop saw signs of God's approval of his decision, so he proceeded to sell his property and to prepare for the move to the land of promise. He also saw portents in what he considered God's "consumption of the natives [of America] with a miraculous plague, whereby a great parte of the country is left voyde of Inhabitants."[12]

The chosen remnant in Israel knew what it was about to accomplish, and set about its task with conviction. God had provided them with a haven and it was their duty and privilege to respond to His election and move westwards to establish His kingdom. To create a Zion in the wilderness, an extra-ordinary faith and a firm belief in divine commission was needed. This faith was often expressed in statements like the one made by Winthrop, describing his understanding of God's commission:

> wee shall finde that the God of Israell is among us, when tenn of us shall be able to resist a thousand of our enemies, when hee shall make us a prayse and glory, that men shall say of succeeding plantacions: the lord make it like that of New England: for wee must Consider that wee shall be as a City upon a Hill, the eies of all people are uppon us.[13]

In addition to his education in the school of the English Bible and in the "noble Hebrew poetry" of the Book of Canticles, Winthrop's imagination was fired by the tremendously gruelling experience he and his fellow immigrants had gone through in the process of removing to the New World. This personal experience lent a visual metaphor to their daily speech. Their everyday behavior was, according to Charles Feidelson, "neither a historical event nor an allegorical fancy but an experience that united the objectivity of history with the meaningfulness of Scripture."[14] They were in the habit of applying biblical metaphors with a sharpness which resulted from an unwavering belief in their assured place in the Scriptures among the prophets and sacred men of old. "The symbolization *process*," says Feidelson, "was constantly at work in their minds. For them, the word 'wilderness' inherently united the forty years of the ancient Hebrews with the trials of the New England forest."[15] For the Puritans, there was a kind of superimposition of the Scriptural story on their own experience. In their minds, as well as in the infinite mind of God, they believed the two were one and the same. The symbolic "wilderness" was invoked not only to represent the New England of the immigrants, but the Atlantic Ocean presented the image of the wilderness of Sinai and the crossing of the Red Sea.

Well into the nineteenth century Americans were listening to political and religious sermons, reminding them of their Hebraic Scriptural identity. Within this visionary framework, Edward Johnson's advice to the Puritan's to "pray continually with that valliant worthy Joshua that the Sun may stand still in Gibean, and the Moone in the vally of Aijalon,"[16] fitting the timeless Scriptural metaphor into their daily existence. Within this framework also, election sermons throughout the seventeenth, eighteenth and nineteenth centuries were given the familiar titles: "The Way of Israel's Welfare" (John Whiting, Boston, 1688), "Moses and Aaron" (Thomas Buckingham, New London, 1729), and "The Prospect of the City of Jerusalem" (Isaac Stiles, New London, 1742).[17]

During the early period of the establishment of the settlements in America, the Puritan immigrants acted according to a firm assumption that they were the chosen few, the remnant in Israel who had defied the corrupt majority and sought refuge in the Canaan of their hopes. And, from the realm of spiritual geography, some visionaries among them sought to localize scriptural places in their new home. Cotton Mather sincerely believed that Mexico City would be the New Jerusalem, the City on the Hill. This epic myth, as enacted in the daily life of the American people, continued and was intensified in Revolutionary and Independent America.[18]

The United States and the Kingdom of God

In fact, when in 1771 Timothy Dwight thought of writing an epic to celebrate America's struggle for independence, he modelled his poem on Milton's *Paradise Lost*. The Book of Joshua supplied Dwight with the bulk of the material for *The Conquest of Canaan*, where he treats the War of Independence in the allegorical context of the wars between the Israelites on the one hand and the peoples of Ai and Gibeon on the other. The most dramatic part of the epic is the victory of the Israelites led by Joshua—America's George Washington—over the Canaanites. The opening of Book One sets the scene of the epic:

> The Chief, whose arm to Israel's chosen band
> Gave the fair empire of the promis'd land,
> Ordained by Heaven to hold the sacred sway,
> Demands my voice and animates the lay....
> ...When now from western hills the sun was driven,
> And night expanding fill'd the bounds of heaven,
> O'er Israel's camp ten thousand fires appear'd
> And solemn cries from distant guards were heard,
> Her tribes, escap'd from Ai's unhappy plain,
> With shame and anguish mourn'd their heroes slain.[19]

A footnote to the first line of the epic explains that "wherever Chief, Hero, Leader, etc., with a capital, respect the Israelitish army, Joshua is intended."[20] Dwight dedicated *The Conquest of Canaan* "to his Excellency, George Washington, Esquire, Commander in chief of the American Armies, The Saviour of his Country, the Supporter of Freedom, And the Benefactor of Mankind."[21]

Even more significant is the letter which Dwight had sent earlier to the American Revolutionary leader asking for permission to dedicate the epic to him. The letter refers to the title of the intended epic as "*The Conquest of Canaan by Joshua.*" The character of Joshua as presented in the "Argument" to Book One could easily be identified with that of Washington and especially relevant is the argument of Hanniel, who attempts to prove the impossibility of fulfillment of the Israelite's design to return to the land of Canaan, "because of the strength, skill, and numerous allies of their enemies." Hanniel informs the Israelites

> that, if they should conquer Canaan, they will be ruined, during the war, by the necessary neglect of arts and agriculture, difficulty of dividing the land, of settling a form of government, and of avoiding tyranny; and concludes with a new exhortation to return to Egypt. Applause. Joshua replies, and beginning to explain the dispensations of providence, is interrupted by Hanniel, who first obliquely, and then openly accuses him of aiming at the usurpation of kingly authority; and asserts the return to be easy. Joshua vindicates his innocence with severity upon Hanniel; and allowing they can return, paints to them the miseries, they will experience from the Egyptian king, lords, people, and manners, and from providential dispensations terminating in their ruin.[22]

The biblical story of the Israelites and their journey to Palestine across the Sinai desert and the Red Sea was used by another poet of Dwight's generation, Joel Barlow. *The Vision of Columbus* (1787) is an epic which celebrates the history of the American nation from its very beginning to the end of time, seen by the great explorer in a vision through which the angel leads him. Book One of *The Vision of Columbus* describes the trip to the New World in a comparison with that of the Israelites to the Promised Land:

> As that great Seer, whose animating rod—
> Raught Israel's sons the wonder-working God,
> Who led, thro' dreary wastes, the murmuring band
> To the fair confines of the promised land,
> Oppress'd with years, from Pisgah's beauteous height,
> O'er boundless regions cast the captured sight;
> The joys of unborn nations warm'd his breast,
> Repaid his toils and sooth'd his soul to rest....[23]

Barlow's preoccupation with this vision of Zion was strong and deep-seated. In 1785 when the General Association of the Congregational Churches of Connecticut decided to undertake a revision of Dr. Watt's version of the Book of Psalmody, they entrusted the job of its revision to him. Barlow applied himself to the task with a good deal of enthusiasm, adding to his version the translation of some Psalms which had not been included by Dr. Watts. One of these additional Psalms, number 137, according to Barlow's biographer, Charles B. Todd, "has never been equalled, not even by Halleck, who attempted it in 1821."[24] Barlow's version clearly shows a personal involvement and feeling for the theme of the Psalm:

> The rivers on of Babilon
>   There where we did sit down,
> Yea, even there we mourned when
>   We remembered Sion.
>
> Our harp we did hang it amid
>   Upon the willow tree,
> Because there them that us away
>   Led in captivitee, etc.[25]

And the following is Barlow's version of the same:

> Along the banks where Babel's current flows
>   Our captive bands in deep despondence strayed,
> While Zion's fall in sad remembrance rose,
>   Her friends, her children, mingled with the dead.
>
> The tuneless harp that once with joy we strung,
>   When praise employed, and mirth inspired the lay,
> In mournful silence on the willows hung,
>   And growing grief prolonged the tedious day....[26]

The persistence of this vision in American thought appears in contradictory application to completely different situations. One example is Timothy Dwight's identification of America not only as the chosen nation in his patriotic optimistic poems, but also in moments of pessimism and disillusionment—in his predictions of its apocalyptic death: "It is the day of the Lord's vengeance; the year of recompenses for the Controversies of Zion. The Earth is utterly broken down, the earth is clean dissolved; the earth is moved exceedingly."[27] The same vision informed both the hopeful and the hopeless situations. In the enthusiasm of the Revolution and Independence, Americans were compared to the chosen people fighting against the Egyptians and Canaanites. But when war against Britain was announced in 1812 and preparations for that battle were underway, David Osgood chided the war party from his church pulpit, quoting the Scriptures, "O children of Israel, fight ye not against the Lord God of your fathers; for ye shall not prosper."[28]

Finally, the situation of the American Indians presents another curious example of the progress of the vision of Zion in American history and thought. During the precarious establishment of the first few continental settlements, the Puritan immigrants, (God's Chosen) saw in the Indians the enemies of Israel: they were analogous to the Egyptians and Canaanites, as we have seen in Chapter 1. During the nineteenth century, however, perhaps as a result of the intensity of millenial thinking, there was an inclination in some American circles to read into the history of the Indians of North America the story of the lost tribes of Israel. Serious scholarly investigations of this subject can be seen in *The Lost Tribes of Israel: Or the First of the Red Men* (Charles Evans? 1861) and *A View of the American Indians: Showing them to Be the Descendants of the Ten Tribes of Israel* (Israel Worsley, 1828).[29]

The argument must have been convincing for some of the Indians themselves to believe it; evidence exists in the following account. In 1818 Levi Parsons was appointed as a missionary and began preparing for his trip to the Holy Land. But, as a nineteenth century historian of the missionary enterprise informs us, "Mr. Parsons had a strong desire to do something more, before leaving the country, for the spiritual interests of the people of Vermont." So Parsons performed the duties of a local missionary, until in September, 1818, when the Prudential Committee of the American Board of Commissioners for Foreign Missions "thought proper to detain him awhile as an agent" to tour the State of New York. He proceeded to visit many towns and give sermons and talks on the missionary enterprise, thus

> giving a fresh impulse to the missionary cause. One of the most interesting circumstances that occurred in connection with his mission, was his meeting with the Stockbridge Indians, then under the care of the missionary, John Sergeant. He preached to them when he was in a state of great weariness and exhaustion...being inspiredby the thought that possibly his audience might be the descendants of

Abraham. When the sermon was over, the Indian chief, a fine, prin-cely-looking fellow, delivered an address to Mr. Parsons, in the best style of Indian oratory. He thanked God that He had sent his servant among them, and had commissioned him to deliver to them 'a great and important talk.' He thanked the preacher also for his excellent counsels, and expressed the wish that theymight answer the pur-pose for which they were designed. He then proceeded to read a 'talk' in Indian and English, which he desired Mr. Parsons to deliver to 'the Jews, their forefathers, in Jerusalem,'...[30]

During the first quarter of the nineteenth century, the timeless vision of America as theCity on a Hill was transferred to a definite geographical location of the Kingdom of God in the Holy Land of Scripture. There were many expressions, often very emotional, by pilgrims, tourists and missionaries bemoaning the present state of Palestine and longing for the day when the land would be peopled by its "rightful inheritors." Ellen Clare Miller looks at the vast area of the Levant in 1871 and says:

Of these lands of the East are some of the most sublime words of prophecy written; and to the missionary there it may be given to ad-vance even the literal fulfilment of the glorious promise made through the prophet Isaiah,—a promise spiritually fulfilled in peace, joy, and blessing, wherever souls are truly converted to God...[31]

Miller then turns her thoughts to the promise "They Shall see eye to eye, when the Lord shall bring again Zion," and looks forward to its ful-fillment:

When the veil shall be uplifted
    From before all nations' eyes,
When the light shall chase the darkness,
    And the lifeless bones arise;

When each kindred, tongue, and people
    Shall go forth to seek the Lord,
When they ask for the way to Zion,
    With their faces thitherward;[32]

Many reasons can be advanced to explain this shift of the American myth of God's Israel from the New World to the Holy Land. One im-portant factor is that during the latter part of the eighteenth and the beginning of the nineteenth century, Americans were introduced to the Orient commercially, diplomatically and militarily, and in that process they rediscovered the Holy Land. During the same period the United States was experiencing a special religious fervor, as seen first in the Great Awakening and subsequent revivalist movements. With this surge of religious interest came the two related phenomena of the missionary enterprise and millenial tendency. Both of these latter movements were instrumental in exciting interest in the Holy Land and in creating a sense of urgency for a rebuilding of Jerusalem.

Millenarian Tendencies and American Interest in the Orient

The concept of the millennium was present in American thinking all along, although the nineteenth century witnessed an intensification of its expectancy. Indeed, there are in American writings many references to the "signs of the times." One of these is relevant to the expectation of the Kingdom and comes from the pen of Increase Mather. He says:

"How often have we prayed that the Lord would divide, infatuate and frustrate the Councils of the Heathen that sought our Ruine. As sometimes David when pursued by Absalom prayed saying..."[33]

Mather's editor recognizes that the "end-of-the-world excitement" was not uncommon at the time. He explains that "for its Reproduction in that singular 'Corner of the World,' we can only account by Presumption that a millenial Excitement then prevailed there....Hence it appears that 'End-of-the-world' Excitements are no new things, and are in a Manner periodical."[34] In fact, the signs-of-the-times excitement can be seen in the title of one of Mather's sermons: "A Sermon shewing, that the present Dispensation of Providence declare that wonderful Revolutions in the World are near at Hand; with an Appendix, shewing some Scripture Grounds to hope, that within a few Years, glorious Prophecies and Promises will be fulfilled" (1713).

Reading "special providence" in current events continued to be a feature of American religious thought in the nineteenth century. "It is remarkable," Niebuhr says, "how under the influence of the Great Awakening the millenial expectation flourished in America."[35] The leading figure in the Great Awakening in America, Jonathan Edwards, says that

> it is not likely that this work of God's Spirit, so extraordinary and wonderful, is the dawning, or at least a prelude of that glorious work of God, so often foretold in Scripture, which, in the progress and issue of it, shall renew the world of mankind.... We cannot reasonably think otherwise, than that the beginning of this great work of God must be near. And there are many things that make it probable that this work will begin in America.[36]

Edwards describes the Great Awakening as "a great and wonderful event, a strange revolution, an unexpected surprising overturning of things, suddenly brought to pass." His observation of current events led him to conclude that this indeed was the time of redemption, "the great end of all the other works of God, and of which the work of creation was but a shadow." Edwards, together with his generation, was witnessing the real "work of creation which is infinitely more glorious than the old." He reached the important conclusion that "the New Jerusalem in this respect has begun to come down from heaven, and perhaps never were more of the prelibations of heaven's glory given upon earth."[37]

Clearly, the millenial tendency in this sense was peculiarly American. A survey of the types of religious movements and denominations which flourished during the nineteenth century in America will show to what extent millenialism affected people's thinking. One such group were the Adventists, whom the contemporary *Hand-Book to All Religions* describes as those who "regard the time and purpose of Christ's reappearance in the light of certain prophecies, which they interpret as predictions of his personal reign upon earth."[38]

A prominent religious leader was William Miller who was born in 1781 in Pittsfield, Massachusetts, and who started a millennial movement, announcing that the date of the Second Coming of Christ was to be the year 1843. His followers, known as the Millerites, grew into a sect of many thousands, and professed to belief in the literal interpretation of the prophecy of the Second Kingdom. When the Rev. George Bush, the Prophet Muhammad's American biographer, edited Buck's *Theological Dictionary* for a revised American edition in 1854, he added an appendix on the "Advent Believers, or Adventists." He describes this group as "a class of Christians connected with nearly all the evangelical denominations in the United States, who derive their name from the peculiar faith in the speedy coming of Jesus Christ, the second time, without sin unto salvation, to them that look for him."[39] Although Bush identifies the religious beliefs of all Adventists with those of "the various sects with which they stand connected," he adds that their peculiar principles were "originally propagated by Mr. William Miller of the Regular Baptist Church in Low Hampton, Washington Co., N. Y."[40]

The special contribution of most of these millenial sects to the American attitude to the Orient, and the Holy Land in particular, is the peculiar position they accorded to the Jewish people. According to the basic tenets of Millenialism, the Jews were the foundations of this Second Kingdom, and their ingathering was a prerequisite of this great event. The *Hand-Book* describes the principles which were held by most millenarians:

> By some writers the notion of Millennium is considered as nothing more than a retention in Christianity of the Judaic idea of an early kingdom, the eventual restoration of the Jerusalem that now is. The Jews hoped for a temporal deliverer, and their hope centered itself in a temporal reign. The anticipation of an earthly reign involves to

some extent a restoration of the Jews. Such anticipations, widened to include the Gentiles in the benefits, might be taken as the foundation of a certain class of Millennial expectations. Wherever the doctrine is confused with merely temporal ideas it may be regarded as unorthodox.[41]

Many of the leading clergymen of these sects felt that the time was ripe for the coming of Christ but some, like William Miller, were more specific and set dates for the event. Miller came to the conclusion that the Second Coming would happen between March 21, 1843, and March 21, 1844."[42] Although that time passed without fulfillment of the prophecy, in April, 1844, his followers nonetheless remained

steadfast in their faith as to the correctness of their principles and mode of computing time, and their general dates for commencing the periods, but conclude there is some slight discrepancy in chronology. But are still in constant expectation of seeing their coming Lord....[43]

In missionary literature, sermons, orations and reports there were constant references to the signs of the times and the millennium. The Constitution of the American Bible Society announced that "every person of observation has remarked that the times are pregnant with great events. The political world has undergone changes stupendous, unexpected, and calculated to inspire thoughtful men with the most boding anticipations." The Society realized especially that "an excitement, as extraordinary as it is powerful, has roused the nations to the importance of spreading the knowledge of the one living and true God, as revealed in his Son."[44] The Constitution concluded that there was no spectacle "which can be so illustrious...as a nation pouring forth its devotion, its talent, and its treasures, for that Kingdom of the Savior, which is righteousness and peace."[45]

Signs of the Times and the Muslem World

Many signs of the times were seen in current natural phenomena and in political international events—especially those which had to do with events in the Islamic World. The contemporary situation of the Ottoman Empire was often cited by millennialists as relevant to the Second Coming. Speaking of the approximate date of the great event in the light of biblical prophecy, Bush says that

the five months, and hour, day, month, and year, or 541 years and 15 days of Rev. ix., are believed to have commenced with the first entrance of Othman, the founder of the Ottoman empire, into Nicomedia, a Greek province, to commence his war, July 27th, 1299.

And then the period ended Aug. 11th, 1840 the day the ultimatum of
the allied powers of Europe was submitted to Mehemet Ali, and the
fate of the empire was sealed.[46]

By far the most comprehensive view of the history of Islam and its current situation in the light of biblical prophecy is that expressed by Henry
Jessup, the influential, life-long missionary. Jessup's universal view of
the world presents everything in the context of a preconceived plan
which extends from the beginning of creation to the end of time—when
the Church of Christ will rule the whole earth. All the "revolutions and
convulsions [,] the wars and upturnings of the past 2,000 years," he says
in an 1884 sermon, have "proved mighty auxiliaries to the advancing
kingdom of our God."[47] Although there are those who are hesitant and
skeptical of the value of missionary efforts, for Jessup "the triumphal
chariot of His Kingly Majesty will move onward....For the kingdom of
God is a growth, an advance, a progress from lower to higher, from foundation to topstone, from seed to fruit, from type to antitype, from
promise and prophecy to glorious fulfillment."[48]

The progressive nature of this advancing kingdom takes in all the
events of history, including the entire progress of Islam. In fact, the rise
and fall of Islam, to its final extinction, is an important factor in the fulfillment of the Divine plan. This thesis is obvious in the title of one of
Jessup's "labours of love," *The Setting of the Crescent and the Rising of the
Cross: or Kamil Abdul Massiah*, and in a more detailed form in the entire
treatment of *The Mohammedan Missionary Problem*. According to Jessup,
the hand of Providence can be seen in the concurrence of two momentous events which took place in the seventh century and which "were
providentially related in the most intimate manner, as bearing upon the
welfare of the race and the future development of Christ's kingdom in
the world."[49] These two events are the rise of Islam and "the Christianization of the Saxon race in Britain."[50] Other events in the history of
Islam also coincided with momentous events in the history of the Christian West. One such event is the overthrow of the Islamic army by Fer-
dinand in Granada in 1492, which led to the extinction or expulsion of
the entire Moslem population of Andalusia. The year 1492, says Jessup,
is "the very year in which Columbus discovered America, and thus
opened a new field for the growth and development of that christianized
Anglo-Saxon race."[51]

In the more recent history of Islam there were events, wars, and revolutions which, though outwardly harmful to the Christian world, were considered to be designed by the hand of Providence to lead to the Coming of
Christ's Kingdom. The Crimean War, for example, "which for a season
convulsed the whole Turkish Empire, exciting latent Mohammedan

fanaticism and threatening to roll backward the rising tide of light and liberty, resulted in guaranteeing protection and a civil autonomy to the evangelical communities in Turkey...[and] gave England the right to insist upon" her prerogative to exercise that protection.[52] The sectarian strife in the whole of Syria, which also threatened the Christian communities there, resulted (according to Jessup) in more liberties and rights for these communities. The same thing happened as a result of the Bulgarian War of 1877 and, more important as an example of the working of the Providential Plan towards the Kingdom of God, is the Arabi Revolt in Egypt in 1882, when

> ...the wild spirit of Mohammedan bigotry broke out once more, and the streets of Alexandria ran with Christian blood....
>
> The interposition of England, the defeat of Arabi, the check upon rising Moslem frenzy, and the shattering of the Pan Islamic league which had become a menace to progress and civilization in the East, all revealed again the working of that hand which makes no mistakes, and that wise and glorious Providence of God, which overrules all things for His own glory.[53]

There were other religious movements whose ideology stemmed from the central notion of the Second Coming. One of the most important is that of the Mormons, or Latter-Day Saints. Their main theology is the belief "the literal ingathering of Israel, the restoration of the Ten Tribes, the personal reign of Christ on earth for a thousand years of Millenial glory, when the saints will reign with him and judge the Gentiles or unbelievers."[54] The notion of the Second Kingdom and of the rebuilding of Jerusalem was paramount, although in a different geographical perspective. The Mormons' final settlement in Salt Lake City came after years of hardship, and the building of the Mormon Temple was in preparation for the Advent of Christ and his Second Kingdom. The structure was so picturesque, "especially when seen in the first glory of spring, that the stranger almost pardons the enthusiasm with which the inhabitants compare it to the New Jerusalem, as the seer of the Apocalypse beheld it."[55]

To the ranks of those movements we should add the Shakers, a sect which also believed in some kind of spiritual adventism. Although their concept of the "human tabernacle" was never clearly defined, they believed that the millennium was close at hand and that the believers had to prepare themselves to enter the heavenly Kingdom.

By the second half of the nineteenth century, the Adventist movements had become quite sizable in America—hundreds of books, sermons, articles and periodicals were written to advocate or refute the notion of the millennium.[56] According to George Bush, there were four or five millions of books and papers circulated during the last three years in the United States, British provinces, and foreign countries, wherever the English language is read. There have also been some of the writings translated into the French and German languages, and widely circulated. There are five weekly papers now published in the United States, devoted to the dissemination of this doctrine; and two in Canada.

There are large congregations of Adventists in nearly all the Eastern, Northern, and Middle States.[57]

Whereas some of these movements believed in a literal interpretation of Scriptural prophecies regarding the Second Kingdom, some insisted on the figurative interpretation. Of the literalists, some considered the Holy Land—Zion Hill overlooking Jerusalem in particular—to be the geographical location of the Advent; others settled for American localities. In any case the myth of America as God's Israel was given a more material vestige, and ultimately the spiritual metaphor of the city on a hill was transferred to a geographical location to be fulfilled in the Promised Land. The venture, however, was still to be an American one: many of the faithful persisted in the belief that they were partners in the Covenant and an important part of the Providential plan to rebuild the Kingdom of God. Americans were ready to help bring the great moment to fruition. So they looked to the "banks of palm" and the Rose of Sharon as goals to be attained in reality.

The Missionaries and the Rebuilding of Jerusalem

In many religious quarters, especially in the missionary establishment, attempts were made to find in the American experience the fulfillment of prophecy regarding the rebuilding of Jerusalem. A sermon entitled "The Promised Land," delivered by Heyman Humphrey at Goshen, Connecticut, in September 29, 1819, essays to establish the analogy. Humphrey introduces the sermon with Joshua xiii, 1: "And there remaineth yet very much land to be possessed." The connection between "possessing the land" and the Biblical promise and prophecy was very clear to Humphrey, although his reference to the Promised Land is at first not presented literally. In fact, the church in his analogy becomes the nation of Israel. His opening statement reveals the obsession with the vision of Zion and the "conquest of Canaan," and shows the identity of the missionary establishment as the bearer of the responsibility:

God, as the supreme Ruler and absolute Proprietor of the world, thought fit to give all the land of Canaan to Abraham and his posterity for an everlasting inheritance. This grant was again and again renewed and confirmed to Isaac and Jacob, as heirs of the promise. But they were not to take immediate possession. While the Canaanites were filling up the measure of their iniquities, the children of Israel sojourned and were oppressed in Egypt; and it was not till the time of Moses, that they were delivered from that terrible bondage…upon the top of a mountain, which overlooked the fertile plain of Jordan, Moses yielded up at once his commission and his life—not, however, till he had, by divine authority, invested Joshua with the supreme command.…

The chronicler continues to tell the story of Joshua, his bravery, his dedication to the conquest of Canaan, and his determination to claim the "promised heritage." With age upon him, Joshua, by dividing the remaining land by lots, still called upon his people to drive out "the heathen." Humphrey's sermon concludes that there is still much land to be claimed and

that immense regions of the earth, which belong to the church, are still unsubdued;

that the ultimate conquest and possession of all these is certain;
that, although the excellency of the power is of God, this great work is to be accomplished by human instrumentality;

that but for lamentable and criminal apathy of the church, it might have been accomplished ages ago;

that as Christendom now possesses ample resources and ability, she is solemnly bound in the name of God, and with the least possible delay to set up her banners in every heathen land. And,

that the aspects of Divine Providence are peculiarly auspicious to the missionary enterprizes of the day.[58]

Humphrey reminds his congregation of the urgency of the divine mission of the American church, saying that the mount on which the church stands, overlooks the whole land of promise.[59] The figure of the church on a mountain overlooking the land of promise wavers between a literal reference to the Holy Land of biblical promise and a general allusion to the tremendous task of evangelizing the whole world. The figure becomes more potent with Humphrey's use of scriptural idiom, in which the church takes on the metaphysical aspect of Zion Hill, addressing its members:

surely the Isles shall wait for me, and the ships of Tarshish, first to bring thy sons from far, their silver and their gold with them, unto the name of the Lord thy God, and to the Holy One of Israel, because he hath glorified thee.[60]

Thousands, says Humphrey, are answering the call of the church and are coming to the aid of the Lord, proclaiming with one voice: "For

Zion's sake we will not hold our peace, and for Jerusalem's sake we will not rest."[61]

Missionary quarters resounded with the trumpet call urging believers to go forth and bring the heathens and Muslems to the light of the Gospel, with the realization of Zion as the ultimate goal. Many of the missionaries were aware of this sacred duty and some advocated the priority of the rebuilding of Jerusalem and the restoration of the Jews. One prominent missionary, J. T. Barclay, says that

> the American Christian Missionary Society (under whose auspices the mission to Jerusalem is conducted), in entering upon the prosecution of the missionary enterprise, resolved—as wisely as u-nanimously—in imitation of apostolic example, to make the offer of salvation to Israel, that noble race from whom it came—for salvation is of the Jews.[62]

Barclay bases this priority for the missionary efforts on the Messiah's address to a Syro-Phoenician heathen when he said "I am not sent but unto the lost sheep of the house of Israel." According to Barclay, Christ gazed at the great city and exclaimed: "O Jerusalem! Jerusalem! how often would I have gathered thy children together, as a hen doth gather her brood!" Christ's instructions to the twelve Apostles were to "go—not into the way of the Gentiles—but rather to the lost sheep of the house of Israel." The missionaries who were commissioned by Christ were charged especially "to witness for him first in Judea, 'beginning at Jerusalem.'" The acts of the Apostles, says Barclay, prove that they showed special preference for the Jews, and the Apostle Paul, in particular, stated that his "heart's desire and prayer to God [are] for Israel."

Thus Barclay recognizes that the first concern for the American Christian society was "to plant its first mission in Jerusalem, mainly in reference to the Jews—not unmindful, however, that Jerusalem possesses various other claims upon our consideration as a field of missionary operations."[63] The first few missionaries and missionary leaders in America were aware of that responsibility. Samuel Worcester, for example, prefaced his "Two Discourses" which he presented in connection with missionary activities with these lines:

> O ye seed of Israel his servant, ye children of Jacob his chosen ones;
> Be ye mindful always of his Covenant, the word which he commanded to a thousand generations;
> Even the Covenant which he made with Abraham, and of his oath unto Isaac;
> And hath confirmed the same to Jacob for a law, and to Israel for an everlasting Covenant.
> David

> That the Gentiles should be fellow heirs, and of the same body, and
> partakers of his promise in Christ by the Gospel.
> Paul.[64]

The combination of the "everlasting Covenant" given to the "chosen ones," and Paul's statement that "the Gentiles should be fellow heirs," reveals the place which American religious leaders felt that Christians had in the Promise, and the responsibility they held to bring about its fulfillment. References in missionary quarters to the exact geographical location of the Promised Land were quite clear from the beginning, unlike the spiritual metaphors of America as "God's Israel." As early as 1819, the active missionary evangelist and theologian Moses Stuart[65] gave a sermon at the ordination of some missionaries who were on their way to the Levant: "Shall the happy days of Christian triumph no more return to bless the earth; to animate the exertions, and exalt the hopes of those who love Zion?" Then Stuart ended his sermon on a more literal reference: he exhorted the prospective missionaries to go to the midst of Jerusalem to plant, once again, the standard of the Cross.[66]

The missionaries were not to labor alone in the cause of Zion. As a result of the factors already described, there also developed a popular zeal among American Evangelists and moderate Christians to prepare for the Coming Kingdom in the Promised Land. There are many examples of Americans who left the United States to establish settlements in Palestine—where the great event was expected to take place. A new surge of activities took place in search of the literal fulfillment of prophecy. There are many references by travelers to colonies in the Levant which were established in the Holy Land in expectation of the coming of the Messiah.[67] One such reference is the humorous account by Robert Barr of his encounter with some "colonists" towards the end of the nineteenth century. Barr meets with a Mr. Rollo Floyd in the Holy Land, and the latter undertakes to guide him through the sacred places. Floyd's interesting career, says Barr, "is a striking example of the genius of this great people." The American nation, to which Floyd belongs, is the most inventive of all nations, "having cut itself loose from the traditions of the old world."[68] Americans are credited by Barr with many new scientific and technical inventions, but,

> when the inventive brain of America disdains anything so material
> as machinery, it turns naturally toward the constructing of religions.
> I suppose there are more religions invented in America in a year
> than exist in all other parts of the world put together....While the
> broad East is content with one or two religions, the broad West numbers
> hers by hundreds. Thus we have Mormonism, Spiritualism,
> Shakerism, and dozens of other isms.[69]

Rollo Floyd, whom Barr met in Palestine, was there because "in his youth he fell a victim to one of the numerous ephemeral religious inventions." The sect to which he belonged started "in cold and stormy Maine, of all places in the world." They believed "that Christ was about to return to the Holy Land, and it was necessary for those who wished to be saved to be there to meet their Redeemer. This was thirty or forty years ago, and enough devotees were got together to equip for themselves and their families a sailing ship.[70] The arrangements for their removal to Palestine were made by the American Consul, who, according to Barr, was a Jew. The pilgrims' hopes were disappointing and many of them had to be taken back to the United States by arrangements made by Secretary Seward, not before augmenting the Consul's "thrifty bank account."[71]

An account of a similar nature is that given by Annie DeWitt Shaw of Baltimore, Maryland, who visited the Holy Land with "Uncle Will" about the year 1897. On arriving at Jerusalem, Annie recites the scriptural description of the city: "Beautiful for situation, the joy of the whole earth, is Mount Zion, on the sides of the north, the City of the Great King."[72] The next morning the party's dragoman took them on a tour of the city, starting with "a house which is the residence of a community that is awaiting the fulfillment of the prophecies as to the restoration of Jerusalem.[73] The community was called "the American Colony," although it included some other nationalities. Shaw, with childlike innocence, says "I had not the least idea of what they were staying in Jerusalem for; and when they said to me that several of their brethren had gone to Chicago, I innocently asked if they were going to form a community of the same kind there. Uncle Will thought that was something to laugh at."[74]

Not all travelers in the Holy Land, however, looked with humor or innocence at these American colonies. The general attitude was that of veneration for the devotion and self-denial showed by the colonists. The author of *The City of the Great King*, for example, informs us that "the unpretending but efficient colony of Americans, first organized under the zealous advocacy of the late Mrs. Minor, has by no means proved an aberration as is sometimes asserted,…"[75] As for the colonists themselves, there is no better expression of their zeal and self-denial than that of a young American woman, Lydia Schuler, who offers in a series of letters to the *Gospel Visitor* a good example of the sentiments of Adventists waiting for the Messiah in the Holy Land.

In simple, almost unlettered language, but with absolute belief in the literal fulfillment of prophecy, Schuler writes to her "Dear brother in

Christ" on May 10th, 1854, from the "Plains of Sharon" explaining the reasons for her removal to Palestine:

> You express a desire to know what has provoked me to forsake my father, mother, brother, sisters and friends and come to this land.— When I felt my sins heavy upon me and no one could take them away but he whose blood was spilt here in this land, he said, come unto me, I will comfort thee; and indeed I found him precious to my soul. I then laid myself and all that was near and dear to me on the altar and prayed that I might only do the Lord's will and be useful in his vineyard.[76]

She goes on to relate how she became inspired by the Scriptures and convinced that the duty of the Gentiles was to restore Israel to the "Lord of the Bible." Through her acquaintance with a Philadelphia nonsectarian group, she made her way to the Holy Land to address what she called "the suffering of the Jews."

Five years later, Schuler, still persistent in her quest for the Kingdom of God, reveals an even stronger belief in the approaching millennium. In July, 1859, she sums up in one letter the conditions which prevailed in the Holy Land seen through the eyes of prophecy. The most important condition to be fulfilled in order to bring about the Coming Kingdom is the restoration of the Jews to Palestine. Schuler says about this:

> The Jews' wailing place was to me the most interesting place in Jerusalem. My dragoman, an East Indian Jew, of Moorish skin, who, by the way, is an English subject, and speaks English well, conducted me thither. We threaded our way through the usual narrow and dirty lanes, misnamed streets, of Eastern cities, and came to an area in the form of a quadrangle, near the bridge where the dwellers in Zion were once wont to pas over, to worship God in the Temple on His holy mount, Moriah. In the ancient foundation wall of the Temple are several courses of large, leveled stones, upon which the Jews lavish their kisses and embraces and through the crevices of which they pour up their prayers to God for the restoration of His Temple, and their early coming triumph in Jerusalem.[77]

Her graphic prose describes her newfound brotherhood with the Jews who bring their prayers to this place which has been defiled by the Muslems, but which will some day be returned as their rightful inheritance.

By the 1850's the transfer of the vision of Zion to the new geographical location in the Holy Land was complete. The second half of the nineteenth century was a period of consolidation of that vision. The number and nature of accounts written by American travellers to the Holy Land are evidence of the process.[78] For example, the "Publishers Announcement" to Barclay's *The City of the Great King* states that the book "is presented to the public, believing that much will be found in it of great interest and value to all classes of the religious world, and to those who would see the hand of Providence in the history and fortunes of Israel, and the nations with whom they have been associated, for more than three thousand years.[79]

All classes of the religious world were interested in Israel and the untiring efforts of travellers in the Levant followed the footsteps of the Tribes of Israel from Egypt to Palestine; these diverse men and women felt compelled to explore that route for themselves. One of these was Samuel Colcord Bartlet, a prominent clergyman and President of Dartmouth College, who first did a good deal of research on the route of the Israelites, then made that trip himself. The result was a work whose title bespeaks his mission: *From Egypt to Palestine, Through Sinai, the Wilderness and the South Country: Observations of a Journey Made with Special Reference to the History of the Israelites* (1879).

Another person who followed the footsteps of Moses to the land of Canaan was Margaret Bottome, a zealous believer, who described her trip in a series of all-but-mystic letters.[80] There was also Beverly Carradine, whose *Journey to Palestine* (1891) reveals the fervor with which a Southern clergyman colors his personal account of his trip from Egypt through Sinai to the Promised Land.

American travelers in the Holy Land heard an irresistible call to trace the path of the Israelites. These pilgrims and travelers identified their past experiences with that of the Hebrews in crossing the wilderness in search of the Promised Land. One distinguished traveler, Stephen Olin, who called himself an enlightened Christian, and looked with scorn on the "superstitious rites of the Christian crowds in Jerusalem during the pilgrimage season, had nothing but praise for a missionary, Leider (whose first name he did not give), who worked diligently "in the discharge of his duties, to visit several places very interesting from their connection with sacred history." Olin describes these efforts with zeal and admiration. He traces Leider's peregrinations in imitation of the route of the Israelites in order to check the historical journeyings which led to the point where they miraculously crossed the Red Sea, and to confirm what he calls "the sacred geography."[81]

The Place of the Jews in the Vision of Zion

Schuler's sentiments towards the Jewish people and their association with the Holy Land were shared by many of her compatriots. These sentiments were an integral part of the Western Christian Judaic heritage, and in this sense they became characteristic of American religious thinking. Gradually, during the nineteenth century, the Jewish people were introduced to the American myth of the vision of Zion whereby Americans began to recognize a central position occupied by the true "chosen people" of Scripture in the Second Kingdom, although still clinging to what they perceived to be their own sacred commission to bring about that Kingdom. There was a noticeable change in the role to be played by America; from "God's Israel". America subsequently became the instrument in the realization of prophecies and in the fulfillment of promises. Perhaps coming in contact with the Holy Land was responsible for the relocation of the Kingdom of God from the New World to Zion Hill, and consequently it brought to the forefront another people who were supposed to be beneficiaries of the promise.

Contemporary opinion on this matter varied from one extreme to the other. For example, the American edition of Buck's *Theological Dictionary* mildly states under the subtitle, "Jews, restoration of," that "from the declaration of Scripture we have reason to suppose the Jews shall be called to a participation of the blessings of the Gospel, Rom. xi; 2 Cor. iii.16; Hos. i.11, and some suppose shall return to their own land, Hos. iii.5; Is. 1xv.17, etc.; Ezek. xxxvi."[82]

The time of the return, says the *Theological Dictionary*, is not certain: "some think about 1866 or 2016; but this, perhaps, is not so easy to determine altogether, though it is probable it will not be before the fall of Antichrist and the Ottoman empire."[83] A similar, though more forceful, view is expressed in the *Hand-Book to All Religions* which sees the "Lands of Judea" in the light of "the promise to the Jews," and the prophecies which were expected to be fulfilled. The *Hand-Book* realizes that the worst obstacle to be overcome was that "the stronghold of Zion" was under the domination of "Turks and Mohammedans."[84]

There were a number of organizations, and many activities, in both America and England, urging the conversion of the Jews as a step towards their restoration. In fact, one of the earliest American missionary ventures was that of the Boston Female Society for the Promotion of Christianity among the Jews. This society sent Josiah Brewer to the Holy Land to investigate the condition of the Jewish people there and the method to be followed for their conversion to Christianity.[85]

The conversion of the Jews, however, was not always insisted upon. Some of these organizations started using the term "amelioration and reformation of the conditions of the Jewish people," and more efforts were directed to the restoration process. The *Theological Dictionary* advises, for example, that Christians should "avoid putting stumbling-block in their [the Jews'] way. If we attempt any thing for their conversion, let it be with peace and love. Let us, says one, propose Christianity to them, as Christ proposed it to them. Let us lay before them their own prophecies....Let us never abridge their civil liberty, nor ever try to force their consciences."[86]

In the Holy Land, the predominant American attitude toward the Jewish people was that of sympathy for their plight and dispersion, and a genuine commitment to the cause of Israel. Schuler's opinions were not those of the extreme Adventists only. An Episcopal minister, Charles Andrews, writes the editors of the *Episcopalian Recorder* from Jerusalem on February 25, 1842, remarking on "the extreme sparseness of the population" in the whole region of the Holy Land. The only occupants he sees are "a few miserable Arabs with their flocks...[in] a rich, extensive and beautiful country." The scene evokes in Andrews a long cultural tradition of religious education. "Where," he asks, "were the many thousands of Simeon and Dan to whom this faithful region was assigned! Alas not one of their descendents [sic] is here to be found. Prophecy is fulfilled [sic]. The country 'without inhabitants' sits solitary. But is it not so kept by providence, waiting for its own people? They are indeed long absent."[87] Andrews' statement was part of the continuing cultural dialogue of the myth of Zion. When writing a historical account of the development of Palestinian explorations, Frederick Bliss said that the history of "the Hebrew conquests" and the "establishment of the Jewish kingdom, its subsequent division, the growing influence of Asyria, the scattering of the tribes in Exile, the return of the Jews to their native land...these points must be at the tip of the tongue of every Sunday-school scholar."[88]

It is not surprising, therefore, that one of the standard activities of American travellers and missionaries in the Holy Land was a visit to the Wailing Wall and to the Jewish quarter in Jerusalem; the persistence and strength of this cultural tradition can be seen in their chronicles. In 1896 Lee S. Smith was on a pilgrimage from Egypt to Palestine and when he arrived in the Land of Canaan he "proceeded 'to do' Jerusalem in true American style."[89] His party first visited the Church of the Holy Sepulchre. But he could not for a moment believe that this was the site of the Crucifixion and Resurrection of the Savior. Yet, he says, "remembering that it has been so considered throughout hundreds of years, and that millions have visited and worshiped there because of that belief; and that the blood of hundreds of thousands had been spilt in fighting for its possession—recollecting all this, we entered it with a feeling of reverence."[90]

Smith was happy to say that the possessors of the church were "Latin and Greek Catholics, and Armenians...no Protestants, not only because of the necessity of a band of [Turkish] soldiers to preserve the peace, but because of the mummery and the foolery surrounding the place."91 The party then proceeded to the "Tower of David, the Jewish Wailing Place, and to David's and Solomon's tombs on the crest of Mount Zion." Smith's reaction to these sites sums up the traditional sacred associations of the Judaic history of the Holy Land:

> What emotions filled our breasts as we stood on Mount Zion, and looked upon the group of buildings known as the tombs of David and Solomon—the sweet singer of Israel, and the wise man who so basely abused his God-given wisdom. In this group of buildings is shown a large upper room in which it is claimed that the Last Supper was eaten. As to this there may be doubts, but as to the tombs of those two mighty kings of Israel being somewhere under these buildings, I think there can be no doubt; but unfortunately, the Turk rules here also, and permits no Christians to do more than enter the buildings.[92]

American encounters with members of the Jewish religion on the sacred soil of the Holy Land during the nineteenth century evoked certain emotions which resulted from that same Hebraic tradition which Bliss talks about. They were especially strong and sympathetic emotions because of the transfer of the original American myth of Zion to the Promised Land of Scripture. Thus Lydia Schuler's sympathetic comments on the Jews at the Wailing Wall[93] are matched by many other accounts of American travelers. The Hebrews occupied a special position in the Western Christian tradition, and travelers to the Levant saw them face to face, not as they had seen and dealt with the Jewish people in their own country. One of those American travelers is Barclay who, in Jerusalem, reflects on the situation of the Jews and their special value, saying: "That the Hebrew race is the noblest that has ever adorned the annals of humanity, will not be questioned even by the proud Anglo-Saxons themselves." But in addition to their racial superiority, Barclay sees their value in other respects. For, he says, there can be no doubt that, "if converted—speaking as they do, all the languages of earth, habituated to all customs, and acclimated to every region—they would make the best missionaries on the face of the globe."[94]

A great deal of this adulatory attitude towards the Jewish people, however, was not utilitarian in nature, but resulted from the religious educational tradition in America. One of the people described by Bliss as "every Sunday school scholar," Marion Harland, devotes two long chapters in her account of travel to the Levant to the condition of the Jews, identifying that same religious education as the source of her feelings. In the chapter entitled "Thine Ancient People the Jews," Harland says "under this name I heard them prayed for every day throughout my infancy and girlhood. The phraseology in which the patriarch of the household remembered them at the family altar varied little in all those years: 'We pray Thee to have mercy upon Thine ancient people the Jews, and bring them into Thine Everlasting Kingdom, together with the fullness of the Gentiles. May they look upon Him whom they have pierced, and acknowledge Him as King of kings and Lord of Lords.'"[95] Harland says this prayer "over to herself" on a murky afternoon as she walks through the Jewish Quarter, not mindful of the "corrugated soles" of her shoes, as she slips and slides "upon the greasy mud of the Jewish quarter in the City of David." She is guided by a Mr. David Jamal (who had been in the service of the Church Missionary Society for twenty years) to the residence of the Chief Rabbi of Jerusalem and then to the house of a lesser rabbi. Both interviews are, each in its own way, enriching to the spiritual well-being of the American lady and have a salutary effect on her belief in biblical prophecy.

Harland exchanges a few ceremonious preliminary remarks and then enters into what she calls "catechizing" with the learned Hebrew. She asks "If he attaches any significance to the influx in late years of the Jews from other lands into Palestine. Also if he can give me an approximate idea of the number who have thus immigrated within ten years." To which the Rabbi answers in a matter-of-fact manner: "If you would know how many have come in the past sixty years, I should answer that there were but one thousand Jews in Jerusalem and the vicinity in 1833. There are thirty thousand now." Harland tries to elicit from the Chief Rabbi an answer which would confirm her understanding of the prophecy. She asks whether they are all drawn by the same motive. He answers, unimpassioned, "The Jews come to Palestine because they love it as the land of their fathers and their country. Some have come expecting the Messiah. They are foolish. When He comes, He will rule the whole earth, not merely this little corner of the globe."

As for the signs that will usher in the Messiah's personal advent, the Rabbi can only suggest that the political horizon is dark and may mean much. But no man can tell. And, anyway, the advent will be prefaced with "the Great Fight of Armageddon....Gog and Magog will appear and be overthrown. There will be a terrible bloody conflict of all nations in the Valley of Decision." The Messiah's first appearance, says the Rabbi, will be upon "Mount Safed, the highest point of Galilee, so say the holy writings." The American lady recalls in an aside that Safed is indeed called the "city set upon a hill." Perhaps the learned man is right, although, she says, "we are told by Zechariah that when 'the Lord shall go forth and fight against those nations as when he fought in the day of battle, His feet shall stand upon the Mount of Olives which is before Jerusalem on the east.'"

The dispute gets a little more heated when Harland suggests that some of America's most learned Rabbis did not actually expect a personal Messiah. "They believe," she tells the Chief Rabbi of Jerusalem, "that the prophecies relative to His comming point to the perfectibility of human nature; to an advanced state of morality and subjugation of whatever is base and vicious in man's nature and conduct; to the cessation of war and crime...."[96] This statement ruffles the dignified Rabbi's complexion for the first time, and he retorts in a nervous, loud voice: "No devout Jew believes such a monstrous thing! The men who assert it are infidels—materialists. The Messiah will be a real personage, great, holy, powerful, perfect, and He shall reign in the Mount Zion, forever and ever."[97]

Harland then is taken to visit another religious leader of the Jewish community. He is a man after her own heart. Says Harland, "far from eluding such queries as I have put to his superior in office and worldly gear, he talks enthusiastically of his belief that the Kingdom of the Messiah is near at hand." His explanation of the prophecy of the battle of Armageddon is interesting to his American visitor. He says that "Gog and Magog are, I am inclined to think, Russia. All nations will be engaged in the Valley of Jehoshaphat. The right will conquer, the God of Israel fighting for it. A congress of nations will be held and decide to restore Palestine to the Jews, who will thence forward possess and cause the waste places to break forth into singing, the desert to bloom as the rose."[98]

Harland, coaxing her host into more predictions, comments that "there is not room in Palestine—or in all Syria, for that matter—for one-half of the Jews now alive upon the earth." The Rabbi "smiled benignantly and with the calmness of his convictions" answers his quest, basing his conviction on the prophecy: "You forget that they have never yet had all the Promised Land—'from the river of Egypt, the Nile, 'unto the great river, the river Euphrates.' The promise is 'ordered in all things and sure.' The whole world will then be at peace; nations shall learn war no more. All will worship one only and true GOD, the GOD of Israel." Putting out her hand "impulsively" and shaking his hand, the American pilgrim says to the Rabbi: "You are a Protestant!" Obliquely, he answers, "We serve the same Lord."[99]

The City of the Great King

During the first half of the nineteenth century, Adventists in the United States of America felt sure of the approaching milennium and called on their fellow countrymen and all Christians to be ready for it. Signs of the times, as we have seen, were unmistakeable, and confirmed their expectations. Americans who went to the Holy Land had committed to memory a great number of prophecies and scriptural statements on the future of the Holy Land. They saw in the current state of affairs a confirmation of these signs of the coming Kingdom, and they pondered with awe and anxiety what was to become of the declining Ottoman Empire.

The most articulate expression of the vision of rebuilding Jerusalem is that voiced by the American doctor and missionary, J. T. Barclay, in 1858. His book *The City of the Great King: Jerusalem As It Was, As It Is, and As It Is To Be* explores with apparent scientific accuracy the geographical and historical realities of the "promise" and prophecies. Barclay, and many of his fellow Americans, recited at the site of the literal Kingdom the prophecies of Isaiah that "the Lord shall arise upon thee, and his glory shall be seen upon thee; and the Gentiles shall come to thy light, and kings to the brightness of thy rising" (ix, 1, 3); and "then the moon shall be confounded and the sun ashamed, when the Lord of Hosts shall reign in Mount Zion, and in Jerusalem, and before his ancients gloriously" (xxiv, 23).[100] Recited by Barclay on Mount Zion, this clearly was no longer a dream of Mexico City or Salt Lake City as the New Jerusalem. It is, as Barclay and others thought, "Jerusalem as it is to be."

The City of the Great King, although not as well known as the works of Robinson, Thomson and Lynch, expressed the beliefs and aspirations of many religious Americans of the time. Its painstaking, seemingly scientific exploration of the sacred sites, the conviction which informed its description of the present state of affairs in the whole area, and the certainty with which it predicted the future, mark the total transformation of a national myth to a vision of the immediate future.

The sacred sites of the coming Kingdom evoked expressions of ecstasy and fulfillment from pilgrims to the Holy Land. Such is the beautiful apostrophe which flowed from the pen of Barclay, the medical doctor working for the cause of Zion:

> Jerusalem! "Name ever dear!" What hallowed memories and entrancing recollections spring at the mere mention of that name! There is music and magic in the very thought! Jerusalem, the joy of the whole earth! The city of the Great King! Zion, the city of solemnities—an eternal excellency! The hill which God desireth to dwell in; yea, will dwell in it for ever!: The theater of the most memorable

and stupendous events that have ever occurred in the annals of the world. Jerusalem! the world-attracting magnet of the devout pilgrim of every age, and the stern warrior of every clime; not the least of whom were the chivalrous Crusaders of our noble ancestry! a spot at once the focus and the radiating point of the strongest emotions of three powerful religions!...

What are the recollections associated with the monuments and antiquities of Memphis, Babylon, Nineveh, Athens, Rome, London, or the cities of the Azteks, compared with those that cluster around the City of the Great King!...where the son of Jesse tuned his soul-stirring harp, and penned his Psalms for the saints of all ages; where Solomon reared a house for the Lord of Hosts to dwell between the Cherubim; where the Son of God suffered and died, and rose again—whence he ascended on high, and whither he will come again on the clouds of heaven in like manner as he went up...and "Jehovah of Hosts shall reign in Mount Zion and in Jerusalem, and before his ancients gloriously," sitting upon his throne in the sublime metropolis (then brought near)—the New Jerusalem above. Then shall the Holy City truly become "the joy of the whole earth!"

"Glorious things of thee are spoken,

Zion, city of God![101]

Similar feelings were often stirred by the sight of the sacred city despite its deteriorating condition and the abuses of its various churches. In an "attempt to discriminate between truth and error with regard to the sacred places of the Holy City,"[102] George Jones, a chaplain in the U.S. Navy, shows great excitement at the first view of Jerusalem,[103] and when visiting the Temple, he loses himself in a reverie of vision and biblical longing. Jones recalls that "the Lord is in his Holy Temple, let all the earth keep silence before Him." The temple represents, says Jones, a "gorgeous edifice," which is "raised to such a stupendous height, wrapped in a splendor that the eye can scarcely look upon."[104] His imagination unites with religious emotion as he visualizes in the depth of the great Temple "a spot of mysterious darkness and solitude" where one feels "the presence of Jehovah." "This Temple," he writes "belongs not to Jerusalem, but to the whole world. And He, the Diety, whose very name is awful, and should be used with reverence, hath blessed this spot with his peculiar presence; and it is meet that man should look upon it with deep and solemn feeling"[105] The scene evokes Jones' memory of the Psalms of David, no doubt part of his early religious training. "How amiable," Jones repeats, "are thy tabernacles, O Lord of Hosts."[106]

It was not only in the City of the Great King that such emotions were evoked in pilgrims and travellers. Every step on the way from Egypt or Syria to the Holy Land was a reminder of a Patriarch or a Scriptural prophecy. Even travelling down the Nile from Luxor to Cairo was a thrilling religious experience for Charles Andrews, Episcopal minister from Virginia. "My dear wife," he writes home, "I can scarcely believe my own eyes when I see myself upon the sacred river."[107] And a fellow countrywoman, Sarah Haight, writes of the view which she has of Cairo from the vicinity of the Citadel which overlooks the city. Her remarks on the view are significant for the perspective which the viewer has:

> From this elevated terrace we had a magnificent view. Beneath our feet lay the whole city, sufficiently distant to prevent its disagreeable details from offending the eye. The domes and minarets of all the mosques were seen at one glance. Beyond the city, towards the west, were the river and the green valley, bounded by the hills of the Libyan desert, on the edge of which rise the mighty Pyramids. To the north was the Land of Goshen, and the solitary obelisk of Heliopolis is all that now remains of *On*, that once proud city of priests, where Moses became "learned in all the wisdom of the Egyptians."...To the east lies the road taken by the Children of Israel at the time of the Exode.[108]

With such a realization of Scriptural analogy and prophecy, Barclay therefore does not find it surprising "that the result of Protestant missionary effort has not been more cheering." However, he takes consolation in the obvious fact that "Moslem opposition, it is confidently believed, is now at an end—indeed, the impression is almost universal among themselves that the days of Islamism are numbered—at least for the present."[109] Barclay cites the Muslim's peculiar views of destiny which "can but prove as certainly paralyzing under the waning moon, as they were irresistibly stimulating under its crescent. It is now far too late in the day for Moslem prestige to avail, as in days of yore!"[110]

From 1843, according to Barclay, the governance of Christians in Jerusalem was in the hands of the consuls of foreign powers, especially those of France, Prussia, and Sardinia. Spain and the United States established official consulates in the 1850's and "as far as his own subjects are concerned, a Consul is virtually 'King of Jerusalem,' and plays the despot with perfect impunity."[111] Describing the results of these developments, Barclay concludes that "as far as *Moslem rule* is concerned in its exercise towards Christians, Jerusalem is no longer trodden down of the Gentiles. Nor can the least doubt be entertained as to the early enfranchisement and complete enlargement of the Jews. A better day has already dawned upon Zion."[112]

A fellow countryman of Dr. Barclay, J.V.C. Smith, who wrote "*A Pilgrimage to Palestine*," and who crossed paths with the doctor in Jerusalem, reached the same Scriptural conclusion based on the moral conditions of the Muslems in the Levant. Smith sees no hope of reforming and converting Muslems because "Christianity offers nothing acceptable to the depraved conquerors of Syria."[113] Smith also notices the analogy with Scriptural history, remarking that,

> the Canaanites were crushed on account of their idolatries, and the cities of the plain destroyed by the fire from heaven for the very abominations now as common here and notorious as possible; and it is certain, that till the present inhabitants are rooted out of the land, and a new race of men introduced in their stead, the gospel will only be precious with a few, who can have little influence in changing the manners and customs of the whole.[114]

Both Smith and Barclay displayed a remarkable compatibility of political and religious thinking.[115] Both of them sought the rebuilding of Zion and both saw the hand of Providence in the social and political, events which were taking place. Furthermore, in common with many other Westerners, Americans not excluded, both saw the prospect for re-establishing Zion as the principal outcome of these events. At the core of the Eastern Question lay the fulfillment of Scriptural prophecies concerning the future of the Land of Promise. Each saw in the power politics of the Western nations clear indications that these nations all agreed, or at least should agree, on the priority of establishing a Jewish commonwealth in the Holy Land. J.V.C. Smith discounted the possibility of individual efforts, and called for collective action by the governments of the Western powers. He says, in part:

> As frequently expressed in the course of preceding observations on the future destiny of the Land of Promise, I fully believe in the final restoration of the Jews, and the re-establishment of the nation. That greatest of all events to the reflecting Christian, who sees the hand of God in the eventful history of the descendants of Abraham, must be brought about by the concurrence and guarantee of all the Christian powers of the earth, who will thus be instrumentalities in fulfilling the intentions of Divine Providence.[116]

Barclay, in turn, quotes the "very just remarks" made by a Dr. Durbin in describing the situation in the Holy Land and the efforts of the foreign consulates to establish a Hebrew diocese in Jerusalem. The statement which Barclay favors is of special significance for the paramount theme of the fulfillment of prophecy within the context of political developments:

> But the prospective *political* bearing of this Hebrew diocese is perhaps a matter of much greater interest than its immediate religious results. It is doubtless intimately connected with the restoration of the Jewish commonwealth in Palestine, chiefly under the auspices of

England and Prussia. It is not to be affirmed that these governments instituted this measure with the sole, or even chief intent to accomplish this great prophetic event; yet without doubt they looked to the state of the Jewish and Christian mind, which these prophecies have produced with regard to the restoration, as a material, perhaps an essential element in their success. That the measure is considered by the five great powers as having an important political bearing, is evident from the fact that, since the organization of the diocese, France, Russia, and Austria have sent their consuls to Jerusalem, where there is neither trade nor commerce to be encouraged or protected....[117]

An earlier account of the political situation in the Holy Land was one by Sarah Haight, the "lady of New York." Haight also saw a unique chance for the Western powers, especially England and France, to intervene and divide the area among them. The ambitious policy of Muhammad Ali in Egypt was a reminder of older days. "A faint parallel" appeared to her "between the ancient Pharaoh and the one who now sways the sceptre of Misraim." Muhammad Ali, "like his prototype," had an insatiable thirst for conquest of other countries, and he had already

subjugated all Ethiopia, Libya, and part of Arabia, and has lately overrun Palestine and Syria. This last conquest was to satisfy his rapacious desire for plunder; and though the treasurers of Tyre and Sidon no longer excite the cupidity of the invader, and the gold of the temple of the Lord has long since disappeared, yet the "golden fleece of Serica" yields a rich and tempting crop....[118]

She goes on to warn that the day will come when he will bring about his premeditated plan to conquer Islam.

These reflections reminded Mrs. Haight of some "remarks" written by her husband, Richard Haight, in correspondence with a friend back home "on the present affairs and future prospects of the East." The extensive excerpts quoted by Mrs. Haight from her husband's remarks show political insight and prophetic wisdom. Richard Haight was a member of the fledgeling American Oriental Society[119] and must have also had some official position, judging from the warm reception accorded him by the American consuls in Alexandria and Cairo. This, and the fact that he wrote his reflections on the state of affairs in the East before the end of the first half of the nineteenth century, give them added significance. Haight says that Russia had an eye on India, and was capable "at any moment she pleased [to] seize upon the key of the Euxine gates, and close them against the combined efforts of all the West, and hold them, too, in spite of all the navies in existence."[120] On another front, Haight warns that "unless some more decided measures be soon taken by England and France conjointly, Russia will have obtained so firm a foothold in Persia and Kurdistan, that the Punjab will offer but a faint resistance to her arms and wiles. Then the Euphrates and Indus will be as free for her myriads as they were for those of Timurlane and Genghis Khan."[121] Haight credits Russia with inciting the Greek rebellion against Ottoman rule "to execute her purpose against the Turk." But when the Greek seemed to be gaining the upper hand, Russia gave secret aid to the Turk, "inciting him to use the most cruel measures in the barbarous warfare, until the people of Christendom...compelled their governments to combine for the rescue of fallen Greece from her cruel oppressor." Thus the Ottomans were weakened and sank deeper in the arms of Russia for protection. Haight adds:

> Russia had accomplished her purpose; she had prostrated Turkey, and therefore made a merit of magnanimously sparing a fallen foe. The seeds of discord have taken too deep root in the great empire of Islam for all the diplomacy of the West ever to eradicate them; and all its members are too much disjointed for England to succeed in reconstructing a powerful empire on the ruins of the one she (so foolishly for herself) assisted in overturning.[122]

All of this, says Haight, went on while the nations of Europe were playing a useless game of diplomacy. What surprised him was that England did not, "seize upon Turkey in Europe, and portion off the remainder of the empire to satisfy the cupidity of the other nations."[123] But Haight's plan is not based on political considerations only and on the power struggle among Western countries. Here and there the proposal reveals the influence of the vision of Zion and the biblical prophecy. In Europe, says Haight, the Turk is a "usurper" anyway, "and there would be no crime in unseating him by any of the powers." And as for the rest of the Ottoman Empire, "the same may be said of him who ruffianly lords it over the land from the Nile to the Euphrates."[124] Haight does not neglect to propose a solution for the population of this area. "From Constantinople to Cairo," he suggests, "the Turks...should be politely escorted across the Euphrates, and there permitted to reconstruct an empire on the former territory of the califs, making old Baghdad's walls once more resound with the glories of Haroun al Raschid."[125]

Haight's analysis of the situation in the East rests both upon his assessment of the political power struggle over the possessions of the Ottoman Empire and on his American Western heritage of the vision of Zion as translated into a geo-political reality. Haight tells his correspondent that if he could not "erect empires in Asia," he could "at least build *chateaux en Espagne*."[126] He then launches on his dream: "I will now carve up the East," he says, "and give to each hungry expectant such a share of it as I think would be most conducive of his own good; after which I will settle the future constitution of Asia as I understand it."[127] England and France, according to Haight, should be the first beneficiaries "of the Eastern banquet which has been so long waiting their pleasure."[128] The proposed division as drawn by Haight gives

> to France all the southern coast of the Mediterranean, from Morocco to the borders of Egypt, with the privilege of making conquests as far into the interior of Africa as she might choose, always excepting the Atlantic coasts. Egypt should be England's, with the right to carry her arms to the Cape of Good Hope. Syria should go to France, as far as the Euphrates on the East and the Taurus on the north. Asia Minor to England, with the right to march to Bucharia if she saw fit.[129]

This accomplished, the Muslem population of these territories should be "politely escorted" across the Euphrates to establish their Caliphate in Baghdad. And once these preliminaries are "settled in secret conclave," Haight would have England occupy Persia, Bucharia, Bengal and the Punjab, "thus surrounding the new calif, and preventing him from communicating with the Moslems of Hendustan."[130]

Haight's vision of the future was obviously a yearning for the fulfillment of the literal prophecy of the New Jerusalem,—an East where

> Throughout all the Holy Land the sacred monuments are surrounded by thousands of pilgrims from the farthest west; and the pious female devotee returning to her home, nourishes her roses of Sharon with the water of Jordan. The descendant of Ishmael now visits in peace the bazars of Cairo and Damascus, and his hand is no longer against every man, nor every man's hand against him.[131]

Richard Haight's design for the Orient, especially the Holy Land, was unique in that it came so early in the American rediscovery of that part of the world. But it was certainly not an isolated dream. It fits in with Smith's scheme of rooting out the local population and planting in its place a superior race of men, with Schuler's personal participation in the preparation for the coming Kingdom, with Barclay's City of the Great King as the core of the solution to the Eastern Question, and with scores of other schemes and dreams by Americans who did or did not visit the Holy Land. Some of these men were practical and some were idealists, but both types had a clear conviction of the possibility, and ultimately in the inevitability, of the realization of their dreams.

William Lynch, navigator of the Dead Sea and the River Jordan, was one of the practical men of action. He came back from his expedition with a detailed official report which he submitted to the Secretary of the Navy, and with an equally detailed narrative of the journey. The latter was printed and reprinted many times. In addition, Lynch led a group of people who advocated the dispatch of excavation and exploration teams to the Levant with an ultimate scheme for the fulfillment of scriptural prophecies—especially those of Isaiah—of populating the desert, restoring the Jews to Zion Hill and making the area a thoroughfare for East-West commerce. As part of this campaign Lynch gave a lecture entitled "Commerce and the Holy Land" which was endorsed by a number of missionaries and prominent Americans.[132]

Barclay's "Millennial Jerusalem," on the other hand, is the pure scriptural vision of Zion, which is nonetheless based on a practical awareness of the political and social conditions in the area. He looks at some current phenomena and events and sees them as containing preliminaries to the ultimate event. Such a phenomenon isCrimean War "the Russo-Turkish war—that most anomalous of wars—the significant issue and results of which will tell mightily upon earth's destiny, and invest the Jews and their capital and country with unspeakable interest."[133] Other signs are just as significant, although some of them are in the nature of internal policy and everyday occurrences. Otherwise, he asks,

> What mean the various lines of streamers now traversing the length and breadth of the Mediterranean and Red Seas—placing Palestine in such direct, constant, and intimate communication not only with other parts of Asia, but with Europe, Africa, America, and the Isles of the Gentiles? What the railways now projected between Jaffa and the Persian Gulf, via Neapolis, with which a branch from Egypt is to unite—passing through Jerusalem, a "highway" from Egypt into Assyria? (S. xix.23.) And what the electric telegraph at the Holy City—the great central metropolis!—to say nothing of the stupendous scheme of converting the great depressed basin of Arabia Deserta into an inland ocean by letting in the waters of the Red Sea![134]

Barclay's vision of the future of the Holy Land agrees totally with the literal interpretation of Scriptural prophecies and promises. To begin with, "the city of cities" will cover more than a hundred square miles and will have millions of inhabitants. There will be railways from Al-Arish, Askalon, and Ghaza. The city will be on the track route between East and West, no doubt the Great Highway to Egypt of Scriptures. To this City of The Great King—the joy of the whole earth—"supremacy is assigned in the coming age by Him who is Governor among the nations—the King of Kings and Lord of Lords."[135] Furthermore, from Zechariah (xiv.8), Barclay learns that "at the coming of the Lord two most copious perennial streams of water shall burst forth from Jerusalem—, one going forth towards the Mediterranean or 'hinder sea,' and the other towards the 'former' or Dead Sea—developed apparently by the great earthquake."[136] An earthquake may have in the past opened the great valley near Jerusalem, and this, says Barclay, may be ready to become the future river-bed. The author, then concludes that although there is no positive information on the size of the river,

> if it be as large as that emptying into the Dead Sea, it may be rendered very serviceable not only for the irrigation of a large district of country, but for internal boat navigation. If it be true that the desert of Arabia was once an inland sea or lake, and is still depressed below the level of the sea, may it not be re-filled either from the sea or by this river? It will be recollected that while Jerusalem is 3927 feet above the Dead Sea, its elevation above the Mediterranean is only 2610 feet; and that Jehovah Shammah will be much more depressed.[137]

Should these two rivers gush forth into the Mediterranean and the Dead Sea, what wondrous prospects of progress awaited this region! According to one of them, running into the Dead Sea "would produce a succession of rapids, cascades, and cataracts unequalled in all the world....What inconceivable power for the propulsion of machinery! What teeming luxuriance must crown the banks of this fertilizing and vivifying stream....!"[138] The barren desert will bloom, and then indeed "the wilderness and the solitary place be glad, and the desert rejoice and blossom as the rose!" The Psalmist's "vision," according to Barclay, had predicted all of this in speaking of the gladdening waters of the river "the streams thereof shall make glad the city of God, the Holy Place of the tabernacles of the Most High. (Ps.xlvi.4.)."[139] As for the river issuing to the West, Barclay does not find positive information that it will have the greatness of the eastern river, but he considers it a "legitimate inference," that it will be similarly endowed. If on the banks of this river

> the Highway of Holiness shall lead from Yehoval Shammah to the Holy City and Temple, through the desert of Tekoah, thus really become "an house of prayer for all nations," what a paradisaical avenue would conduct the millennarian pilgrim up to the House of the Lord! Thus shall "the ransomed of the Lord return, and come to Zion with songs and everlasting joy upon their heads!"[140]

The temporal blessings of this millenial age will be great: Satan will be bound, the Lord's presence will be felt, the waters of the Dead Sea will be healed, its evaporation will be restricted, and there will be considerable geological changes. Truly, concludes Barclay, as he envisions this millenial age, "how glowingly is the prosperity of the land and nation of Israel set forth by the prophets, when Judah and Israel shall have been restored and brought in complete subjection to their prince, David—the Beloved —i.e. the Prince Messiah. (Is.1x, etc.)."[141]

These, however, are only a few of the glorious events of the millennium. The last few pages of Barclay's *City of the Great King* present a picture of the ideal state over which the Messiah will rule upon his second coming.

> There is no aspect in which the Millennial age can be regarded, that is not richly suggestive of the most pleasing and profitable themes of contemplation. Satan being bound, and man brought into complete subjection to Jesus Emmanuel, the whole creation, which had hitherto groaned in travail on account of man's sin, is vocal with praise—"the times of the restitution of all things" having now arrived! Who, that has a heart to feel, can refrain from praying and laboring for "a consummation so devoutly to be wished.!"[142]

Barclay's is the ideal religious picture of the realization of the vision of Zion, as interpreted literally from Scriptural passages, and applied with total conviction to future developments in the lands of the Bible.

8

THE DREAM OF BAGHDAD
The Orient of the Romantic Imagination

"Indeed, as we stop to lunch, and the Commander hands
us the bread, cheese and dates, which are our morning
refreshment, we seriously consider whether the romances of
the Arabian Nights are not veritable history.
'Or the veritable history a romance of the Arabian Nights,'
says the cold-blooded Pasha."

George William Curtis, *The Howadji in Syria*, 1852

"Strictly speaking, Orientalism is a mode of speech." With this sentence
a writer in *The Knickerbocker* of June, 1853, introduced a long and interesting essay on "Orientalism."[1] But the statement is not altogether accurate
or complete. The writer's analysis of the American concept of the Orient
shows that Orientalism is actually a "mode of thought" as well. The
essay reveals all the elements upon which the American missionary
treatment of the Orient was based, as well as the aspirations for fulfillment of the American vision of Zion. In addition, the essay recognizes
the "pictorial" image of the Orient "as it first flashes upon the mind,"
absorbing "all the colors of the chromatic scale" and violating all the
rules of "artistic unity." This pictorial image of the Orient and of the
Orientals is basically a fanciful concept which derives from a long,
cumulative tradition of the imaginary world of the *Arabian Nights*, of the
literature written in imitation of that popular work, and of the many
accounts and stories brought home by American travelers.

The Popular Picture of the Orient

The Knickerbocker essay sums up the popular concept of Orientalism:

We frame to ourselves a deep azure sky, and a languid, alluring atmosphere; associate luxurious ease with the coffee-rooms and
flower-gardens of the Seraglio at Constantinople; with the tapering
minarets and gold- crescents of Cairo; with the fountains within and
the kiosks without Damascus—settings of silver in circlets of gold.

> We see grave and reverend turbans sitting cross-legged on Persian carpets in baths and harems, under palmtrees or acacias, either quaffing the cool sherbet of roses, or the aromatic Mocha coffee, sipped from the fingan poised in the zarf; we picture the anxious Armenian in busy bazaars, offering the customer the amber mouthpiece of the chibouque, while he commends his ottar of roses and gold-cloth; we see the smoke of the Latakia—the mild, sweet tobacco of Syria—whiffed lazily from the bubbling water-pipe, while the devotee of back-gammon listlessly rattles the dice; we hear the musical periods of the story-teller, relating the thousand-and-one tales to the ever-curious crowd...
>
> This is is Orientalism, not as it is, but as it swims before the sensuous imagination. It is too unreal to be defined. The idea partakes of the extravagance of the Oriental mind, and would fain be invested with poetic imagery. To analyze it is to dissolve the charm.[2]

Obviously, this picture drew as much upon the Orient as it did upon the American imagination. Thus when Americans left for the Orient they carried with them, besides the "sacred associations," an exotic picture of what they were about to experience there. That picture was of an Orient of the imagination, a world of fantasy and of dreams, and just as the dreamer of Zion sought to rebuild the Orient according to "prophecy," the romantic traveller tried to revive the dream of Baghdad.

The fantastic picture of the Orient had been a long time in the making. For a long time Americans remained dependent for their literary entertainment and taste on England. The novels of Sir Walter Scott were very popular with the public, and when Washington Irving wanted to establish himself as an American author he used the exotic Orient as one source of material for his works. *The Arabian Nights,* as the *National Union Catalogue* shows, was frequently printed in the United States during the nineteenth century, either complete or in selections.

In 1873, Harriet Beecher Stowe edited a collection of the nine works of fiction most popular with the American public. Significantly, two of these works were Oriental: *Vathec* and some tales from *The Arabian Nights.*[3] But even more important as an indication of the popularity of these works are Stowe's introductory remarks. "The boundaries of this present life proved too narrow and too poor for the wants of the soul." The story-teller, she explains, has been a popular person everywhere, and in Arabia he "holds enchanted crowds about him by the evening camp-fire."[4]

"Even in the strictest households," Stowe continues, there were always "Certain permitted works of fiction, which have taken such hold on the human heart that every member of the family who knew the English language read them, not as a matter of course, but as one of the choicest delights of life." Stowe continues: "We pity the child who has passed through the impressible, believing age of childhood...[and] who has not read 'Pilgrim's Progress,' 'Robinson Crusoe,' 'Aladin's Lamp,' and 'Sinbad the Sailor.'" These books of fiction are the best which could give "such a start to the imagination, such a powerful impulse to the soul."[5] Stowe finally makes special mention of the magic effect of *The Arabian Nights* on the tender minds of young readers:

> Not less wonderful was the blissful season when, as a homesick child in a lonely farm-house, all became things of naught. A golden cloud of vision encompassed us, and we walked among genii and fairies, enchanted palaces, jewelled trees, and valleys of diamonds. We became intimate friends with Sinbad the Sailor; we knew every jewel in the windows of Aladdin's palace, and became adepts in the arts of enchanting and disenchanting.[6]

Readings from *The Arabian Nights* and similar literature preconditioned the American traveler even before journeying to the Orient and definitely shaped his attitude to things Oriental. Such was the case of the writer of *Letters from Asia* who said:

> The pleasing reflections arising from having perused Eastern Tales, which had so often beguiled many of my leisure hours, causing the mind to dwell on scenes that can exist only in the imagination, almost led me to fancy that they would be realized in Asia—those beautiful compositions often executed, at our theatres, under the title of *"Turkish Music,"* tending to strengthen the illusion.[7]

Very often an American traveller in the Orient was reminded of *The Arabian Nights* by a scene in a street in Damascus or in a Bedouin encampment. Even the most austere Christians among the pilgrims could not fail to read into a scene their boyhood memories of those romantic tales. David Millard remarked upon one such occasion that "frequent reading of Eastern scenery had greatly interested me from the days of boyhood. Often had I contemplated the grandeur of objects along the great river Nile—the city of the Califs... Often, too, had I fancied the picturesque appearance of a caravan traveling over the deserts of Arabia."[8] And William Lynch referred on frequent occasions to the world of *The Arabian Nights*. Once in Damascus he was tempted to walk through the covered bazaars which were lined with cafes on both sides. Hundreds of little lamps were suspended above the pavements, "under which, on broad benches and low stools, squatted and sat, those visitors who preferred the sensual indulgence of coffee and chibouque; while those whose tastes were more intellectual, listened silently within, as one read or related some tale of the East. The scene brought the days of our boyhood back, and we remembered the Arabian Nights,—Haroun al Raschid, and his excursions in disguise."[9]

And another traveller, Sarah Haight, was torn between the "sacred associations" of the Orient and its charm. Reluctantly and gradually, while sailing by Constantinople, she was so awed by the novelty and charm of the scenery, that she said, "I could scarcely believe it to be reality; and I confess I could only think of scenes of the Arabian Nights, or fancy myself dreaming over a page of Hadji Baba."[10] Haight consciously drifted into the dreamlike world of Oriental romance, but not before warning her reader of the danger of indulging the dream and forgetting the reality. For the first time, she allowed these feelings to come over her "like angels' visits, few and far between," and she confessed that it was a pity "to shut one's heart against the sweet intrusion, but rather to court the ecstatic pleasure they induce, and by gentle embraces endeavor to arrest their fleeting course. The sad and sober realities of life are but too apt to claim dominion over us, and chase away those bright and pleasant dreams. Not caring to divest myself of the delightful emotions I experienced, I floated down the Bosphorus with Europe and Asia on either hand, having fresh in my mind the reminiscences of Greek and Persian struggles which these shores once beheld, of crusading armies with pike and pennon, lance and oriflamme."[11] On the plains of Acre, and while Haight brooded over the bloody wars which were fought there between the armies of the crescent and the cross, she remarked that "independent of all other associations connected with this interesting locality, it has been converted into classic ground by the 'Talisman'-ic pen of the immortal bard of Scotland. On every side I fancied I could recognize some spot so graphically described in his Tale of the Crusaders."[12]

Other travellers in the Orient did not have such reservations to spoil their romantic dream.[13] And some Americans—like George William Curtis, Bayard Taylor, Richard Stoddard, and William Alger—were ideal examples of the inveterate romantic dreamers who drifted down with complete abandon into the Oriental world of the imagination. Curtis, who indicated early in his narrative that he had been made aware of the vast difference between the Western world which he had just left and the Orient to which he looked forward, mused as he sat on his balcony in Cairo:

> I held a letter in my hand. It was dated several weeks before in Berlin, and its incredible tales of cold, thin twilight for day, of leafless trees, and of bitter and blasting winds, were like ice in the sherbet of the oriental scene my eyes were draining. Beneath the balcony was the rounded fullness of accacia groves, and, glancing along the lights

and shadows of the avenues, I marked the costumes whose pic-
turesqnuess is poetry....

I read another passage in the wintry letter I held, and remembered
Berlin, Europe, and the North, as spirits in paradise recall the glacial
limbo of the Inferno.[14]

Curtis had set the stage for his fancy to lead him. The rest is poetry:

> It is impossible not to feel here, as elsewhere in the East, that the
> national character and manners are influenced by the desert, as
> those of maritime races by the sea. This fateful repose, this strange
> stillness, this universal melancholy in men's aspects, and in their
> voices, as you note them in quiet conversation, or in the musical
> pathos of the muezzin's cry—the intent but composed eagerness
> with which they listen to the wild romances of the desert, for which
> even the donkey-boy pauses, and stands, leaning upon his arms
> across his beast, and following in imagination the fortunes of Aboo
> Seyed, or the richer romances of the Thousand and One Nights—all
> this is of the desert—this is its silence articulated in art and life.[15]

Oriental bazaars, Curtis said, are "so exciting to the imagination," and of
his experience in the bazaars of Cairo he recorded that

> The merchant, gravely courteous, reveals his treasures, little
> dreaming that they are inestimable to the eyes that contemplates
> them. His wares make poets of his customers, who are sure that the
> Eastern poets must have passed life in an endless round of shop-
> ping.[16]

Curtis serenely wore "away the day in this delightful traffic." The
whole experience was for him "a rhetorical tilt. We have talked, and
lived, and bought, poetry."[17]

The Orient of the Imagination

The imagination was at work very often in the daily experiences of
travelers to the Orient. Herman Melville's use of the imagination at the
harbor of Constantinople is another example of the way the traveller com-
pensated for any inability to see things clearly. On approaching the city,
the ship's captain decided that the fog was too thick to dock, so the ship
had to wait at a distance, thus thwarting Melville's hopes of seeing the
magnificent city for the first time. Melville's fancy, however, penetrated
the thick fog and supplied the details of what he could not see with his
bare eyes. "The fog," he said, "only lifted from about the skirts of the city,
which being built upon a promontory, left the crown of it hidden
wrapped in vapor....It was a coy disclosure, a kind of coquetting, leaving
room for imagination and heightening the scene. Constantinople, like her

Sultanas, was thus seen veiled in her 'Ashmack.' Magic effect of the lifting up of the fog disclosing such a city as Constantinople."[18] Through fog or darkness, the traveler was in an "Oriental" state of mind and was consequently willing to let loose his imagination to supply the details.

It was also on a night of "truly *Egyptian* darkness" that "an American lady" sat in an enclave in one of the Pyramids of Cairo watching an Arab encampment:

> ...In the distance, a few dying embers served to throw an uncertain light on sundry forms lying about, so like the human as easily to be mistaken for man or mummy. In the foreground were several campfires, around which were seated the half-naked Bedouins, silently and voraciously devouring some fragments of food.
>
> While gazing at these hideous creatures, my imagination transformed the hooded females who flitted by the blaze into Hecates and witches, the swarthy myrmidons into devils incarnate, and the half-consumed mummy-fuel into some victim they were tormenting. Now and then a shrill ejaculation from a female, or a coarse laugh from the savage-looking beings by the fire, with their lank bodies, shaved heads, sunken eyes, and endless mouths, gave the whole a more sepulchral and demoniacal appearance than anything I had ever seen before in real life, or in the mockhorrors of *Der Freischutz*.[19]

The Orient supplied the darkness, the fog, the narrow covered streets,[20] or the veil, and the imagination of the traveller took care of the rest. In Haight's imagination she was able to see the sharpest details, down to the shaven heads, the sunken eyes and the endless mouths—all through the Egyptian darkness!

The traveller was often faced with the forbidding walls which enclosed the dwellings of Damascus, or the veils which hid the visage of an Oriental beauty. The walls, as well as the veil, were but invitations, to peer through and discover what lay hidden beyond. Curtis expressed the situation in concrete but poetic terms: "Damascus is a dream of beauty as you approach it. But the secret charm of that beauty, when you are within the walls, is discovered only by penetrating deeper and farther into its exquisite courts, and gardens, and interiors, as you must strip away the veils and clumsy outer robes, to behold the beauty of the Circassian or Georgian slave."[21]

The veil of mystery which covered the face of the Orient was as baffling as it was inviting, especially when the face behind it was that of an Oriental female. American travellers were not deterred by that veil, but tried to see through it. When curiosity prompted a deeper searching for the face behind the veil, the result was quite characteristic of the workings of the imagination. The black American slave, David Dorr, was one of those who had encounters with veiled Oriental women. In Constantinople, Dorr was provoked by the dogs and veiled women. It was "a source of low spirits to a man from off the waters...to see women moving about like spirits or shadows, and cannot be seen."[22] But once he sat close to "one nymph-like lady [who] was so witty in her manner of talking to her black maid, and so full of good humor, that I knew she must have been pretty." They, Dorr and the veiled lady, looked at each other for one hour, Dorr fixing his gaze at her eyeslits and "would have given five pds to lift her veil; I knew she was pretty, her voice was so fluty, and her hands so delicate, and her feet so small, and her dress so gauzy; she was like an eel. I do not believe she had any bones in her."[23] For all intents and purposes, the veil was not there. Dorr's imagination showed him the essence of the Oriental beauty; so clear was he about this that he asked his guide to buy her for him, offering 25 dollars as her price, and an additional 25 dollars for the guide's services. But, alas, this was not to be; the damsel was not for sale, especially since he "was no Mohammedan."[24]

Even when the traveller did not see any women, his imagination convinced him that they were somewhere there. George Lloyd Stephens, while in Constantinople, noticed the absence of women in the streets, except that, "occasionally I caught a glimpse of a white veil or a pair of black eyes sparkling through the latticed bars of a window."[25] By a strange turn of the imagination George Jones, Chaplain of the *Delaware*, after journeying up the Nile to Cairo, said that of all that they had sailed past at night they "got but an imperfect view; soon after several other large white edifices came in sight, and our imaginations, excited by the glimpses of splendor which we had caught, by the time, and the country, worked each into a scene of eastern enchantment, and we pictured in each of them fair captives from other countries, gazing through the lattice and sighing for their distant native hills."[26] And the author of *Pencillings By the Way* almost got into trouble with the Turks on the Dardanelles because he wanted to look more closely at some women who were hidden from men's sight behind a latticed window.[27]

When the veil dropped and the traveler came literally face to face with Turkish beauty, he still could not erase from his fantasy a continued speculation of the Oriental woman in distress. At one point Stephens met a party of five men and three women and had a meal with them. The women were pretty and unveiled, and, what is more, they seemed quite happy with their "state of servitude....Notwithstanding their laughing faces, their mirth, and the kind treatment of the men, I could not divest myself of the idea that they were caged birds longing to be freed. I could not believe that a woman belonging to a Turk could be otherwise than unhappy."[28] Stephens tried his best "to procure from them a signal of distress; I did all that I could to get some sign to come to their rescue," but all was in vain. Stephens had to part ways with them without fulfilling his heroic feat, still convinced that he had left "two young and beautiful women, leading almost a savage life, whose personal graces would have made them ornaments in polished and refined society. Verily, said I, the Turks are not so bad after all; they have handsome wives, and a handsome wife comes next after chibouks and coffee."[29]

In Istanbul Willis had a still closer encounter with an unveiled female. This time the shock received by the American traveler was stronger, because it shattered many of his preconceptions, as well as the image he had drawn for himself of Oriental society. There was something about the behavior and looks of the lady which did not conform to those ideas derived from *The Arabian Nights* and other stories of the exotic Orient. Willis was at a shop in the Grand Bazaar of Constantinople when he became the object of curiosity for a certain female who had entered just as he was examining a turquoise ring. Then, wrote Willis,

> a woman plumped down upon the seat beside me, and fixed her great, black unwinking eyes upon my face, while an Abyssinian slave and a white woman, both apparently her dependants, stood respectfully at her back. A small turquoise ring (the favourite colour in Turkey) first attracted her attention. She took up my hand, and turned it over in her soft, fat fingers, and dropped it again without saying a word. I looked at my interpreter, but he seemed to think it nothing extraordinary, and I went on with my bargain. Presently my fine-eyed friend pulled me by the sleeve, and, as I leaned toward her, rubbed her forefinger very quickly over my cheek, looking at me intently all the while. I was a little disturbed with the lady's familiarity, and asked my Jew what she wanted. I found that my rubicund complexion was something uncommon among these dark-skinned Orientals, and she wished to satisfy herself that I was not painted![30]

The whole event was very unusual, if only because of the forward behavior of this woman who was thought to be veiled, coy, and a passive object of pleasure for the Turk. It is in situations like this that the traveler's Oriental dream was interrupted by something not so "Oriental." The traveler, we feel, was constantly looking for something to confirm the dream, or to aid the imagination. And seldom was he or she disappointed. Just after his encounter with the two beautiful unveiled women, Stephens had another, more Oriental experience; his narrative reveals the enjoyment of the dream and the fear of its interruption.

> If before I had occasionally any doubts or misgivings as to the reality of my situation; if sometimes it seemed to be merely a dream, that it

could not be that I was so far from home, wandering alone on the plains of Asia, with a guide whom I never saw till that morning, whose language I could not understand, and upon whose faith I could not rely;…the party which I met now was so marked in its character, so peculiar to an oriental country, and to an oriental country only, that it roused me from my waking dreams, fixed my wandering thoughts, and convinced me, beyond all peradventure, that I was indeed far from home, among a people 'whose thoughts are not as our thoughts, and whose ways are not as our ways;' in short, in a land where ladies are not the omnipotent creatures that they are with us.

This party was no other than the ladies of a harem. They were all dressed in white, with their white shawls wrapped around their faces, so that they effectually concealed every feature, and could bring to bear only the artillery of their eyes. I found this, however, to be very potent, as it left so much room for the imagination; and it was a very easy matter to make a Fatima of every one of them. They were all on horseback, not riding sidewise, but *otherwise*; though I observed, as before, that their saddles were so prepared that their delicate limbs were not subject to that extreme expansion required by the saddle of the rougher sex. They were escorted by a party of armed Turks, and followed by a man in Frank dress, who, as I after understood, was the physician of the harem. They were thirteen in number, just a baker's dozen, and belonged to a pacha who was making his annual tour of the different posts under his government, and had sent them on before to have the household matters all arranged upon his arrival....[31]

Playfully, Stephens wished that some change would take place in Western social habits, especially in the conventions of courting and the relations between men and women. Instead of having twelve men follow in the train of one lady, "what a goodly spectacle," it would be to see twelve fair maids follow one man! "Our system of education is radically wrong," he teased; in the Orient women are trained since childhood in such a manner as to "become as gentle, as docile, and as tractable as any domestic animal. I say again, there are many exceeding good points about the Turks."[32]

The Primitive Arab of the Desert

There was something about the primitive state of the Oriental, especially the Bedouin society, that appealed to American travelers. Perhaps the Arab of the desert was a reminder of the past innocence of America before the advent of political, cultural and industrial maturity. In a sense the Arab provided an outlet, an escape to the world of romance and

simplicity. The Bedouins were lovingly described by Curtis as sober creatures, whose "eyes are luminous and lambent, but it is a melancholy
light. They do not laugh. They move with easy dignity, and their habitual
expression is musing and introverted, as that of men whose minds are
stored with the solemn imagery of the desert."[33] Curtis rose to the height
of his romantic sympathy when he pictured the nobility of the primitive
dweller of the desert:

> The Bedoueen is mild and peaceable. He seems to you a dreamy
> savage. There is a softness and languor, almost an effeminacy of im-
> pression, the seal of the sun's child. He does not eat flesh—or rarely.
> He loves the white camel with a passion. He fights for defence, or for
> necessity; and the children of the Shereefs, or descendants of the
> Prophet, are sent into the desert to be made heroes. They remain
> there eight or ten years, rarely visiting their families.[34]

The character of the noble savage was an object of sympathetic admiration for many American travelers. Even the hardy William Lynch,
who was normally hostile to the local population, stopped at times to admire "the magnificent savage" whom he described as "the most handsome man."[35] And at one point he watched the Arabs cook and eat their
food offering quite a "pastoral" spectacle which evinced from him expressions of tender sympathy despite his physical revulsion.[36] Bayard
Taylor, more romantically inclined, saw in the Arabs of Spain an "elegant
and refined race" whose demise he sincerely regretted.[37] On other occasions he described the Bedouin as a passionate, brave warrior.[38]

The desert setting and the simple, primitive life of Muslims, especially
the Bedouins, made them particularly attractive to the traveler. In his
eyes they were the direct descendants of Ishmael, retaining all the wild
nature, purity and simplicity associated with that original prototype.
Sarah Haight saw this in the amazed reaction of the Arabs of Egypt when
she showed them a compass and explained that they could tell by it
where to turn their faces when they prayed.[39] And Millard spent a evening watching the Arabs reaction to an eclipse. When he tried to explain
to them that natural phenomenon in scientific terms, Millard realized
how removed they were from the civilized world.[40] The same innocence
was displayed by the Arab Sheikh who was taken by Henry Jessup on a
tour of the printing press which the missionaries established in Beirut,[41]
by the hundreds of Arabs who flocked to see the *U.S.S. Delaware* in every
Islamic port,[42] and by the group of Arabs from Muscat who visited the
United States of America in April, 1840, and were taken by train to upper
New York.[43] The responses of all of these groups to Western society, as
described by Americans, similarly revealed the Muslim as a primitive,
simple man, still in communion with nature.

The collective life and character of the Arabs, as observed by American travellers, confirmed this picture. The pages of travel accounts are punctuated with observations of the unsophisticated lifestyles of the natives. Millard, among others, gave a good deal of attention to the collective life of the Bedouin Arabs in their natural habitat, following their regular daily routine. To him they seemed like "the sons and daughters of Ishmael" whose life represented the fulfillment of prophecy.[44] And when Millard got to know the Bedouins well, he did not mind their company; in fact, he began to think they were "good fellows."[45] Close, prolonged association often resulted in a better understanding and appreciation of these primitive people and of their simple nature. Lynch's official *Report*, which he submitted to the Secretary of the Navy on his return from the Orient, praised the courage, hospitality, and the assistance of his native companions, saying that "the Arabs were our guides and messengers; they brought us food when nearly famished, and water when parched with thirst. They had thus been perfectly tractable, and I know not what we should have done without them."[46] On another occasion, Lynch recorded that he and his party were "saved by the Bedouin" when they were attacked by Christian pilgrims in the Holy Land.[47]

This collective image of the Muslems, Arabs or Bedouins was characteristic of the Western concept of these primitive and remote peoples. One of the most fascinating and idealistic descriptions of the Arabs appeared in Irving's analysis of the Prophet Muhammad's social and cultural setting. Describing the Arab of the desert, Irving said:

> The necessity of being always on the alert to defend his flocks and herds made the Arab of the desert familiar from his infancy with the exercise of arms. None could excel him in the use of the bow, the lance and the scimiter, and the adroit and graceful management of the horse. He was a predatory warrior also; for though at times he was engaged in the service of the merchant, furnishing him with camels and guides and drivers for the transportation of his merchandise, he was more apt to lay contributions on the caravan or plunder it outright in its toilful progress through the desert. All this he regarded as a legitimate exercise of arms; looking down upon the gainful sons of traffic as an inferior race, debased by sordid habits and pursuits.

> Though a restless and predatory warrior, he was generous and hospitable. He delighted in giving gifts; his door was always open to the wayfarer, with whom he was ready to share his last morsel, and his deadliest foe, having once broken bread with him, might repose securely beneath the inviolable sanctity of his tent.[48]

Ralph Waldo Emerson echoed this in an entry of his *Journal* where he said that "Arabia is the country of the horse—fleeter and gentler there than elsewhere; of the camel—happily named the ship of the desert...; of the Bedoween, who from the first year of recorded time up to this moment has preserved his savage Ishmaelitish independence, who is lavishly hospitable and a ferocious robber, nominally the subject, yet insults the town and plunders the caravans of the Turk. The Arab neither laughs nor weeps."[49]

Thomas Carlyle, with whom Emerson felt a great affinity, and who devoted one of his *hero* essays to the Prophet Muhammad, described the Arab in similar terms. "Left alone with the Universe; by night the great deep Heaven with its stars," he said, the Arabs acquired the habits of nobility, generosity, meditation and enthusiasm. They are, furthermore, taciturn, but eloquent, gifted when they do speak. Muhammad, having been born and raised in this setting, uttered words "as no other man's words. Direct from the Inner Fact of things;—he lives, and has to live, in daily communion with that." Such a man, said Carlyle, "is what we call an *original* man; he comes to us first hand." His words are "a fiery mass of Life cast-up from the great bosom of Nature herself. To *kindle* the world; the world's Maker had ordered it so."[50]

Naturalness, or daily communion with nature, was what Stephens also observed in the character of the Turk and consequently he thought of the Turkish community as the descendants of the Patriarch. The wandering tribes of the Turks, he said

> come out of the desert, and approach comparatively near the abodes of civilisation. They are a pastoral people; their riches are their flocks and herds; they lead a wandering life, free as the air they breathe; they have no local attachments; to-day they pitch their tents on the hill-side, to-morrow on the plain; and wherever they sit themselves down, all that they have on earth, wife, children and friends, are immediately around them. There is something primitive, almost patriarchial, in their appearance; indeed, it carried one back to a simple and perhaps a purer age, and you could almost realize that state of society when the patriarch sat in the door of his tent and called in and fed the passing traveller.[51]

It is quite significant that the aspect of Arabian life which impressed HenryThoreau, Henry David David Thoreau most of all was its simplicity, austerity, and closeness to nature. Thoreau himself held to the principles of simplicity; he ventured into nature "to front the essential things in life"; and he called on his fellow citizens to "simplify, simplify." It is for this reason that what he admired in the Prophet Muhammad was the fact that his mother ate dried meat. He also had words of praise for

some of the Arab leaders who were known for their austerity and un-
pretentiousness. Thoreau entered in his *Journal* of May 1, 1851:

> Khaled would have his weary soldiers vigilant still; apprehending
> a midnight sally from the enemy, 'Let no man sleep,' said he. 'We
> shall have rest enough after death.' Would such an exhortation be
> understood by Yankee soldiers?

> Omar answered the dying Abu Beker: 'O successor to the apostle
> of God! spare me from this burden. I have no need of the Caliphat.'
> 'But the Caliphat has need of you!' replied the dying Abu Beker.[52]

The Arab and the American Red Indian

A number of Americans traveling in the Orient were struck by the
similarity of the Bedouin to the American Indian. While Millard watched
an Arab feast he mused over the commonalities of the songs, dances and
food and those of "our Indians."[53] Lynch, on several occasions, made the
same remark, presenting comparisons of the lives,[54] warfare,[55] and
"walking gait of the two races." Lynch was invited by an Arab Sheikh to
visit his tents:

> What a patriarchal scene! Seated upon their mats and cushions
> within we looked out upon the fire, around which were gathered
> groups of this wild people, who continually reminded us of our In-
> dians. Then came their supper, consisting of a whole sheep, en-
> tombed in rice, which they pitched into without knives or forks, in
> the most amusing manner. There was an Arab bard withal, who
> twanged away upon his instrument, and sung or rather chanted
> mysterious Arabic poetry. He will never
>> 'Make a swan-like end,
>> Fading in music.'[56]

Interestingly enough, Lynch recorded that at the request of Dabney Carr,
the American Consul in Constantinople, he presented the Ottoman Sultan (in the name of the President of the United States) some "biographies
and prints, illustrative of the character and habits of our North American
Indians."[57]

Perhaps the most poetic of comparisons came from the pen of George
William Curtis, who sympathetically reconstructed the pattern of Oriental life, and its sad demise, along the lines of the romantic life and death
of the American Indian. He said:

> Strangely and slowly gathers in your mind the conviction that the
> last inhabitants of the oldest land have thus a mysterious sympathy
> of similarity with the aborigines of the youngest.

> For what more are these orientals than sumptuous savages?

As the Indian dwells in primeval forests...so lives the Oriental, the pet of natural luxury, in a golden air, at the foundations of History, and Art, and Religions; and yet the thinnest gleanings of stripped fields would surpass his harvest....

Nor does the Oriental fail in dignity and repose. His appearance satisfies your imagination no less than your eye. No other race has his beauty of countenance, and grace of costume; nowhere else is poetry the language of trade. His gravity becomes tragic, then, when it seems to you a vague consciousness of inadequacy to his position, the wise silence of a witless man.

—We have, then, a common mother, and the silence of the western is kin to that of the eastern sky.[58]

Simplicity of Muslem Devotions

Another aspect of Muslem life which impressed some American travellers in the Orient is the simplicity of Muslem worship and prayers. The call to prayer in a rough, unmusical human voice sounded unaffected to Western ears. Many travellers enjoyed recording in their accounts their own English versions of the Mu'azin's call to prayer. In his *Clarel*, Melville wrote a description of the morning prayer which he entitled "Under the Minaret":

But ere they might accost or meet,
From minaret in grounds hard by
Of Omar, the muezzin's cry—
Tardy, for Mustapha was old,
And age a laggard is—was rolled,
Announcing Islam's early house
Of orison...

...But, promptly, still
Each turban at that summons shrill,
Which should have called ere perfect light,
Bowed—hands on chest, or arms upright;
While over all those fields of loss
Where now the Crescent rides the Cross,
Sole at the marble mast-head stands
The Islam herald, his two hands
Upon the rail, and sightless eyes
Turned upward reverent towards the skies....[59]

Echoes of this call could be heard also in poems by William Alger and Bayard Taylor, among other American poets. One of Alger's poems entitled "The Call to Evening Prayer" describes the enchanting atmosphere of Oriental devotion, concluding with the beautiful, though inaccurately rendered, lines

'In the Prophet's name, God is God, and there is no other.' On roofs, in streets, alone, or close beside his brother, Each Moslem kneels, his forehead turned towards Mecca's shrine,
And all the world forgotten in one thought divine.[60]

The Islamic prayer was as exotic and baffling as the Arab's strange language and the mysterious face behind the veil. The traveler often tried to penetrate that mystery and to interpret, within the context of his Western thinking, the meaning behind the physical motions of Muslem prayer. Many travelers were not able to divest themselves of preconceptions; to them the prayers performed by Muslems were mere physical gesticulations without meaning. Haight made fun of the Arab sailors on the Nile who stopped everything when called to prayer, and described the Arab "swinging his arms, and prostrating and striking his forehead." The Arab, according to the American Lady, left his breakfast untasted in order to satisfy his conscience, but in reality he was "whetting his appetite by an extra half-hour's gymnastics."[61]

What the traveler saw in these motions was only their outward appearance and in many cases he insisted on the "seeming" aspect of the act of worship. A good example of the stubborn incredulity of travelers is the description of these prayers given by William Thomson, author of *The Land and the Book*. Muslem prayers, Thomson said, are a subject for a most "interesting study—a scene not witnessed in all places in such perfection." The men stood on an elevated terrace, having spread their cloaks and rugs, and, Thomson said,

They are Moslems preparing to say prayers—*perform* them rather, in this most public place, and in the midst of all this noise and confusion.

Let us stop and watch the ceremony as it goes on. The man next to us raises his open hands till the thumbs touch the ears, exclaiming aloud, *Allah hu-Akbar*—'God is great.'

Thomson continued to describe the seemingly calisthenic nature of the ceremonies in detail, and then observed that "they seem to be wholly absorbed in their devotions, and manifest a power of isolation and abstraction quite surprising."

That is the result of habit and education; small children imitate it to perfection. There is certainly an air of great solemnity in their mode of worship, and, when performed by a large assembly in the mosques, or by a detachment of soldiers in concert, guided in their genuflections by an imaum or dervish, who sings the service, it is quite impressive. I have seen it admirably enacted by moonlight on

the wild banks of the Orontes, in the plain of Hamath, and the scene
was something more than romantic. But, alas! it was by as villanous
a set of robbers as could be found even in that lawless region.[62]

Observing some Bedouins at prayer from a distance, another
American traveller, Charles Leland, thought they resembled sheep, especially when they "rise and put their heads together and begin ba'aing."[63]
William Lynch, on the other hand, stood amazed at the devotion of
Arabs at prayer. He also witnessed the early morning prayers and, like
other American travellers looking at the outward physical signs, exclaimed over the obvious pride of the worshippers in their religion and
in the "open avowal of" their faith.[64] Lynch also displayed a certain degree of incredulity, leading him to muse somewhat cynically that "if outward observance be indicative of inward piety, the Turk is the most
devout of human beings."[65] He suggested that the Turk was too primitive and unsophisticated, too "savage," to partake of the "inward piety"
of the civilized, i.e. Christian.

Significantly, however, certain more romantic travellers were impressed by the devotion and sincerity of a Muslim at prayer. A sympathetic description of these prayers came from the anonymous writer of
Letters from Asia, who said

> When a Turk once commences his prayer, nothing but the immedi-
> ate preservation of his life would tempt him to cease before he has
> ended it; and I frequently see them in the Baths, Bazars, Khans, and
> even in the streets, offering up their vows to the Deity with the ut-
> most devotion.[66]

Willis[67] and Taylor were also understanding, the latter showing his
recognition of the exotic but touching devotion of the Muslim in two
poems which he included in his *Poems of the Orient*. In "Arab Prayer" the
Arab character is presented in all its aspects: the romantic, the fierce, and
the devout.[68] Some of the verses follow:

ARAB PRAYER

"La illah il' Allah!" the muezzin's call
Comes from the minaret, slim and tall,
That looks o'er the distant city's wall.

"La illah il' Allah!" the Faithful heed,
With God and the Prophet this hour to plead:
Whose ear is open to hear their need.

The sun is sunken; no vapor mars
The path of his going with dusky bars.
The silent Desert awaits the stars.

> I bend the knee and I stretch the hand,
> I strike my orehead upon the sand,
> And I pray aloud, that He understand.
>
> Not for my father, for he is dead;
> Not in my wandering brother's stead—
> For myself alone I bow the head.
>
> God is Great, and God is Just:
> He knoweth the hearts of the children of dust—
> He is the Helper; in Him I trust.

In his poem, "The Sheikh," there emerges the character of a mystic as devout and profound as any Hindu or Buddhist. It is a translation from the Arabic:

> Not a single
> Star is twinkling
> Through the wilderness of cloud:
> On the mountain,
> In the darkness,
> Stands the Sheikh, and prays aloud:—
>
> God, who kindlest aspiration,
> Kindlest hope the heart within,—
> God, who promisest Thy mercy,
> Wiping out the debt of sin,—
> God, protect me, in the darkness,
> When the awful thunders roll:
> Evil walks the world unsleeping,
> Evil sleeps within my soul
>
> Keep my mind from every impulse
> Which from Thee may turn aside;
> Keep my heart from every passion
> By Thy breath unsanctified....

The remaining verses also call upon God to send his saving spirit to one who is impervious to his compassionate presence.[69]

George Lloyd Stephens, a keen observer and a traveler who delighted in mixing with the native population, enjoying their Turkish baths, sleeping in their hostels and smoking their chibouqs, also stood frequently at the entrances of the mosques and observed closely how the Muslems performed their prayers. He tried to penetrate the world of the "seeming," and of outward gestures, probing instead the inner meaning of Muslim devotions. He admired what he saw. In Foggi once he heard the mu'ezzin

> call all good Mussulmans to prayer. The door opens toward Mecca, and a little before dark the muezzin comes out, and, leaning over the

railing with his face toward the tomb of the Prophet, in a voice, every tone of which fell distinctly upon my ear, made that solemn call which, from the time of Mohammed, has been addressed five times a day from the tops of the minarets to the sons of the faithful. 'Allah! Allah! God is God, and Mohammed is his prophet. To prayer! to prayer!'[70]

Thomson's obvious rejection of the prayers as meaningless "outward' manifestations, as well as Stephen's guarded admiration of the intense devotion of Muslims, are both immediate reactions to their physical appearance and experience. Both are colored by preconditioned beliefs and attitudes towards Muslims which were shared by most Americans of the nineteenth century. Thomson saw physical phenomena—the outward signs—as the only reality: that which looked sincere was not always so in fact. The only quality which Thomson was able to appreciate, even remotely, in the religious performance was its romanticism. Stephens, in turn, recognized some genuine, albeit romantic, devotion in the performance, all the more unbelievable to him because of the "polluted fountain" of Islam.

Thus it is obvious that the American traveller who went to the Orient hoping to partake of exotic experiences, and to indulge in the ecstatic romance of *The Arabian Nights,* was able to achieve some degree of satisfaction merely by observing the Oriental at prayer. This led him to believe he also took part in the imaginative fulfillment of the dream of Baghdad.

CONCLUSION
American Orientalism

"The East had given its message to the World, and must retire."

Moncure Conway,
"East and West," 1859

The profundity, as well as the breadth of the American emotional and intellectual attachment to an Oriental perspective during the first three centuries of the European presence in North America, is greater than commonly supposed. This attachment, which is still the basis for America's involvement in the Orient, was in the making from the founding of the colony at Plymouth; it became a mature constituency by the end of the Civil War. And although the establishment of the American Oriental Society in 1842 marked the beginning of a more active stage in the development of American Orientalism, there had been a number of Orientalist activities throughout the history of the American people.

When the early Puritan colonies were founded, the immigrants based their conduct in life on the firm belief that they occupied a special position in a Providential plan. They, as the "chosen", were heirs to a covenantal promise and were entrusted with the task of rebuilding the Kingdom of God, the "little American Israel." This Kingdom became the symbol of their spiritual and temporal labors in the New World. The Puritans strove, collectively, to bring about the New Jerusalem, the ultimate city of Protestant Christianity.

When America became an independent political state, its citizens continued to use the same symbol to refer to their ideal community. To make their argument more poignant, they added comparisons with the Travellers, Ameri Europe and with "corruption" in the "Romish" church. The combination and interaction of these factors in America thinking, together with later developments on the American scene during the nineteenth century, gave a new direction to the energy of the American people towards the Orient, and the Holy Land in particular. During that period, Islam was introduced to the American nation both as a rival force and as an alien religion. Furthermore, America witnessed a surge of religious enthusiasm marked by the ascendancy of adventist and millenarian churches and expectations. The missionary movement also gained momentum, and American men and women went out to "spread the word of God" throughout the world, especially in the Orient.

In addition, during the nineteenth century, the American nation was operating within the continent on the principle of Manifest Destiny, which in practical political terms meant expansion to the West and annexation of territories. It was then that the symbolic Kingdom of God was transferred into a concrete endeavor in the Holy Land, and thus the Orient became for many Americans the field of action for both the political and religious sides of Manifest Destiny.

Many Americans strove to reach this sacred goal in obedience to the will of God. This group included missionaries, colonizers, diplomats, travellers, researchers, scholars and many others. Some Americans, enchanted by the world of the *Arabian Nights,* tried to realize the Dream of Baghdad, or, more often, bemoaned the passing away of that world. In either case, the Orient was a field of labor open to Americans. Back home, hundreds of books and articles were written on the Orient and on Islam and the Prophet Muhammad, a definite sign of continued interest in the affairs of the region. This is the essence of the American Orientalist dialogue which was so alive in the nineteenth century, and which continues to be a major American concern today.

Orientalism was characterized by a continuing involvement with the East, often amounting to personal identification with the region and an assertion of ownership. And the Orientalist's argument, his claim to the region, was in part seen as the will of God that he should "stand as sure in Asia as in America." This was the divine order which Eli Smith and many religious as well as lay Americans obeyed. It was their expression of Manifest Destiny.

The Orientalist political claim was just as well documented as that of the missionary and the laborer in the cause of Zion. David Porter and Dabney Carr, Consuls in the Ottoman domains, William Lynch, leader of an official expedition to the Holy Land, Richard Haight, traveller in the Orient, and scores of other Americans based their claim to proselytize and incite "revolt" on the American Constitution which guaranteed the right of free expression, political and religious, to every American. The American flag was to be a beacon of light in a land engulfed in darkness, and American naval forces were to aid in spreading that light if need be. The call to "stand on the Heights of Calvary and proclaim to the followers of the Pseudo-Prophet" was as much a political Orientalist expression as it was that of a missionary.

Indeed, there was a constant overlapping of religious, political, and purely humanistic idiom in the Orientalist dialogue. The land was "sitting in darkness," "benighted," under despotic rulers; the people were "degraded," "enslaved," "backward" ("primitive" in more sympathetic statements). "We," said the American benefactors, will "possess," "occupy," and "reclaim" the land; "we" will teach them the principles of American education and politics. To decide the future of the Orient and the fate of the Orientals was not only a privilege, but an obligation both for the missionary and the layman. No national boundaries, no international treaties, and no principles of self-determination were relevant in the case of the Orient and the Oriental. The Orient was an object to be dealt with; the Oriental a passive, mute recipient of the treatment. The benign death sentence by Moncure Conway, "the East has given its message to the world and must retire," and the mournful death announcement by George William Curtis are expressions of this Orientalist dialogue. But there were other statements, less sympathetic and more authoritarian. The practice of "carving up" the Orient, restructuring and dividing it among the European powers, was a common exercise. The Orientalist also was to decide whether Orientals were capable of being converted, or, better still, to be "removed," and a better race to be gathered in the land.

There were overtones of racial superiority and prejudice in many of the statements made by Orientalists. Jessup and Lynch provide two obvious examples, but they were representatives of the general attitude of Americans. To "Anglo-Saxonize" and to "Americanize" the Orient meant to raise it from a state of abject ignorance and heathenism.

American Orientalism has developed in the present century into a full-grown independent idiom whose relations with its European counterparts are not those of a satellite. Its activities now take many directions: intellectual, academic, political, religious, and others. The Middle East Studies Association of America is the umbrella organization of many academic institutions which have made great strides in the various fields of Orientalist studies. These modern academic interests in the Orient were preceded on a limited scale in works published as early as the beginning of the nineteenth century in the *Transactions of the American Philosophical Society*, the *Journal of the American Oriental Society*, the *Proceedings of the American Numismatic Society*, the *North American Review*, the *Methodist Review*, and other learned journals. There were also other individual effort such as those by William Thomson, Edward Robinson, William Lynch, to name only a few. It is evident that many popular journals and periodicals published (almost on a daily basis) articles of Orientalist concerns in order to satisfy the increasing public interest in the subject.

It is evident that American political and religious involvement in the affairs of the Orient is still part of the Orientalist dialogue and has increased tremendously during the last fifty years. Only a naive journalist, a highly specialized academician, or a politician could venture to analyze the complicated nature of the factors—social and political—which have brought about these developments. In any case, these factors fall outside the scope of the present work. Modern considerations notwithstanding, one has to turn a blind eye to America's cultural history not to see in the contemporary situation the continuation of certain aspects of the American Orientalist dialogue described in the previous chapters. A few examples will illustrate this.

The recent propelling to an American presidential race of an Evangelical preacher who openly supported Israel was significant since it came at a crucial time in the Arab-Israeli dilemma. The support given to Israel by the American evangelical churches (Jerry Falwell's is an obvious example) and by certain political figures are reminders of American zeal in the cause of Zion in the nineteenth century. Central to this, of course, is the application of fundamentalist thinking which equates the language of scriptural prophecies with modern political developments.

Another instance of the existence of an American Orientalist dialogue is the unwavering support by successive American administrations of Israeli violations of international conventions on human rights and of International Law. The constant use of the veto in the Security Council to block any censure of Israeli atrocities, including crushing the bones of young Arabs, demolishing homes, and displacing the Arab population, all show a persistence of Zionist dominance in the American Oriental dialogue as well as callousness to the plight of the Arab victims. America's refusal to grant the Palestinians the right to self-determination and free expression is also reminiscent of the age-old practice or representing the Arab as a silent recipient of Western mistreatment. In effect, the efforts of the nineteenth-century American political planner and religious enthusiast to "remove" the inhabitants—"occupiers"—of the land and replace then with a "better race" are still at work today. The all-but-universal American public support of Israeli policy and practices, and heartless disregard of the plight of over two million Palestinian Arabs, flies in the face of traditional American concern for human rights and sense of justice. The stereotyping and stigmatizing of the Arab and Muslim in the media, in school text books, and in popular literature, about Islam have their precedents in nineteenth century America. References of this type to other religions, even if less sinister, would have been a *casus belli* and would have called forth claims of anti-Semitism.

The author of "Orientalism" in the June, 1853 edition of the *Knickerbocker* summed up the many variations of the American Orientalist dialogue by describing the romantic world of the *Arabian Nights*, the "heathenism of the Mahometan imposture," the rebuilding of New Jerusalem, and the plan to elevate the Orient to a civilized state. "God," he said,

> gives the intelligent and civilized *power*, not to prey upon the weaknesses of his creatures, but to elevate them in the scale of being, to rescue from eternal anarchy, stagnation, and despotism, the magnificent domains of the East. By the same right, American may unfurl the stripes and stars in the harbor of Jeddo, and open Japan to the world. By the same right, western powers may divide the Mohametan world, displace sterility with cultivation, ignorance with refinement, and rapine with protection, but not the converse.

The destiny of the Orient was perceived to be firmly locked to that of America and the part to be played by the United States was drawn by the hand of God. The Orient, like the American West, seemed "to have been reserved by Providence to be the meeting-place of the Anglo Saxon on his eastern and western path of empire." As for the argument for annexation, here again there was no need for justification. Annexation, with the seal of prophecy, is its own justification. "Our nation has increased six millions since the last census, and has annexed within a few years a territory nine times the size of France...and no power but the Almighty conceivably prevent the Democratic element of American from making its impress upon the Orient." And how could the Almighty conceivably prevent such a destiny when everything tended to point toward the fact that "the prophecy of Isaiah is approaching fulfillment in the East"?

This is American Orientalism of mid-nineteenth century. It is a fabric, a mosaic, of many threads and pieces, with an intense involvement in the Orient as the principal motif. It includes religious zeal to fulfill the vision of Zion, nostalgic yearning for the Dream of Baghdad, continual official interest in the internal affairs of the Orient, the increasing popularity of travel in Orient, missionary concern for the "lost" Muslim souls, and the urgency of the task of spreading the benefits of the American experience. These, and more, are given added poignancy, and made peculiarly American, by the Puritan rhetoric of the Jeremiad which distinguished the American experience from the beginning.

ENDNOTES

Introductory Essay

1. Lanigan probably knew Edward Lear's the "Akoond of Swat," printed in his *Laughable Lyrics* (1877). Actually, the long obituary in London Times, 22 January 1878, p. 4, gave much political and historical detail. The bare announcement ran on 18 January.

2. See the entry under Lanigan in Alan Gribben, *Mark Twain's Library: A Reconstruction* (Boston: G. K. Hall, 1980), 1:396–97.

3. Petroleum Vesuvius Nasby, *The Morals of Abou Ben Adhem* (Boston: Lee and Shepard, 1875), 14.

4. Horace Perry Jones, "Southern Editorial Humor and The Crimean War," *Studies in American Humor*, NS 2 (Winter 1983–84), 171–84.

5. For a definitive survey, see Waldemar Zacharasiewicz, "National Stereotypes in Literature in the English Language," *Yearbook of Research in English and American Literature*, 1 (1982), 75–120. Mahadev L. Apte, *Humor and Laughter: An Anthropological Approach* (Ithaca, N.Y.: Cornell University Press, 1984), 113–14, sums up the cross-cultural research into the humorous, denigrating use of ethnic stereotypes.

6. George William Curtis, Nile Notes of a Howadji (New York: Harper, 1851), 43–44.

7. Page Smith, *The Rise of Industrial America* (New York: McGraw-Hill, 1984), 554.

8. See Richard D. Mosier, *Making the American Mind: Social and Moral Ideas in the McGuffey Readers* (New York: King's Crown Press, 1947), 164–65. The Readers invariably glorified missionaries (90–91).

9. C. Eric Lincoln, *Race Religion, and the Continuing American Dilemma* (New York: Hill and Wang, 1984), 131–32.

10. *Mark Twain's Travels with Mr. Brown*, ed. Franklin Walker and G. Ezra Dane (New York: Russell and Russell, 1971), 85–86.

11. *The Innocents Abroad* was based upon newspaper letters now collected in *Traveling with the Innocents Abroad*, ed. Daniel M. McKeithan (Norman: University of Oklahoma Press, 1958). Though significant, the revisions are not crucial here. Dewey Ganzel, *Mark Twain Abroad: The Cruise of the "Quaker City"* (Chicago: University of Chicago Press, 1968), is helpful. More generally, see Franklin Walker, *Irreverent Pilgrims: Melville, Browne, and Mark Twain in the Holy Land* (Seattle: University of Washington Press, 1974).

12. The letters, which ran in the *New York Herald* on 1, 4, 9, 11 and 19 July 1873, were reprinted in *Europe and Elsewhere*, ed. Albert Bigelow Paine (New York: Harper, 1923). For Twain's later comment, see Everett Emerson, *The Authentic Mark Twain: A Literary Biography of Samuel L. Clemens* (Philadelphia: University of Pennsylvania Press, 1984), 76.

13. Now available in *Mark Twain's Satires and Burlesques*, ed. Franklin R. Rogers (Berkeley: University of California Press, 1967). Incidentally, Huck Finn, on Tom Sawyer's advice, tries to summon up "genies" by rubbing an "old tin lamp" Of course, the harem and its rumored customs lurked behind "1,002[d] Arabian Night." In "Autobiography of a Damned Fool" (1877), the American speaker, having converted to the "religion of Mahomet," saw a "plain religious duty, now, that I should have a harem" and issued invitations to several spinsters—*Twain's Satires and Burlesques*, 145–46.

14. For identification of the five tales, see "Explanatory Notes" in *The Adventures of Tom Sawyer; Tom Sawyer Abroad; Tom Sawyer, Detective*, ed. John C. Gerber, Paul Baender, and Terry Firkins (Berkeley: University of California Press, 1980).

15. *Mark Twain's Rubaiyat*, Introduction by Alan Gribben (Austin, Texas; Santa Barbara, Calif.: Jenkins Publishing Co., 1983).

16. *Christian Science* (New York: Harper, 1907), 96.

Preface and Acknowledgments

1. Edward W. Said, *Orientalism* (New York: Random House, 1978), 3.
2. Ibid., 73.

Chapter One

1. Sydney E. Ahlstrom, "Theology in America." In Smith and Jamison (eds.), *Religion in American Life*. (Princeton, NJ, 1961) I:236.

2. For further information on the subject see the works by Vernon Parrington, Charles Feidelson, H. Richard Niebuhr and Perry Miller.

3. The concepts of manifest divine favor and "Manifest Destiny" are important factors which often influenced American political and diplomatic thought, dealings with Indians, and relations with other nations. This theme is more fully explored in the treatment of the American missionary tendencies in Chapter V of this volume.

4. John Cotton, "God's Promise to his Plantation," *Old South Leaflets* III(53):title page.

5. Ibid., 5.

6. Cotton Mather, *Magnalia Christi Americana*. (Hartford, 1855), I:69.

7. John Winthrop, "Conclusions," *Old South Leaflets* II(50):10.

8. Roger Williams, "Letters of Roger Williams to Winthrop," *Old South Leaflets* III(54):4.

9. Increase Mather, "Prevalency of Prayer," *Early History of New England* (Albany, NY, 1864), 255.

10. Cotton Mather, *Magnalia Christi Americana*, I:131.

11. George Washington, "Washington's Addresses to the Churches," *Old South Leaflets* III(56):15.

12. Perry Miller, "From the Covenant to the Revival." In Smith and Jamison, (eds.) I:325.

13. Ahlstrom, Ibid., 240–41.

14. Ibid., 241.

15. Cotton Mather, *Magnalia Christi Americana*, I:71.

16. Ibid., 71–73.

17. Ibid., I:10–12, 28.

18. Samuel Worcester, *Two Discourses*. (Salem, 1805), 5–6.

19. Ibid., 8.

20. Ibid., 40.

21. See also the theme of life as a spiritual journey from captivity in sin to freedom in faith, as in Thomas Carleton's *The Captives' Complaint* (1668) and Thomas Bayle's *A Relation of a Mans Return and His Travails Out of a Long and Sore Captivitie* . . . [London? 1677]. *Zyons Travellers* (1677). Here again freedom and true belief are represented by the symbolic Holy Land. For these and other references on this theme, see Marcia J. Pankake, *Americans Abroad*. (Unpublished Ph.D. dissertation, 1975), 9–12.

22. As quoted by Vernon L. Parrington, "The Puritan Divines, 1620–1720," *Cambridge History of American Literature*, I:41.

23. William Bradford, "History of Plymouth Plantation," *Old South Leaflets*, 7(153):12–13.

24. Ibid., 13–14.

25. Cotton Mather, *Magnalia Christi Americana*, I:60.

26. Vernon L. Parrington, "The Puritan Divines," 32.

27. As quoted by H. Richard Niebuhr, *The Kingdom of God in America*, 48.

28. Ibid., xii.

29. Ibid, 48.

30. Stephen Olin, *The Works*. I:61.

31. Ibid., 62.

32. John Winthrop, "Conclusions," 4.

33. Stephen Olin, *The Works*. I:114–15.

34. John Winthrop, "Conclusions," 1.

35. Stephen Olin, *The Works*. I:62.

36. Frederick Merk, *Manifest Destiny and Mission* (New York, 1963), 3.

37. "The U. S. A Commissioned Missionary Nation," *The American Theological Review*, I (January 1859): 166–67.

Chapter Two

1. Joel Barlow, *The Works*. (Gainesville, Fla., 1970), I:527.

2. William Ray, *Poems*. (Auburn, 1821), 56.

3. Timothy Dwight, *The Major Poems*. (Gainesville, Fla., 1969), 511.

4. Ezra Stiles, *The United States Elevated to Glory and Honor*, in John Wingate Thornton, *The Pulpit of the American Revolution* (Boston, 1860), 440. Stiles, President of Yale College, stated that he chose this text from Deuteronomy "as introductory to a discourse upon the political welfare of God's American Israel, and as allusively prophetic of the future prosperity and splendor of the United States" (Thornton, 473).

5. David Humphreys, quoted by James A. Field, *America and the Mediterranean World 1776–1882* (Princeton, 1969), 14. That the establishment of the new state was part of the Providential plan can be seen in many sermons and political speeches, as in George Duffield's *"Sermon Preached in the Third Presbyterian Church of Philadelphia:" December 11, 1783*. The day of Independence, for Duffield, was "a day whose evening shall not terminate in night; but introduce that joyful period, when the outcasts of Israel, and the dispersed of Judah, shall be restored; and with them, the fulness of the Gentile world shall flow to the standard of redeeming love" (16–18).

6. Joel Barlow, *Works*. I:4.

7. Ibid., 9.

8. William Ray, *Poems*, 20–21.

9. Thus when he spoke of the Constitution of the new nation, John Adams said that American's "have now the best opportunity and the greatest trust in their hands that Providence ever committed to so small a number since the transgression of the first pair." *A Defence of the Constitutions of Government of the United States of America*. (London, 1987).

10. Joel Barlow, *Works*. I:527.

11. Perry Miller, "From Covenant to Revival." In Smith and Jamison (eds.), I:332.

12. Quoted by Edward M. Burns, *The American Idea of Mission* (New Brunswick, N.J., 1957), 141.

13. *New York Times*, March 29, 1955.

14. *The Constitution of the American Bible Society* (New York, 1816), 13. The same tendency to see the hand of Providence in the political events and in Independence led Samuel West to say in 1776 "that Providence has designed this continent to be the asylum of liberty and true religion; for can we suppose that the god who created us free agents, and designed that we should glorify and serve him in this world that we might enjoy him forever hereafter, will suffer liberty and true religion to be banished from off the face of the earth?" (Thornton, 311). See also American Board of Commissioners for Foreign Missions (ABCFM), 7th *Annual Report*, 8–9, 13; and Moses Stuart, 26–27.

15. Enoch, Lincoln, "An Oration, Pronounced at Worcester in Commemoration of American Independence, July 4th, 1812" (Worcester, Mass., 1812), 14.

16. Sydney E. Ahlstrom, I:241.

17. Quoted by Alice Felt Tyler, *Freedom's Ferment* (Minneapolis, 1944), 1.

18. "The United States: A Commissioned Missionary Nation," *American Theological Review*, I (1859): 153–54.

19. Ibid., 154.

20. Governor Morris, as quoted by Burns, 61–62.

21. Hamilton, Alexander, *The Works*. (New York, 1850–1851), VII:152–53.

22. "The United States: A Commissioned Missionary Nation," 154.

23. Ibid.

24. Ibid., 155.

25. Joel Barlow, *Works*. I:526–27.

26. Ibid., I:12.

27. Timothy Dwight, "Greenfield Hill," *The Major Poems*, 516.

28. H. Richard Niebuhr, *The Kingdom of God in America* (New York, 1937), 178–79.

29. "The United States: A Commissioned Missionary Nation," 153.

30. Ibid., 156.

31. Ibid., 156–57.

32. William Swain, *Philadelphia Public Ledger* (October 25, 1847).

33. Ezra Stiles, *The United States Elevated*, 18.

34. Joel Barlow, *Works*. II:348.

35. See H. Richard Niebuhr, 123 ff.

36. William Ray, 54, 57.

37. Sydney E. Ahlstrom, 332.

38. David F. Dorr, *A Colored Man Round the World*. (Cleveland, 1858), 12.

39. William F. Lynch, *Narrative* (Philadelphia, 1853), 126.

40. Ibid., 119.

41. Joel Barlow, *Works*. I:527.

42. Thomas Paine, *Common Sense*, as quoted by David Burner, et al., *The American People* (St. James, NY, 1980), 72.

43. Joel Barlow, *Works*. I:4. See also p. 532.

44. Timothy Dwight, *The Major Poems*, 500.

45. Ibid., 511.

Chapter 3

1. L. K. Washburn, "Who are Christians," *The Index* (Oct. 31, 1878), 519.

2. Ibid.

3. Theodore Dwight, "Condition and Character of Negroes in Africa," *Methodist Quarterly Review*, XLVI (Jan. 1864), 77.

4. Ibid., 7. Description of the Christian world as "civilized" and the non-Christian world as "uncivilized" was a prevalent tendency among most European and American writers. "The others," so to speak, are this way categorized and distinguished from "us."

5. Ibid., 7.

6. Ibid., 78. Many other writers recognized the unifying influence of Islam. See, for example, Charles Forster, *Mohammetanism Unveiled*: 2 vols. (London, 1829), I:7; and Ralph Waldo Emerson, *Journals*, I:60, Jan. 12, 1822.

7. Ibid., 78–79.

8. Ibid., 79.

9. "Catalogue of the books belonging to Salem Athenaeum, with the bylaws" (Salem, Mass., 1811), in *Early American Pamphlets, Massachusetts*, Vol. 26, 1785–1819.

10. See Harriet Silvester Topley, *Salem Imprints, 1768–1825* (Salem, Mass., 1927), 230–240. Other useful references which have been consulted on the subject include: Thomas G. Wright, *Literary Culture in New England, 1620–1730* (New Haven, 1920); Samuel E. Morison, *Harvard College in the Seventeenth Century* (Cambridge, Mass., 1930); *A Catalogue of the Library of Yale College* (New Haven, 1743); *A Catalog of Curious and Valuable Books Belonging to the Late Reverend and Learned Mr. Ebenezer Pemberton* (Boston, 1717).

11. Alexander Ross' translation of *The Koran* was included in first American edition issued as *The Koran: Commonly Called Alcaron of Mahomet* (Springfield, Mass., 1806). George Sale, *The Koran: Commonly Called the Alcoran of Mahomet* (London: 1850)

12. Ross, "The Translator to the Christian Reader." In Knolle, *Turkish History*, II:a2.

13. Sale, "To the Reader," *The Koran*, v–vi.

14. Some works on the subject which are frequently mentioned in American writings include Ockley's *History of the Saracens*, which included a biography of the Prophet Muhammed; Gibbon's *The Decline and Fall of the Roman Empire*, Boulainvilliers' *Life of Mahomet*, Carlyle's *On Heroes and Hero Worship*, "The Hero As Prophet, Knolles, *The Turkish History* and Sale's translation of *The Koran*.

15. Washington Irving, *Mahomet and His Successors* (New York, 1849), 15.

16. Ibid., 16

17. George Bush, *The Life of Mohammed* (New York, 1847), 5.

18. Ibid.

19. Ibid., 5–6

20. Ross. In Knolle, *Turkish History*, II:a2.

21. Ibid.

22. Ibid.

23. Sale, "To the Reader," *The Koran*, v.

24. Ibid.

25. Ibid.

26. Ralph Waldo Emerson, "Heroism," *The Collected Works*, II:147. (Cambridge, Mass., 1971-).

27. [Anonymous Biographer], *The Life of Mahomet; or, the History of that Imposture*, 2nd American ed. (New York, 1813), ii. Further references to this work will be to the anonymous biographer.

28. Ibid., iii–iv.

29. Ibid., iv.

30. Ibid., v.

31. Ibid., v.

32. Bush, 6.

33. John Hayward, *Book of Religions* (Boston, 1843), 220.

34. Ibid., 223.

35. Hannah Adams, *Dictionary of All Religions and Religious Denominations* (Boston, 1817), 156.

36. Hayward, 221.

37. [Anonymous Biographer], 9.

38. Ibid., 8–9.

39. Ibid., 9.

40. Ibid.

41. Ibid., 11.

42. Ibid., 14.

43. Ibid., 16–17.

44. Adams, 157; see also Alexander Ross's statement on this subject, "The Translator to the Christian Reader." In Knolle, II, ii.

45. Hayward, 226–27.

46. "Our Arabian Visitors," *New York Morning Herald*, August 5, 1840.

47. Ross, II:a2.

48. Bush, 234–40.

49. Adams, 156.

50. Ibid., 158.

51. Ibid., 161. See also Jessup's *Mohammedan Missionary Problem*, 27–28.

52. Adams, 157.

53. Ibid., 157–58.

54. Josiah Brewer, *A Residence at Constantinople* (New Haven, Conn., 1830), 378. Brewer (p. 327) says that Muhammad had no knowledge of the Christian Scriptures.

55. Ross, II:1.

56. [Anonymous Biographer], 28.

57. See, for example, Ross, II:1.

58. Hayward, 220.

59. See [Anonymous Biographer], 39, and Ross, II:1.

60. Jessup, *The Mohammadan Missionary Problem*, 62–63.

61. Ibid., 65.

62. Edward Forster, *Mohammedanism Unveiled*. (London, 1829), I:vi.

63. Ibid., viii.

64. Ibid., 19–21.

65. Ibid., 21.

66. Adams, 157. Jessup agrees with Adams on both points, but Sale and Bush are more reserved. See also Emerson's note in his journal quoting Muhammad as saying: "Paradise is under the Shadow of the Swords." *Journals*, VI:186. The same quotation is used by Emerson at the beginning of his essay on Heroism.

67. Hayward, 229.

68. Bush, 12. Note also that Bush (19) recognizes that "an enlightened Christian estimate of the prophet of Arabia and his religion is, we believe, seldom formed, simply because the subject has seldom been so presented as to afford the means of such an estimate."

69. Ibid., 49–50.

70. Ibid., 12.

71. Ibid., 54.

72. Jessup, *The Mohammedan Missionary Problem*, 13.

73. Ibid., 13.

74. Ibid., 17.

75. Ibid., 13–14.

76. Ibid., 14–15.

77. Nicholas De Cusa, *Cribratio Alcorani*, (Rome, 1461–1462.) For a good presentation of De Cusa's career and ideas, see Nicholas Rescher, *Studies in Arabic Philosophy*, (Pittsburgh, 1966).

78. Jessup, *The Setting of the Crescent*, 5.

79. Sale, "To the Reader," *The Koran*, x.

80. Ross, II:xi.

81. Jessup, *The Setting of the Crescent*.

82. Ibid., 7.

83. Ibid.

84. Ibid., 11.

85. For opinions of Melville, J.V.C. Smith and others, see Chapter V of this volume.

86. *Letters from Asia*, (New York, 1819), 19.

87. Jessup, *The Setting of the Crescent*, 5.

88. Ibid.

89. Ibid.

90. Ibid., 12–13. See also Sale, iv, and Ross, II:a2, for similar views. These writers also did not fear for a good Christian to be influenced by reading the Quran. On the contrary, such reading would serve as "tonic to the Christian" (Ross's "antidote"), as proof of the universal application of the gospel, and as a means to show the beauty of Christianity.

91. Ibid., 20. See also Lynch, 50, and Haight, I:100–102 on formal but, to them, meaningless Islamic devotions.

92. Jessup, *The Mohammedan Missionary Problem*, 28–29.

93. Jessup, *The Setting of the Crescent*, 20–21.

94. Ibid., 21. Jessup elaborates on this point in *The Mohammadan Missionary Problem*, 51, by listing all the "mis-representations and perversions" by Islam of the person and teachings of Christ. There a semblance of a dialogue is carried out, again Jessup speaking for both sides.

95. Ibid. In *The Mohammadan Missionary Problem*, 137–38, Jessup deals with the absence of an equivalent of the idea of atonement by salvation in Islam. Muslems work for atonement by outward signs of devotion and personal effort. What they need is to "feel the enormity of sin against a just and holy God." See also *The Setting of the Crescent*, 145–147.

96. Jessup, *The Setting of the Crescent*, 131.

97. Jessup, *The Mohammedan Missionary Problem*, Preface, p. 9.

98. Ibid., 23–24.

99. Ibid., 27–28.

100. Ibid., 30. See also Jessup's "*Sermon*" on this comparison.

101. Ibid., 43. 26–27, 34.

102. Ibid., 55.

103. Ibid., 47.

104. Ibid.

105. Ibid., 49.

106. Ibid., 59.

107. Ibid., 61–62.

108. Ibid., 70.

109. Ibid., 73.

110. Ibid., 75.

111. Ibid., 75. Other Christian writes on Islam had different views of this feature. See Chapter VIII of this volume.

112. Royal Tyler, *The Algerine Captive*. (London, 1802), II:129–30.

113. Ibid., 131.

114. Ibid.

115. Ibid., 130.

116. Ibid., 130–31.

117. Ibid., 131–32.

118. Ibid., 133.

119. Ibid., 134.

120. Ibid.

121. Ibid., 142–43.

122. Ibid., 143.

123. Ibid., 144.

124. Ibid., 144–45. Chapter 27 also includes a curious presentation of a "Mahometan Sermon" attended by the hero. The subject of the sermon was the "attributes of Deity" and "it was received by his audience with a reverence better becoming Christians than infidels." The attributes are the immortality, omnipresence, omnipotence, mercy, justice and unity of God.

125. For examples of "Christians Turned Turk," see Ray, 233–235, and Foss, 15.

126. Ibid., 43.

127. Although the voice is Tyler's, there is a certain degree of objectivity exercised in presenting the Muslim point of view.

128. Tyler, 46.

129. Ibid., 49.

130. Ibid., 49.

131. Ibid., 49–50.

132. Ibid., 50.

133. Ibid.

134. Ibid., 52–53.

135. Ibid., 53.

136. Sale, 28.

137. Ibid.

138. Ibid.
139. Carlyle, 43.
140. Ibid., 43–44.
141. Ibid., 44.
142. Ibid., 45.
143. Ibid., 56.
144. Margaret Fuller's, article in *Dial*, II (July 1841): 131.
145. Ibid.
146. Ibid.
147. *Dial*, I, 2 (Oct. 1840): 161.
148. Ibid., 162–63.
149. "Was Mohammed an Imposter or an Enthusiast," *North American Review*, 63 (Oct., 1846): 497.
150. Ibid., 497.
151. Ibid., 500.
152. Ibid., 501-03.
153. George H. Miles, *Mohammed, the Arabian Prophet*. (Boston, 1850), "Preface," v.
154. Ibid.
155. Ibid., vii.
156. Ibid., vii–viii.
157. Irving, 241–42.
158. Ibid., 242.
159. Ibid., 242–43.
160. Moncure Daniel Conway, *The Sacred Anthology* (New York, 1874), v.
161. Ibid., v–vi.
162. James Freeman Clarke, *Ten Great Religions*. (Boston, 1871), II:24.
163. Ibid., I:30.
164. For the image of the Arab and Muslem in America, see Edmund Ghareeb, *Split Vision: The Portrayal of Arabs in the American Media* (Washington D.C.: American-Arab Affairs Council, 1983); Janice Terry, *Mistaken Identity: Arab Stereotypes in Popular Writing* (Washington, D.C.: American-Arab Affairs Council, 1985); and Edward Said, *Covering Islam* (New York: Pantheon, 1981).

Chapter 4

1. Council Papers, North Carolina State Archives, Raleigh, N.C., X79.1154.1.
2. Ibid.
3. House of Lords Manuscript, 1678–1688, 137.
4. Edgar Stanton Maclay. A History of American Privateers (New York, 1899), 30.
5. "Mediterranean Trade: Report of the Secretary of State relative to the Mediterranean Trade. Communicated to the House of Representatives, December 30, 1790, and to the Senate, January 3, 1791," 1st Congress, 3d Session, Document No. 44, 104-05.

6. "Morocco and Algiers: Message from the President of the United States, communicating a Report from the Secretary of State, in relation to Morocco and Algiers," 3d Congress, 1st Session, Document No. 66 [67], 290.

7. "Mediterranean Trade," 107.

8. "Barbary States," 3d Congress, 2d Session, Document No. 105, [p. 11]. Letter with Treaty from Stephen Decatur and William Shaler to Secretary of State, James Monroe from *U.S.S. Guerriere*, Bay of Algiers, July 4, 1815.

9. Ibid.

10. David Humphreys, "A Poem on the Future Happiness of America." Quoted in *A Short History of Algiers*, 3rd ed. (New York, 1805), 99.

11. *The Algerine Captive*, II, 146–148.

12. See Ray W. Irwin, *The Diplomatic Relations of the U.S. With the Barbary Powers* (Chapel Hill, NC, 1931), 49.

13. *The Algerine Captive*, II:148–49.

14. Humphreys, *Works*, 54.

15. See Irwin, 24 ff. on the anonymous *Letters from Barbary*.

16. Quoted by Irwin, 24–25.

17. "Report by Adams and Jefferson," 2nd Congress, May 29, 1786.

18. "Letter from the Secretary of State in Relation to the Prisoners at Algiers," 2nd Congress, 1st Session. Philadelphia, December 9, 1791.

19. See Charles Burr Todd, *Life and Letters of Joel Barlow* (New York, 1886), 120–21.

20. Charles Forster, *Mahometanism*, I:16, attests to the popularity of this work.

21. "Interior of Africa," *North American Review*, V (May, 1817): 11–12.

22. Charles Ellms, *Voice of Adventure*, "Preface."

23. John I. Foss, 1.

24. Ibid., 2.

25. Ray, 79–81.

26. Ray, "Elegy on the Death of Lieutenant James Decatur," *Poems*, 75–76.

27. Ibid., 73–74. A similar picture emerges in many contemporary accounts. Barlow, for example, describes Hassan Pasha as "the beast," (Todd, 123; Irwin, 55); a popular textbook of geography by John Hibbard, *The Rudiments of Geography*, 6th ed., (Burnard, Vermont, 1841) describes the "governments of the States of Barbary" as despotic, cruel, inhuman, and the manners of their peoples as the worst "which human depravity can invent or perpetrate." Hibbard says that there is no law or justice in these states (202).

28. "Prisoners at Algiers: Message from the President of the United States to Congress, communicating a report of the Secretary of State, in relation to American prisoners at Algiers," 1st Congress, 3d Session, December 30, 1790.

29. Ibid.

30. Ibid., "Speech by President Washington," Wednesday, December 8, 1790. See also Ibid., the "Address by the Senate to the President, Monday, December 13, 1790.

31. "Barbary States," 3d Congress, 2d Session, Communicated to Congress March 2, 1795.

32. Humphreys as quoted in *A Short History of Algiers*, 99.

33. See Foss, p. 78.

34. William Shaler, *Esquisse de l'etat d'Alger* (Paris, 1830) Shaler had made similar suggestions for British occupation of North Africa in his *Sketches of Algiers* (Boston, 1826).

Chapter 5

1. The best account of American missionary activities in the Orient is A. L. Tibawi's *American Interests in Syria, 1800–1901*. (Oxford, 1966). See also American Board of Commissioners for Foreign Missions, W. E. Strong and O. W. Elsbree.

2. ABCFM, *Report of the Prudential Committee to the Tenth Annual Meeting* (Boston, 1819), 29.

3. In his treatment of Orientalism in Emerson's writings, Frederic I. Carpenter rightly notes that "the Bible has been the book of Christianity, and Christianity has been the religion of the Occident; and so, for all Westerners and for Emerson, the Bible has formed a part of Occidental literature." *Emerson and Asia* (Cambridge, Mass., 1930), ix–x.

4. Tibawi, 4.

5. "Divinity of Missions," *The American Theological Review*, I (Nov., 1859): 607.

6. Ibid., 607.

7. Ibid.

8. Josiah Brewer, 6.

9. For the concept of Americans as the people of the Covenant, see Chapter I of this volume: "A Place for My People."

10. Samuel Worcester, *Two Discourses*. (Salem, Mass., 1805), 9.

11. Ibid., 12.

12. Ibid., 40.

13. "The United States A Commissioned Missionary Nation," *The American Theological Review*, I (January, 1859): 152–73.

14. Ibid., 152–53.

15. Cotton Mather, *A Pillar of Gratitude* (Boston, 1700), 32.

16. Cotton Mather, *The Diary of Cotton Mather*. Entries for May 26, August 11, 1716 and March 6, 1717.

17. William Bradford, The History of Plymouth Plantation. (New York, 1908), 46.

18. "The United States A Commissioned Missionary Nation," 156.

19. Frederick Merk, *Manifest Destiny and Mission in American History* (New York, 1963), 3. See also Chapters I and II on the Providential plan and the duty of Americans.

20. Ahlstrom, I:255.

21. For a succinct, detailed account of this stage of the development of the American missionary enterprise, see Tibawi, "The Pioneers," *American Interests in Syria*, Chapter I.

22. Ahlstrom, I:255.

23. William Lee Miller, "American Religion and American Political Attitudes," in Smith and Jamison, II:92.

24. Ahlstrom, I:235.

25. ABCFM, *Report of Prudential Committee,* 28–29.

26. Ibid., 30.

27. "A Memoir of Asaad Esh Shidiak." In ABCFM, *Missionary Paper* 8 [7], 1.

28. Ibid., 3.

29. Acts, xx, 22.

30. ABCFM (1819), 112.

31. J. V. C. Smith, *A Pilgrimage to Palestine,* (Boston, 1853), 108.

32. Ibid., 109.

33. William M. Thomson, *The Land and the Book,* (London, 1905), 278.

34. See "Report of Prudential Committee," 29.

35. T. G. Appleton, *Syrian Sunshine* (Boston, 1877), "Preface."

36. Eli Smith, *Trials of Missionaries,* (Boston, 1832), 7.

37. F. G. Hibbard, *Palestine.* (New York, 1851), 317.

38. "Jerusalem," *The Ladies Companion,* X (April, 1839): 31.

39. "Instructions," ABCFM, *Report of Prudential Committee...*Section 9, 14.

40. Ibid., 29.

41. "News of the Churches and Missions," *American Theological Review,* II (Feb. 1860): 202.

42. Ibid., 204.

43. Ibid., 394.

44. Ibid., 394.

45. Ibid., 201.

46. Henry H. Jessup, *Women of the Arabs,* (New York, 1873), 180.

47. Ibid., 182.

48. Charles Wesley Andrews, *Private Correspondence,* letter from the Nile, (Duke University Manuscript Department, December 14, 1841).

49. Herman Melville, *Journal of a Visit to Europe and the Levant.* (Princeton, 1955), 58.

50. J. V. C. Smith, 118–19.

51. "Our Arabian Visitors," *New York Morning Herald,* August 3, 1840.

52. "Interior of Africa," *North American Review,* V (May, 1817): 24.

53. J. V. C. Smith, 19–20.

54a. ABCFM, "Summary View of Protestant Missions," *Missionary Paper, No. 4,* February 1823, 17.

54b. James Brooks, "A Letter from Jerusalem," *The Gospel Visitor* IX,7 (July, 1859): 209.

55. Stephen Olin, *Travels in Egypt, Arabia Petrea and the Holy Land.* (New York, 1844), II:108-09.

56. Brooks, "A Letter from Jerusalem," *The Gospel Visitor,* IX,7 (July, 1859): 209.

57. Ibid., 210.

58. [McI.] Robertson, [Journal of Travel], an unpublished manuscript, 110–113.

59. John L. Stephens, "Incidents of Travel in Greece, Turkey, Russia, and Poland," *In Remarkable Voyages and Travels*. (London, n.d.), 171.

60. J. V. C. Smith, 126.

61. Charles Andrews, November 17, 1821, from Alexander to the editors of the *Episcopal Recorder*.

62. ABCFM, *Missionary Paper No. 8 [7]*, 4.

63. Quoted by James A. Field, *America and the Mediterranean World; 1776–1882*, (Princeton, NJ, 1969), 288.

64. Ibid., 290.

65. Lynch, 88.

66. David Porter, *Constantinople and Its Environs*. (New York, 1835), II:311. See also Stephen's *Incidents of Travel In Greece, Turkey...*, 168, for a similar event.

67. This is discussed further in Chapter VI of this volume.

68. As quoted by David H. Finnie, *Pioneers East*. Cambridge, Mass., 1967), 200.

69. Quoted by Field, 210; Squadron Letters: Smith to Secretary of the Navy, April 19, 1845, September 11, 1845.

70. Finnie, 127.

71. Ibid., 128–29.

72. Porter, II:317–18.

73. Finnie, 129.

74. Moncure D. Conway, *My Pilgrimage to the Wise Men of the East*. (Boston, 1906), 138–39.

75. Eli Smith, 15.

76. John L. O'Sullivan, *The Democratic Review* (July and Aug. 1845).

77. Ahlstrom, I:256 ff.

78. John Cotton, "God's Promise to his Plantation," *Old South Leaflets* I(53):14–15.

79. *Public Ledger*, Oct. 25, 1847.

80. *Boston Times*, Oct., 1847.

81. *The Pennsylvanian*, Dec. 20, 1847.

82. Joel Barlow, I:526.

83. John L. O'Sullivan, *The Democratic Review* (July and Aug., 1845).

84. For the contemporary American concept of missionary work, see *The Great Commission*, (Hartford, 1856).

85. Frederick Merk, *Manifest Destiny*. (New York, 1963), 24.

86. Ibid., "Preface."

87. Moses Stuart, *A Sermon* (Andover, 1819), 25–27.

88. ABCFM, *Report*, 3rd Annual Meeting, (Hartford, September 16, 1812): 31.

89. Merk, "Preface," ii.

90. Ibid., iii.

91. "The United States A Commissioned Missionary Nation," 167.

92. ABCFM, *Report of Prudential Committee...Tenth Annual meeting*, 28.

93. Ibid., 29.

94. "Instructions," ABCFM, *Report of Prudential Committee...*3rd Annual Meeting, 13.

95. Ibid., 14.

96. ABCFM, *Missionary Paper*, No. 4, 1823, 2.

97. Ibid., 22.

98. Eli Smith, 6. See also ABCFM, *Missionary Paper No. 8 [7]*, "A Memoir of Asaad Esh Shidiak," 4, entitled "Ignorance and Sin"; and J.V.C. Smith, 118, entitled "Debased Morals."

99. "The United States A Commissioned Missionary Nation," 153, 157.

100. Stuart, 26–27.

101. Brewer, title page.

102. Ray, 20–21.

103. Eli Smith, 4.

104. Ibid., 8–9.

104a. "The United States A Commissioned Missionary Nation," 153.

105. Eli Smith, 15.

106. Quoted by Finnie, 130.

107. See Tibawi, 255.

108. Ibid.

109. Jessup, *The Mohammedan Missionary Problem*, 94.

110. Ibid.

111. Ibid.

112. Ibid., 107.

113. Ibid.

114. Ibid., 108.

115. Ibid., 130.

116. Ibid., 134–36.

117. Henry Jessup, *Fifty-Three Years in Syria*. (New York, 1910), II:768.

118. Sarah Rogers Haight, *Letters from the Old World by A Lady of New York*. (New York, 1840), 263.

119. J. V. C. Smith, 118. See also "Vision of Zion," Chapter VII of this volume.

120. Quoted by Merk, 125.

121. "The United States: A Commissioned Missionary Nation," 164–165. See also William T. Stead, *The Americanization of the World*. (New York, 1972).

122. Ibid., 154, 156.

123. Heman Humphrey, *The Promised Land*. (Boston, 1819), 7.

124. Ibid., 8.

125. Ibid., 8–9. See also Eli Smith, 14; ABCFM, "A Memoir of Asaad Esh Shidiak," *Missionary Paper No. 8 [7]*, 3–4.

Chapter 6

1. *The New York Herald*, May 4, 1840.

2. Stephens, *Incidents of Travel in Greece, Turkey...*, 175.

3. Charles Edwin Bergh, *Private Correspondence*, (Duke University Manuscript Department). Letter to his father from London, August 25, 1841.

4. Ibid., Sept. 20, 1841.

5. Some lists are to be found in contemporary accounts such as those kept by the Gliddens in Egypt; *Fifty-Three Years in Syria*, Bliss' *Encyclopaedia of Missions*. Of the modern works which deal with the subject of travel, I have made use of the lists provided by Finnie, *Pioneers East*; Metwalli, *The Lure of the Levant*, unpublished Ph.D. dissertation; Smith, *American Travellers Abroad*. (1969).

6. John Lloyd Stephens, *Incidents of Travel in Egypt, Arabia Petraea, and the Holy Land*. (Norman, Oklahoma, 1970), I:v.

7. Lynch *Narrative*, vi. The demand for Oriental travel accounts can be seen also in a notice by the publishers of one of the earliest missionary travel works written by Josiah Brewer. The notice says that the second edition of Brewer's A Residence at Constantinople, (New Haven: Durrie & Peck, 1830), had to be printed even before the distribution of the first edition because it was discovered that there were not enough copies for the actual subscribers in the immediate vicinity. Brewer, "Note by the Publishers," 4.

8. Stephens, *Incidents of Travel in Egypt...*, xxxix.

9. Ibid., xl. See also George Jones, *Excursions to Cairo, Jerusalem, Damascus and Balbec*, (New York, 1836), i.

10. Metwalli, 6.

11. Haight, I:iv.

12. Ibid., I:v.

13. Lynch, v.

14. George William Curtis, *The Howadji in Syria*, (New York, 1856), iii.

15. Haight, I:91.

16. Charles Wesley Andrews, *Private Correspondence*, (University Manuscript Department); Bergh, Private Papers (Duke University Manuscript Department).

17. Metwalli, 8. Taylor also edited collections of travel literature which were very popular.

18. See for this aspect of American involvement in the Orient, William B. Hasseltine and Hazel C. Wolf's *The Blue and the Gray on the Nile*, (Chicago, 1961); and William M. Thayer's *From Tannery to the White House: The life of Ulysses S. Grant*, (Boston, 1885).

19. David Porter, *Constantinople and Its Environs*, 2 vols., (New York, 1835), II:7–8.

20. Haight, I:33.

21. Ibid., I:42.

22. Lynch, 64 (Monday, Feb. 21, 1848).

23. Ibid.

24. Porter, II:311–12.

25. Haight, I:45–46. See also Marion Harland, *Under the Flag of the Orient*, (Philadelphia, 1897), 289–290 on the work of two American missionaries in Jerusalem.

26. Ibid., II:72.

27. Ibid., I:298.

28. Lynch, 489.

29. Ibid., 504.

30. Ibid., 506-07.

31. Haight, I:120–21.

32. Bergh, letter to his mother, Jerusalem, February 13, 1842.

33. Andrews, Grand Cairo, November 20, 1841.

34. *New York Morning Herald*, May 4,1840.

35. Andrews, *Private Correspondence*, letter to his wife, Paris, September 6, 1841. See also David Millard, *A Journal of Travels in Egypt, Arabia Petrea, and the Holy Land*, (New York, 1853), 11–12.

36. Melville, Herman, *Journal of a Visit to Europe and the Levant*. (Princeton: 1955), [4].

37. Ibid., [6].

38. Ibid., [4].

39. See James Eliot Cabbot, *A Memoir of Ralph Waldo Emerson*, (Boston, 1887), 659.

40. Melville, *Journal*, [4–5].

41. Haight, I:13.

42. Ibid., I:27–28.

43. Bergh, letter to his father, Berlin, September 28, 1842.

44. Robinson, I:1.

45. Lynch, 18.

46. Robinson, I:46.

47. Lynch, v.

48. Millard, 11–12.

49. Andrews, letter to his wife, Paris, September 6–7, 1841.

50. Jones, 29–30.

51. Brewer, 13.

52. W. M. Thomson, *The Land and the Book*. (London: 1905), 46.

53. Ibid., xx.

54. Ibid., 19, Jan. 24, 1857 [Gen. xiii. 17].

55. Andrews, Sept. 24, 1841.

56. Bergh, *Private Correspondence*, letter to his father Beirut, Mar. 6, 1842.

57. A good example of this feeling of belonging to the Orient is Bayard Taylor's Poem "The Poet in the East."

58. Stephen Olin, *The Life and Letters of Stephen Olin*. (New York, 1853), II:112.

59. Ibid., 329. See also Millard, 249, for similar emotional expressions.

60. [McI] Robertson, [Journal of Travel], 30.

61. Haight, II:34.

62. Brewer, 77.

63. Thomson, xi.

64. Ibid., xii.

65. Ibid., xiii.

66. Haight, I, 245.

67. Ibid., 246.
68. Ibid., 307.
69. Stephens, *Incidents of Travel in Egypt...*, 138.
70. Edgar Allan Poe, *New York Review* 18 (Oct. 1837).
71. *Graham's Magazine* (Aug. 1841).
72. Ibid.
73. Haight, II:97–98.
74. Olin, *Travels in Egypt...*, II:117.
75. Bergh, Letter, March 6, 1842.
76. Lynch, 153.
77. Brewer, 94.
78. Ibid., 65.
79. Haight, I:43.
80. Ibid., 26.
81. Haight, I:80.
82. Ibid., 31.
83. Ibid.
84. Haight, I:31–32.
85. Ibid., 39–40.
86. David Dorr, *A Colored Man Round the World*, (Cleveland, 1858), 180.
87. Ibid., 184.
88. [McI] Robertson, [*Journal of Travel*], 110.
89. Ibid.
90. Ibid., Jerusalem, Wed., April 29, 1854, 110.
91. J. V. C. Smith, *A Pilgrimage to Palestine*, (Boston, 1853), 120.
92. Ibid., 123.
93. Millard, 267.
94. Bergh, letter to his mother, Jerusalem, February 13, 1842.
95. Andrews, December 8, 1841.
96. Bergh, letter to his mother, Jerusalem, February 13, 1842. See also Olin, II:52–53.
97. Bergh, letter to his father, Beirut, March 6, 1842.
98. Millard, 97.
99. Ibid., 98.
100. Ibid., 107.
101. Ibid., 107-08.
102. Ibid., 109.
103. Ibid., 186.
104. Ibid., 191.
105. Ibid., 191–92. See also Stephens, *Incidents of Travel in Egypt...*, 187.
106. Stephens, *Incidents of Travel in Egypt...*, 234.
107. Ibid., 234–35.
108. Ibid., 235.
109. Ibid., 235–36.
110. Ibid., 237.

111. Ibid., 259.
112. Ibid., 258–59.
113. Ibid., 259–60.

Chapter 7

1. John Pierpont, *Airs of Palestine*. (Baltimore, 1816), 5–6.
2. The American Adam (R. W. B. Lewis' phrase), as it will be clearly seen was not, after all, so "emancipated from history and undefiled by the usual inheritances of family and race" (Lewis, *The American Adam*, 3rd. ed., Chicago, 1961, p. 5). The American Adam was indeed deeply immersed in the religious past of his race, carrying the burden of the original sin and the responsibility of preparing for the Second Kingdom.
3. Lewis, 2.
4. Emerson, "American Civilization," *The Collected Works*, XI:299.
5. Herman Melville, *Redburn*. (London, 1924), 217.
6. Vernon L. Parrington, *Main Currents in American Thought*. (New York, 1927–30), 23.
7. Quoted by Cotton Mather, *Magnalia Christi Americana*, I:265.
8. See for an example of this thought, an article entitled "The Flight of Imagination," *Graham Magazine* (*The Casket*), (1826), I:105–107, where Milford Bard extolls the power of the imagination which, with "invincible, and irresistible power" leaves "its natal age and shore, and travels back to the remotest periods of antiquity."
9. Parrington, I:40.
10. Ibid.
11. Quoted by Parrington, Ibid.
12. John Winthrop, *Papers*. (Boston, 1929–1947), II:117.
13. Ibid., II:295.
14. Charles Feidelson, Jr., *Symbolism and American Literature*, (Chicago, 1953), 78.
15. Ibid., 78–79.
16. Ibid., 79.
17. Similarly, funeral sermons had such titles as "A Great Man Fallen in Israel" (Nathaneal Appleton, Boston, 1724). Samuel Willard referred to John Hull's death as "a public loss, and deserves *the tears* of Israel." (*New England Funeral Sermons*, xvii.)
18. There were many references to "God's people" and the "chosen" and "Israel" in the arguments for and against the war with Britain.
19. Timothy Dwight, "The Conquest of Canaan," *The Major Poems*, 21.
20. Ibid.
21. Ibid.
22. Ibid., 20. According to Kenneth Silverman *Timothy Dwight* (New York, 1969), Dwight's readers were used to comparing Washington to Joshua, 31–32.
23. Barlow, II:29–30.
24. Charles Burr Todd, Life and Letters of Joel Barlow, LL.D., (New York, 1886), 8.

25. Ibid., 48–49.

26. Ibid., 49.

27. Quoted by Silverman, "Preface."

28. David Osgood, *A Solemn Protest Against the Late Declaration of War*, a Sermon, (Medford, 1812), 3.

29. The Mormon's belief in the descent of the Indians from the Israelites is another example which will be dealt with later.

30. *The Great Commission*, 388–89.

31. Ellen Clare Miller, *Eastern Sketches* (New York, 1977), 209–10.

32. Ibid., 205-06.

33. Increase Mather, "Prevalency of Prayer," *Early History of New England* (Boston, 1864), 253.

34. *The Illustrated Hand-Book to All Religions: From the Earliest Ages to the Present Time* (Philadelphia, 1877).

35. Niebuhr, 141.

36. Ibid.

37. Ibid, 141–42.

38. *The Illustrated Hand-Book to All Religions*, 17.

39. Charles Buck, *A Theological Dictionary.* (Philadelphia, 1854), 478. See also 282–83 on the "Millenium".

40. Ibid.

41. *The Illustrated Hand-Book to All Religions*, 19.

42. Buck, 479.

43. Ibid.

44. *The Constitution of the American Bible Society* (New York, 1816), 14.

45. Ibid., 15.

46. Buck, 479. There were frequent references to the connection between the fall of Islam and the Millennium, especially by Henry Jessup, Barclay, Harland and Haight.

47. Jessup, *Sermon Delivered at the Opening of the General Assembly of the Presbyterian Church*...at Saratoga. May 15th, 1884. (Saratoga, 1884), 22.

48. Ibid., 21.

49. Jessup, *The Mohammedan Missionary Problem*, 13.

50. Ibid.

51. Ibid., 17.

52. Ibid., 23. See also Barclay, xiv–xx.

53. Jessup, *Sermon Delivered...*, 25. See also Jessup's Fifty-Three Years in Syria, 790 ff. for a detailed survey of the method of reaching this goal in the Orient.

54. *The Illustrated Hand-Book to all Religions*, 340.

55. Ibid., 339. On the building of New Jerusalem in America, there is no better illustration than Chapter 13 of *The Book of Mormon*.

56. Examples of these periodicals are *The Signs of the Times* (Boston), *Midnight Cry* (New York), and *The Millennial Star* (Salt Lake City). One of the best expres-

sions of the millennial tendency is the *Millennial Harp*, 1843, a hymn book for the millennarians. (See Buck, *Theological Dictionary*, 479 ff.)

57. Buck, 479.

58. Heman Humphrey, 3–6.

59. Ibid., 19.

60. Ibid.

61. Ibid.

62. J. T. Barclay, *The City of the Great King* (Philadelphia, 1858), 580.

63. Ibid., 580–81.

64. Samuel Worcester, *Two Discourses*, title-page.

65. Stuart was a member of the American Oriental Society and a noted Hebraist at Andover Seminary.

66. Moses Stuart, 44.

67. Travelers speak of these colonies in accounts of their visits to Palestine. See, for example, Harland's chapter 32, "The Box Colony," 288–93.

68. Robert Barr, *The Unchanging East.* (Boston, 1900), 207.

69. Ibid., 208.

70. Ibid., 208-09.

71. Ibid., 209.

72. Annie DeWitt Shaw, *Will, Annie, and I: Travellers in Many Lands* (New York, 1889), 115.

73. Ibid., 117.

74. Ibid.

75. Barclay, xiii.

76. Lydia Shuler, "A Letter from the Holy Land," *The Monthly Gospel-Visiter*, V,12 (Dec. 1855): 286.

77. Shuler, "A Letter from Jerusalem," *The Monthly Gospel-Visitor*, IX,7 (July, 1859): 210–211. Barclay, xiii and 590, gives an account of the work done by the Dickson's for the sake of the Jews in Palestine.

78. See the list of travel books in the forthcoming bibliography of American travel literature by the present writer.

79. Barclay, 3.

80. For this aspect of American journeys in the Holy Land, see chapter 6 of this volume.

81. Olin, 348–349.

82. Buck, 213.

83. Ibid.

84. *The Illustrated Hand-Book to All Religions*, 240–241.

85. Brewer, however, found more Jews in Turkey and proposed that effort should be directed there rather than to the Holy Land. See Brewer, 67 ff.

86. Buck, 213.

87. Andrews, "Letter from Jerusalem," *Private Correspondence*, February 25, 1842.

88. Frederick Jones Bliss, *The Development of Palestine Exploration Being the Ely Lectures for 1903* (New York, 1977), xiv.

89. Lee S. Smith, *Through Egypt to Palestine* (Chicago, 1896), 114.

90. Ibid.

91. Ibid.

92. Ibid., 117.

93. See also Shaw, 141. Shaw vividly remembered her visit to the Wailing Wall on Friday when Jews prayed and wept, "others were reading from the Psalms and chanting the Lamentations of Jeremiah."

94. Barclay, 582.

95. Harland, 281.

96. Ibid., 286.

97. Ibid.

98. Ibid.

99. Ibid., 286–287.

100. Barclay, 619.

101. Ibid., xii.

102. George Jones, *Excursions to Cairo, Jerusalem, Damascus and Balbec*, (New York, 1836), title-page.

103. Ibid., 161.

104. Ibid., 263–264.

105. Ibid., 264.

106. Bliss is awed by visiting places where holy men of the past had trod and had "held converse with the Most High," "Key-Note" to his *Development of Palestine Exploration*, (New York, 1906).

107. Andrews, "On the Bosom of the Nile," letter to his wife, November 18, 1841.

108. Haight, I:115.

109. Barclay, 598.

110. Ibid., 599.

111. Ibid.

112. Ibid., 601.

113. J. V. C. Smith, 118.

114. Ibid., 118–19.

115. Ibid. As far as it is possible to tell from internal evidence, there is no indication that either of the two American travelers knew of the other's work.

116. Ibid., 328–29.

117. Barclay, 601-02. See also Barclay's quotation from a Dr. Tyng, 603.

118. Haight, I:255.

119. *Journal of the American Oriental Society*, I:xi (1849): List of members. Haight presented some books to the collection of the Society.

120. Haight, I:256.

121. Ibid., 257.

122. Ibid., 259–60.

123. Ibid., 260.

124. Ibid.

125. Ibid., 263.

126. Ibid., 261.
127. Ibid.
128. Ibid., 262.
129. Ibid., 261–63.
130. Ibid., 263–64.
131. Ibid., 266–67.
132. Mentioned by Field, 284.
133. Barclay, xii.
134. Ibid., xii–xiii.
135. Ibid., 614.
136. Ibid.
137. Ibid., 615.
138. Ibid., 616.
139. Ibid., 617.
140. Ibid.
141. Ibid., 618–19.
142. Ibid., 619–21.

Chapter 8

1. "Orientalism," *Knickerbocker*, 41 (June 1853) 479.
2. Ibid., 479–80.
3. H. B. Stowe (ed.), *A Library of Famous Fiction*. (New York, 1873).
4. Ibid., vii.
5. Ibid., viii.
6. Ibid.
7. *Letters from Asia*, 1819.
8. David Millard, *A Journal of Travels in Egypt, Arabia Petrea, and the Holy Land* (New York, 1853), 11–12.
9. Lynch, 487.
10. Haight, I:26.
11. Ibid., I:28.
12. Ibid., II:35.
13. [McI.] Robertson, [Journal of Travel] 10; Bayard Taylor, *A Journey to Central Africa;* (New York, 1872), 60, 238 ff.; Charles Edwin Bergh, Private Correspondence, (Duke University Manuscript Department), Letter from Beyrouth, March 6th, 1842.
14. Curtis, 1–2.
15. Ibid., 3–4.
16. Ibid., 8–10.
17. Ibid., 11.
18. Melville, *Journal*, 76–77.
19. Haight, I:135.
20. While these streets gave Curtis an atmosphere of poetry, Melville's imagination worked in a different direction. On arrival in Constantinople Melville

took a walk, dined, and then: "Staid in all night. Dangerous going out, owing to footpads and assassins. The curse of the places. Can't go out at night, and no places to go to, if you could....Whir of the spinning jennies. Terrible place to be robbed or murdered in....Great curse that of Babel....The horrible grimy tragic air of these streets. The rotten and wicked looking houses. So gloomy and grimy as if a suicide hung from every rafter within." Melville, *Journal*, [78 ff.].

21. Curtis, 2–3.

22. Dorr, 122.

23. Ibid., 122–23.

24. Ibid., 124.

25. Stephens, *Incidents of Travel in Greece*..., 156.

26. George Jones, *Excursions to Cairo, Jerusalem, Damascus and Balbec*, (New York, 1836), 40.

27. N. P. Willis, *Pencillings by the Way*. (Philadelphia, 1836), II:40.

28. Stephens, *Incidents of Travel in Greece*..., 172.

29. Ibid.

30. Willis, II:100-01.

31. Stephens, *Incidents of Travel in Greece*..., 173.

32. Ibid.

33. Curtis, 5.

34. Ibid., 59.

35. Lynch, 127, 280–81 and his *Official Report of the United States' Expedition to Explore the Dead Sea and the River Jordan*, 17, for his attitude towards the Arabs.

36. Ibid., 205.

37. Taylor, 409–10.

38. Ibid., 86.

39. Haight, I:100-04.

40. Millard, 186–88.

41. Jessup, *Women of the Arabs*, 183.

42. Jones, 382 ff.

43. See *New York Herald*, Apr. 30, 1840-Aug. 5, 1840.

44. Millard, 122. See also 163–179 for a description of bedouin life and character.

45. Millard, 121.

46. Lynch, *Report*, 17.

47. Lynch, *Narrative*, 260.

48. Irving, 23–24.

49. Emerson, *Journals*, I:327-8.

50. Carlyle, 45–47.

51. Stephens, *Incidents of Travel in Greece*..., 176. See also Curtis, *Syria*, 62.

52. Henry David Thoreau, *Journal*, (New York, 1962): 189–190.

53. Millard, 298.

54. Lynch, 428 ff.

55. Ibid., 220.

56. Ibid., 150.

57. Ibid., 76.

58. Curtis, *Nile Notes*, 12–14.

59. *Clarel*, 49.

60. Included in Longfellow's *Poems of Places*, Vol. 21, *Asia*, 12–13. See also Alger's "The Kibla and the Devotee," *The Poetry of the Orient*, 221.

61. Haight, I:100 ff.

62. Thomson, *The Land and the Book*, 24–25.

63. Leland, 7. See also Leland's story of Mecca, and his sarcastic treatment of the fast of Ramadan, 12.

64. Lynch, 50.

65. Ibid.

66. *Letters from Asia*, 18.

67. Willis, II:43.

68. Taylor, 41–43.

69. Ibid., 121–22.

70. Stephens, *Incidents of Travel in Greece…*, 157–58.

BIBLIOGRAPHY

ABCFM. See American Board of Commissioners for Foreign Missions.

Adams, Hannah. *A Dictionary of Religions and Religious Denominations*. Boston: Cummings and Hilliard, 1817.

Adams, Henry. *Letters of Henry Adams (1858–1891)*; edited by Worthington Chauncey Ford. Boston: Houghton Mifflin, 1930.

———. *Letters to a Niece and Prayer to the Virgin of Chartres, with a niece's memories by Mabel La Farge*. Boston: Houghton Mifflin, 1920.

Adams, Robert. *The Narrative of Robert Adams, an American Sailor*, in *Robinson Crusoe's Own Book; or, The Voice of Adventure*. Boston: Joshua V. Pierce, 1846.

Ahlstrom, Sydney E. "Theology in America: A Historical Survey." In James W. Smith and A. Leland Jamison (eds.), *Religion in American Life*. Princeton, N.J.: Princeton University Press, 1961.

Alger, William Rounseville. *The Poetry of the Orient*. 4th ed. Boston: Roberts Bros., 1874.

Ali Bey [pseud.] *Travels of Ali Bey in Morocco, Tripoli, Cyprus, Egypt, Arabia, Syria and Turkey between the years 1803 and 1807*. 2 vols. London: Longman [etc.] 1816.

American Board of Commissioners for Foreign Missions. *First Ten Annual Reports*, 1810–1820 (issued in one vol.). Boston, 1834.

———. "A Memoir of Asaad Esh Shidiak," *Missionary Paper*, No. 8, (7).

———. *Memorial Volume of the First Fifty Years of the American Board of Commissioners for Foreign Missions*. Boston: 1861.

———. "Summary View of Protestant Missions," *Missionary Paper*, No. 4 (February 1823).

Andrews, Charles Wesley. *Private Correspondence*. Duke University Manuscript Department.

Appleton, T. G. "Preface," *Syrian Sunshine*. Boston: Roberts Bros., 1877.

Barclay, J. T. *The City of the Great King; or, Jerusalem as it was, as it is, and as it is to be*. Philadelphia: James Challen, 1858.

Bard, Milford. "The Flight of the Imagination," *Graham Magazine* I. (1826): 105–107.

Baritz, Loren, *City on a Hill*. N.Y.: John Wiley, 1964.

Barlow, Joel. *The Works of Joel Barlow*. With an Introduction by William K. Bottorff and Arthur L. Ford. 2 vols. Gainesville, Fla.: Scholars' Facsimiles & Reprints, 1970.

Barr, Robert. *The Unchanging East*. 2 vols. Boston: L. C. Page, 1900.

Beard, Charles A. and Mary R. Beard. *The Rise of American Civilization*. New York: Macmillan, 1937.

Bell, Gertrude. *The Letters of Gertrude Bell*. Edited by Lady Bell. 2 vols. New York: Horace Liveright, 1927.

Belloc, Hilaire. *The Great Heresies*. London: Sheed & Ward, 1938.

Bergh, Charles Edwin. *Private Correspondence*. Duke University Manuscript Department.

Bliss, Frederick Jones. *The Development of Palestine Exploration; Being the Ely Lectures for 1903*. New York: Arno Press, 1977.

Bosco, Ronald A. (ed.) *The Puritan Sermon in America, 1630–1750*. Vol. 2: *Connecticut and Massachusetts Election Sermons*. Delmar, N.Y.: Scholar's Facsimiles & Reprints, 1978.

Boulainvilliers, Count of. *The Life of Mahomet*. London: T. Longman, C. Hitch & L. Hawes, 1752.

Brackenridge, Hugh Henry and Philip Freneau. *Father Bombo's Pilgrimage to Mecca, 1770*. Ed. by Michael Davitt Bell. Princeton, N.J.: Princeton University Library, 1975.

Bradford, William, *The History of Plymouth Plantation, 1606–1646*. Edited by William T. Davis. New York: Charles Scribner's Sons, 1908.

Bradford, William. "History of Plymouth Plantation." *Old South Leaflets*. Vol. 7 (No. 153). Boston, n.d.

Brewer, Josiah. *A Residence at Constantinople*, in the year 1827. 2nd ed. New Haven: Durrie & Peck, 1830.

Buck, Charles. *A Theological Dictionary*. New American Edition, revised and improved...George Bush and Will D. Howe. Philadelphia: Crissy & Markley, 1843.

Burke, William J. *American Authors and Books 1640–1940*. New York: Gramercy, 1943.

Burner, David, Eugene D. Genovese, and Forrest McDonald. *The American People*. St. James, N.Y.: Revisionary Press, 1980.

Burns, Edward McNall. *The American Idea of Mission*. New Brunswick: Rutgers University Press, 1957.

Bush, George. *The Life of Mohammad, Founder of the Religion of Islam, and of the Empire of the Saracens*. New York: Harper, 1847.

Bushnell, Horace. "American Politics," *The American National Preacher*. XIV, 12 (Dec. 1840).

Cabot, James Elliot. *A Memoir of Ralph Waldo Emerson*. Boston: Houghton Mifflin, 1887.

The Cambridge History of American Literature. 4 vols. William Peterfield Trent, [et al.] ed. New York: G. P. Putnam, 1917–21. (Reprinted: New York, McMillan, 1972, 3 v. in 1)

Cameron, Kenneth Walter. *Emerson Among His Contemporaries*. Hartford: Transcendental Books, 1967.

————. *Emerson and Thoreau As Readers*. Hartford: Transcendental Books, 1972.

Canot, Theodore. *Adventures of an African Slaver*...Edited by Malcolm Cowley. New York: Garden City Pub. Co., 1928.

Carlyle, Thomas. *On Heroes and Hero-Worship, and the Heroic in History*. Edited with an introd. by Carl Niemeyer. Lincoln: University of Nebraska Press, 1966.

Carnes, J. A. *Journal of a Voyage from Boston to the West Coast of Africa*. Boston: John P. Jewett, 1852.

Carpenter, Frederic Ives. *Emerson and Asia*. Cambridge, Mass.: 1930.

Chrisman, Lewis H. *The Message of the American Pulpit*. New York: Richard R. Smith, 1930.

Christy, Arthur E., (ed.) *The Asian Legacy and American Life; Essays*...New York: John Day, 1945

Christy, Arthur. *The Orient in American Transcendentalism; a Study of Emerson, Thoreau, and Alcott*. New York: Columbia University Press, 1932.

Clark, William Bell. *Ben Franklin's Privateers; a Naval Guide of the American Revolution*. Baton Rouge: Louisiana State University Press, 1956.

Clarke, James Freeman. *Ten Great Religions: An Essay in Comparative Theology*. Boston: Houghton Mifflin, 1871.

Conway, Moncure Daniel. "East and West," *Virginia Pamphlets*, I (1-20). Cincinnati: 1859.

————. *My Pilgrimage to the Wise Men of the East*. Boston: Houghton Mifflin, 1906.

————(ed.) *The Sacred Anthology; a Book of Ethical Scriptures*. New York: Henry Holt, 1874.

Cotton, John. "God's Promise to his Plantation." *Old South Leaflets* III, (51-57). Boston, n.d.

Curtis, George William. *The Howadiji In Syria*. New York: Harper, 1856.

————. *Niles Notes of a Howadiji*. New York: Harper, 1851.

Daniel, Norman. *Islam and the West; the Making of an Image*. Edinburgh: University Press, 1966.

Daniel, Robert L. *American Philanthropy in the Near East, 1820-1960*. Athens: Ohio University Press, 1970.

Dearborn, Henry A. S. "The Trade of the Black Sea," *North American Review* X (Jan. 1820): 108–183.

DeConde, Alexander. *A History of American Foreign Policy*. New York: Charles Scribner's, 1963.

De Cusa, Nicholas. *Cribratio Alcorani*. Rome, 1461–1462.

DeForest, J. W. *Oriental Acquaintances; or, Letters from Syria*. New York: Dix, Edwards, 1856.

DeKay, James Ellsworth. *Sketches of Turkey in 1831 and 1832 by An American*. New York: J. J. Harper, 1833.

"The Divinity of Missions," *American Theological Review* I (Nov. 1859): 605–618.

Dorr, David F. *A Colored Man Round the World, By a Quadroon*. [Cleveland?]: Printed for the Author, 1858.

Dunlop, William. *Four Plays (1789–1812)*. Delmar, N.Y.: Scholars' Facsimilies & Reprints, 1976.

Dwight, Theodore. "Condition and Character of Negroes in Africa," *Methodist Quarterly Review* XLVI. (Jan. 1864): 77–90.

Dwight, Timothy. *The Major Poems of Timothy Dwight (1752–1817)*...With an Introduction by William J. McTaggart and William K. Bottorff. Gainesville, Fla.: Scholar's Facsimile & Reprints, 1969.

Eilts, Herman F. "Ahmad Bin Na'aman's Mission to the U. S. in 1840; the Voyage of the Sultanah to N. Y. City," *Essex Institute Historical Collections* XCVIII, 4 (Oct. 1962): 219–278.

Ellms, Charles. *Robinson Crusoe's Own Book, or, The Voice of Adventure*...Boston: J. V. Pierce, 1846.

Elsbree, O. W. *The Rise of the Missionary Spirit in America 1790-1815*. Williamsport, PA, 1928.

Emerson, Ralph Waldo. *The Collected Works of Ralph Waldo Emerson*. Introductions and notes by Robert E. Spiller. Text established by Alfred R. Ferguson. Cambridge, Mass.: Belknap Press of Harvard University Press, 1971–.

———. *The Correspondence of Emerson and Carlyle*. Edited by Joseph Slater. New York: Columbia University Press, 1964.

———. *The Journals of Ralph Waldo Emerson*. Edited by Edward Waldo Emerson, and Waldo Emerson Forbes. 10 vols. Boston: Houghton Mifflin, 1909–1914.

Feidelson, Charles, Jr. *Symbolism and American Literature*. Chicago: The University of Chicago Press, 1953.

Field, James A. *America and the Mediterranean World: 1776–1882*. Princeton, N.J.: Princeton University Press, 1969.

Finkelstein, Dorothee Metlisky. *Melville's Orienda*. New Haven: Yale University Press, 1961.

Finnie, David H. *Pioneers East: The Early American Experience in the Middle East*. Cambridge, Mass.: Harvard University Press, 1967.

Forster, Charles. *Mahometanism Unveiled*. 2 vols. London: A. & R. Spottiswoode, 1829.

Foss, John. *A Journal, of the Captivity and Sufferings of John Foss; Several Years a Prisoner in Algiers*...Newburyport: Printed by A. March, [1798?]

Gibbon, Edward. *The Decline and Fall of the Roman Empire*. 2 vols. New York: The Modern Library, 1932.

———. *Life of Mahomet*. Boston: Houghton, Mifflin, 1859.

The Great Commission. Hartford: Silas Andrus, 1856.

Haight, Sarah Rogers. *Letters from the Old World by a Lady of New York*. 2 vols. New York: Harper, 1840.

Hamilton, Alexander. *The Works of Alexander Hamilton*...Edited by John C. Hamilton. 7 vols. Vol. VII: Political essays 1792–1804. New York: J. F. Trow, printer, 1850–1851.

Harland, Marion *Under the Flag of the Orient*. Philadelphia: Historical Pub. Co., 1897.

Hart, James D. *The Popular Book: A History of America's Literary Taste*. Berkley: University of California Press, 1963.

Hasseltine, William B. and Hazel C. Wolf. *The Blue and the Gray on the Nile*. Chicago: The University of Chicago Press, 1961.

Hayward, John. *The Book of Religions; Comprising the Views, Creeds, Sentiments, or Opinions, of All the Principal Religious Sects in the World…*Boston: John Hayward, 1843.

Hibbard, F. G. *Palestine: Its Geography and Bible History*. Edited by D. P. Kidder. New York: Lane & Scott, 1851.

Hibbard, John. *The American Reader*. 5th edition. Walpole, N.H.: 1811.

Holt, Arthur E. *The Nation Under God*. Chicago: Willett, Clark, 1939.

Hubbard, John. *The Rudiments of Geography*. 6th Edition. Burnard, VT: 1814.

Hudson, Frederic. *Journalism in the United States, from 1690 to 1872*. New York: Harper, 1873.

Hughes, Langston and Arna Bontemps (eds.) *The Book of Negro Folklore*. New York: Dodd, Mead, 1958.

Humphrey, Heman. *The Promised Land: A Sermon, delivered at Goshen, (Conn.) at the ordination of the Rev. Messrs. Hiram Bingham & Asa Thurston, as missionaries to the Sandwich Islands, Sept. 29, 1819*. Boston: Samuel T. Armstrong, 1819.

Huntress, Keith. *A Checklist of Narratives of Shipwrecks and Disasters at Sea to 1860, with Summaries, Notes and Comments*. Ames: Iowa State University Press, 1979.

Huntington, J. *Right Hand of Fellowship*. Andover: 1819.

Hutton, Lawrence. *Plays and Players*. New York: Hurd & Houghton, 1875.

The Illustrated Hand-Book to All Religions: From the Earliest Ages to the Present Time. Philadelphia: John E. Potter, 1877.

Inge, Milton Thomas (ed.) *Handbook of American Popular Culture*. New York: Greenwood Press, 1988.

"Interior of Africa." *North American Review*, V (May, 1817).

Irving, Washington. *Mahomet and His Successors*. New York: The Co-operative Publication Society, 1849.

Irwin, Ray W. *The Diplomatic Relations of the United States With the Barbary Powers 1776–1816*. Chapel Hill: University of North Carolina Press, 1931.

Isani, Mukhtar Ali. *The Oriental Tale in America Throught 1865: A Study in American Fiction*. Unpublished Ph.D. dissertation. Princeton University, 1962.

Jessup, Henry Harris. *Fifty-Three Years in Syria*. 2 vols. New York: Fleming H. Revell, 1910.

———. *The Mohammedan Missionary Problem*. Philadelphia: Presbyterian Board of Publications, 1879

———. Foreign Missions: Sermon Delivered at the Opening of the General Assembly of the Presbyterian Church America at Saratoga, May 15th, 1884. [n.p.] Published by Friends of Foreign Missions, 1884.

————. *The Setting of the Crescent and the Rising of the Cross, or Kamil Abdul Massiah: a Syrian Convert From Islam to Christianity.* Philadelphia: The Westminster Press, 1898.

————. *Women of the Arabs.* With a chapter for children...New York: Dodd & Mead, 1873.

Jones, George. *Excursions to Cairo, Jerusalem, Damascus and Balbec.* New York: Van Nostrand & Wright, 1836.

Kallen, Horace M. *Cultural Pluralism and the American Idea*...Philadelphia: University of Pennsylvania Press, 1956.

The Koran: The Koran Commonly Called the Alcoran of Mohammed. Translated by George Sale. London: William Tegg, 1850.

————. *The Koran Commonly Called the Alcaron of Mahomet.* First American edition. Springfield: Henry Brewer, 1806.

————. *The Alcoran of Mahomet,* translated by Alexander Ross. In Richard Knolles, *The Turkish History.* London: Randal Taylor, 1688.

Lee, Alfred McClung. *The Daily Newspaper in America; the Evolution of a Social Instrument.* New York: Macmillan, 1937.

Leland, Charles G. *The Egyptian Sketch Book.* New York: Hurd & Houghton, 1874.

Letters from Asia. New York: A. T. Goodrich, 1819.

Lewis, R. W. B. *The American Adam.* 3rd ed. Chicago: The University of Chicago Press, 1961.

The Life of Mahomet; or, the History of that Imposture which was begun, carried on, and finally established by him in Arabia...2nd American ed. New York: Evert Duyckinck, 1813.

Lincoln, Enoch. *An Oration, Pronounced at Worcester in Commemoration of American Independence July 4th, 1812.* Worcester, Mass.: Printed by Henry Rogers, 1812.

Longfellow, Henry Wadsworth (ed.) *Poems of Places.* 31 vols. (v. 21-23: Asia). Boston: J. R. Osgood, 1876–79.

Lowell, James Russell. *The Poetical Works of James Russell Lowell.* Boston: Houghton Mifflin, 1887.

Lynch, William F. *Narrative of the United States' Expedition to the River Jordan and the Dead Sea.* 9th ed., rev. Philadelphia: Blanchard and Lea, 1853.

————. *Official Report of the United States' Expedition to Explore the Dead Sea and the River Jordan.* Baltimore: John Murphy, 1852.

Maclay, Edgar Stanton. *A History of American Privateers.* New York: D. Appleton, 1899.

Mather, Cotton. *The Diary of Cotton Mather* in *Collections of the Massachusetts Historical Society.* Seventh Series, Vol. 7. May 26, 1716, Aug. 11, 1716, Mar. 6, 1717.

————. *Magnalia Christi Americana; or, The Ecclesiastical History of New-England, From its First Planting, in the Year 1620, unto the year of Our Lord 1698.* 2 vols. Hartford, 1853–1855 [v. 1, 1855]

————. *A Pillar of Gratitude.* Boston, 1700.

Mather, Increase. *Early History of New England.* Albany, N.Y.: J. Munsell, 1864.

McKey, Richard H., Jr. "Elias Hasket Derby and the Founding of the Eastern Trade, (Part I)," *Essex Institute Historical Collections*, Vol. XCVIII, No. 1 (Jan. 1962): 1–25.

Melville, Herman. *Clarel: A Poem and Pilgrimage in the Holy Land*. Edited by Walter E. Bezanson. New York: Hendricks House, 1960.

————. *Journal of a Visit to Europe and the Levant. Oct. 11, 1856-May 6, 1857*. Edited by Howard C. Horsford. Princeton: Princeton University Press, 1955.

————. *Redburn: His First Voyage*. London: Jonathan Cape, 1924.

Merk, Frederick. *Manifest Destiny and Mission: in American History*. New York: Alfred A. Knopf, 1963.

Metwalli, Ahmed Mohamed. *The Lure of the Levant*. Albany, Unpublished Ph.D. dissertation. State University of New York, 1971.

Miles, George H. *Mohammed, the Arabian Prophet. A Tragedy, in Five Acts*. Boston: Phillips, Sampson, 1850.

Millard, David. *A Journal of Travles in Egypt, Arabia Petrea, and the Holy Land*. New York: Lamport, Blakemann & Law, 1853.

Miller, Perry. *Errand into the Wilderness*. Cambridge, Mass.: Belknap Press of Harvard University Press, 1956.

————. *The New England Mind: From Colony to Province*. Cambridge, Mass.: Harvard University Press, 1953.

————. *The New England Mind: The Seventeenth Century*. Cambridge, Mass.: Harvard University Press, 1954.

Miller, Ellen Clare. *Eastern Sketches*. New York: Arno Press, 1977.

Milne, Gordon. *G. W. Curtis and the Genteel Tradition*. Bloomington: Indiana University Press, 1956.

Mott, Frank Luther. *American Journalism*. New York, 1962.

————. *Golden Multitude; the Story of Bestsellers in the United States*. New York: Macmillan, 1947.

Mueller, Roger Chester. *The Orient in American Transcendental Periodicals* (1835–1886). Unpublished Ph.D. dissertation. University of Minnesota, 1968.

Murdock, J. E. *The Stage*. Philadelphia. 1880.

Nichols, Roy F. *Advance Agents of American Destiny*. Philadelphia: University of Pennsylvania Press, 1956.

Niebuhr, H. Richard. *The Kingdom of God in America*. Chicago, New York: Willett, Clark, 1937.

Niebuhr, Reinhold. *The Children of Light and the Children of Darkness, a Vindication of Democracy and Critique of its Traditional Defence*. New York: Charles Scribner, 1944.

Ockley, Simon. *The History of the Saracens*. 2 Vol., 2d ed. London, 1718.

Olin, Stephen. *The Life and Letters of Stephen Olin…Late President of the Wesleyan University*. 2 vols. New York: Harper, 1854.

————. *Travels in Egypt, Arabia Petrea and the Holy Land*. 2 vols., 4th ed. New York: Harper, 1844.

————. *The Works of Stephen Olin*. 2 vols. New York: Harper, 1852.

Oliphant, Laurence. *The Land of Gilea;d, with Excursions in the Lebanon*. New York: D. Appleton, 1881.

"Orientalism." *The Knickerbocker*. 41 (June 1853).

Osgood, David. "A Solemn Protest against the Late Declaration of War." *A Sermon. Medford, 1812*.

O'Sullivan, John L. *The Democratic Review*. July and Aug., 1845.

Pankake, Marcia Jean. *Americans Abroad: A Bibliographical Study of American Travel Literature 1625-1800*. Unpublished Ph.D. dissertation. University of Minnesota, 1975.

Parrington, Vernon Lewis. *Main Currents in American Thought*. New York: Harcourt, Brace, 1927–1930.

Parrington, Vernon Lewis. "The Puritan Divines, 1620–1720," *Cambridge History of American Literature*, Vol. I. New York: G. P. Putnam, 1917–21. 4 vols.

Paulin, Charles Oscar. *Diplomatic Negotiations of American Naval Affairs 1778–1883*. Baltimore: The Johns Hopkins Press, 1912.

Pearce, Nathaniel. *Life and adventures during a residence in Abyssinia from 1810 to 1819...2* vols. Edited by J. J. Halls. London: H. Colburn, 1831.

———. "The Perilous Life of Nathaniel Pearce" in Charles Ellms, *Robinson Cruso's Own Book*.

Pierpont, John. *Airs of Palestine: A Poem*. Baltimore: B. Edes, 1816.

Poe, Edgar Allen. *The Complete Works of Edgar Allen Poe*. Vol. X. Edited by James A. Harrison. New York: AMS Press, 1965.

Poe, Edgar Allen. *New York Review*. August, 1841.

Poe, Edgar Allen. "Review of Stephens' Arabia Petraea." *New York Review*. Oct., 1837.

Porter, David. *Constantinople and Its Environs*. 2 vols. New York: Harper, 1835.

Prideux, Humphry. *The True Nature of Imposture Fully Displayed in the Life of Mahamet*. London: W. Rogers, 1697.

Ray, William. *Poems on Various Subjects*. Auburn: U. F. Doubleday, 1821.

Rescher, Nicholas. *Studies in Arabic Philosophy*. Pittsburgh: University of Pittsburgh Press, 1968.

Robinson, Edward. *Biblical Researches in Palestine and the Adjacent Regions*. 3 vols. 3rd ed. London: John Murray, 1867.

Ross, Alexander. *The Alcoran of Mahomet*, in *Richard Knolles The Turkish History*. Vol. II. London: Randal Taylor, 1688.

Said, Edward W. *Orientalism*. New York: Vintage Books, 1979.

Sale, George. *See* Koran.

Sealts, Merton M., Jr. *Melville's Reading: A Check-List of Books Owned and Borrowed*. Madison: The University of Wisconsin Press, 1966.

Setton, M. Kenneth. *Europe and the Levant in the Middle Ages and the Renaissance*. London: Variorum Reprints, 1974.

Shaler, William. "Sketches of Algiers," *North American Review*. Vol. 22. (April 1826): 409–431.

Shaw, Annie Dewitt. *Will, Annie, and I: Travellers in Many Lands*. New York: L. A. Skinner, 1898.

Shuler, Lydia. "A Letter from the Holy Land." *The Monthly Gospel-Visiter*. Vol. V., No. 12 (July 1859)
———. "A Letter from Jerusalem." *The Monthly Gospel-Visiter*. Vol. IX, No. 7 (July 1859).
Silverman, Kenneth. *Timothy Dwight*. New York: Twayne Publishers, 1969.
Smith, Eli. *Trials of Missionaries; an Address Delivered in Park Street Chruch on Oct. 24, 1832*. Boston: Crocker and Brewster, 1832.
———. *An Address on the Missionary Character*. Boston, 1840.
Smith, Harold F. *American Travellers Abroad: A Bibliography of Accounts Published Before 1900*. Carbondale-Edwardsville, Ill.: The Library, Southern Illinois University, 1969.
Smith, James Ward and A. Leland Jamison (eds.) *Religion in American Life*. 2 vols. Princeton, N.J.: Princeton University Press, 1961.
Smith, J. V. C. *A Pilgrimage to Palestine*. Boston: David Clapp, 1853.
Smith, Lee S. *Through Egypt to Palestine*. Chicago: Fleming H. Revell, 1896.
Smith, Lucius E. (ed.) *Heroes and Martyrs of the Modern Missionary Enterprise*. Providence, R.I.: O. W. Potter, 1857.
Smith, Sarah L. Huntington. *Memoirs of Mrs. Sarah L. Smith Huntington*. 3rd ed. New York: American Tract Society, 1845.
Southern, R. W. *Western Views of Islam in the Middle Ages*. Cambridge, Mass.: Harvard University Press, 1962.
Stead, William T. *The Americanization of the World; or, the Trend of the Twentieth Century*. New York: Garland, 1972.
Stephens, John Lloyd. *Incidents of Travel in Egypt, Arabia Petraea, and the Holy Land*. Edited by Victor Wolfgang von Hagen. Norman: University of Oklahoma Press, 1970.
Stephens, John Lloyd. *Indicdents of Travel in Greece, Turkey, Russia, and Poland* in *Remarkable Voyages and Travels*. 2 vols. 7th ed. New York: Harper, 1854.
Stiles, Ezra. *The United States Elevated to Glory and Honor*. 1783.
Stoddard, Richard Henry. *The Book of the East, and Other Poems*. Boston: James R. Osgood, 1871.
Stowe, H. B. (ed.) *A Library of Famous Fiction: Embracing the Nine Standard Masterpieces of Imaginative Literature*. New York, 1873.
Strong, W. D. *The Story of the American Board*. Boston, 1910.
Stuart, Moses. *A Sermon Preached in the Tabernacle Church, Salem, Nov. 5, 1818*...Andover: Flagg and Gould, 1819
Taylor, Bayard. *Egypt and Iceland in the Year 1874*. New York: G. P. Putnam, 1874.
———. *The Lands of the Saracens*. New York: G. P. Putnam, 1871.
———. *A Journey to Central Africa; or, Life and Landscapes from Egypt to the Negro Kingdoms of the White Nile*. New York: G. P. Putnam, 1875.
———. *Poems of the Orient*. 5th ed. Boston: Ticknor and Fields, 1856.
Taylor, Fitch W. *A Voyage Round the World*. New Hampshire, NY: 1851.
Thayer, William M. *From Tannery to the White House: The Life of Ulysses S. Grant*. Boston: James H. Earle, 1885.

Thomson, William. *The Land and the Book, or Biblical Illustrations Drawn from the Manners and Customs, the Scenes and Scenery of The Holy Land*. London, 1905.

Thoreau, Henry D. *Journal*.

Thornton, John Wingate. *The Pulpit of the American Revolution*. Boston, 1860.

Tibawi, A. L. *American Interests in Syria 1800-1901: A Study of Educational, Literary and Religious Work*. Oxford: Clarendon Press, 1966.

Tillman, Seth P. *The U. S. in the Middle East: Interests and Obstacles*. Bloomington: Indiana University Press, 1982.

Todd, Charles Burr. *Life and Letters of Joel Barlow…with Extracts From His Works and Hitherto Unpublished Poems*. New York: G. P. Putnam, 1886.

Tyler, Alice Felt. *Freedom's Ferment*. New York: Harper & Row, 1944.

Tyler, Royall. *The Algerine Captive*. Edited by Jack B. Moore. 2 vols. Gainesville, Fla.: Scholars' Facsimiles & Reprints, 1967.

"The United States a Commissioned Missionary Nation," *American Theological Review*. I (1859): 152–173.

Verrill, A. Hyatt. *The Real Story of the Pirates*. New York: D. Appleton, 1927.

Warner, Charles D. *That Fortune*. New York: Harper, 1969.

"Was Mohammed an Imposter or an Enthusiast," *North American Review* 63 (Oct. 1846): 496–97, 513.

Washburn, L. K. "Who Are Christians?" *The Index*. (Oct. 31, 1878): 518–520.

Washington, George. "Washington's Addresses to the Churches," *Old South Leaflets*, III (65). Boston.

Williams, Roger. "Letters of Roger Williams to Winthrop," *Old South Leaflets*, III (53). Boston.

Willis, Nathaniel Parker. *Prose Writings of Nathaniel Parker Willis*. Edited by Henry A. Beers. New York: Charles Scribner, 1885.

———. *Pencillings by the Way*. 2 vols. Philadelphia: Carey, Lea, and Blanchard, 1836.

Winthrop, John. *Papers*. Edited by A. B. Forbes. Vol. II. Boston, 1929–1947.

———. "Winthrop's Conclusions for the Plantation in New England," *Old South Leaflets* II (50). (Boston, n.d.)

Worcester, Samuel. *Two Discourses, on the Perpetuity and Provision of God's Gracious Covenant with Abraham and His Seed*. (Salem: Haven Pool, 1805).

INDEX

A

A Pilgrimage to Palestine, 169
Abdurrahman, 69, 75
Abraham, 7, 39, 86
Abu-Taleb, 39
Abyssinia, 113
Adams, Hannah, 35, 37–38, 42
Adams, Henry, 116
Adams, John, 68–69, 73
Adams, John Quincy, 99
Adams, Robert, 77, 95
Adventists
    and location of Advent, 155
    and millenialism, 151, 167
    sizable movements of, 154
    sympathize with Jews, 163
Adventures of Huckleberry Finn, xix
Africa, 113, 173
    civilization in, 28
    Islam in, 29
Age of Reason, 36
Ahlstrom, Sidney, 6, 19, 24, 29, 88–89, 104
Airs of Palestine, 212
Akhoond of Swat, 1
Alcott, Bronson, 61
Alger, William, 180, 190
The Algerine Captive, 47, 52, 55, 57, 73
Algiers, 66, 69–71, 73, 75, 78
    See also Barbary States
America
    in beginning of creation, 17
    as center of world, 20
    as City on a Hill, 143–144, 149, 212
    claim of ownership of East, 196
    concern for mankind, 21
    directed by Providence, 22, 43, 85, 87,
      105, 107, 112, 199, 261
    as empire, 21, 106
    first encounters Muslim world, 112
    first seminaries in, 88
    immigrants to, 20
    independence of, 45, 68
    initiated into diplomacy, 72
    as instrument of fulfillment, 162
    insularity of, xv
    as Israel, 16, 43, 143–146, 149, 155, 212,
      261
    as Kingdom of God, viii, 17, 106, 127, 145,
      149, 261
    liberty in, 24
    and Manifest Destiny, 16, 19, 21, 23, 45,
      80, 85, 104–105, 109, 196, 199
    missionary spirit of, 21, 23, 85, 87–88, 104,
      134
    Orientalism in, 196, 199, 261
    prophets in, 4
    Puritan influence on, 29, 261
    slavery in, 53
    as unique experiment, 16, 19
    wealth of, 20
    westward expansion of, 23
American Bible Society, 18, 152
American Board of Commissioners for
    Foreign Missions (ABCFM), 89, 101,
    106, 148
American Christian Missionary Society, 157
American Episcopal Mission, 120
American Evangelic Mission, 121
American Oriental Society, 171, 261
American Presbyterian Mission, 121
American Theological Review, 19–20, 22,
    85, 87–88, 93–94, 107, 112
Andover, 88
Andrews, Charles, 94, 98, 119, 122, 126,
    134–135, 163, 169
Anglo-Saxons, 22, 44–45, 107, 112, 153, 164,
    197, 199
Anti-Semitism, xviii
Antichrist, 12
Arabian Nights, xv, xviii, 1, 178–179, 194,
    196, 199
The Arabs in the Mind of America, ii
Austria, 171